T0348417

Rating Based Modeling of Credit Risk
Theory and Application of Migration Matrices

RATING BASED MODELING OF CREDIT RISK

Theory and Application of Migration Matrices

Stefan Trueck

Svetlozar T. Rachev

AMSTERDAM • BOSTON • HEIDELBERG • LONDON
NEW YORK • OXFORD • PARIS • SAN DIEGO
SAN FRANCISCO • SINGAPORE • SYDNEY • TOKYO
Academic Press is an imprint of Elsevier

Academic Press is an imprint of Elsevier
30 Corporate Drive, Suite 400, Burlington, MA 01803, USA
525 B Street, Suite 1900, San Diego, California 92101-4495, USA
84 Theobald's Road, London WC1X 8RR, UK

Library of Congress Cataloging-in-Publication Data
Application submitted

British Library Cataloguing-in-Publication Data
A catalogue record for this book is available from the British Library.

ISBN: 978-0-12-373683-3

For information on all Academic Press publications
visit our Web site at: *http://www.elsevierdirect.com*

Printed in the United States of America
08 09 10   9 8 7 6 5 4 3 2 1

To my parents and Prasheela
(S.T.)

To Svetlozar Todorov Iotov
(S.T.R)

Contents

Preface

Credit risk has become one of the most intensely studied topics in quantitative finance in the last decade. A large number of books on the topic have been published in recent years, while on the excellent homepage maintained by Greg Gupton there are more than 1200 downloadable working papers related to credit risk. The increased interest in modeling and management of credit risk in academia seems only to have started in the mid-1990s. However, due to the various issues involved, including the ability to effectively apply quantitative modeling tools and techniques and the dramatic rise of credit derivatives, it has become one of the major fields of research in finance literature.

As a consequence of an increasingly complex and competitive financial environment, adequate risk management strategies require quantitative modeling know-how and the ability to effectively apply this expertise and its techniques. Also, with the revision of the Basel Capital Accord, various credit risk models have been analyzed with respect to their feasibility, and a significant focus has been put on good risk-management practices with respect to credit risk. Another consequence of Basel II is that most financial institutions will have to develop internal models to adequately determine the risk arising from their credit exposures. It can therefore be expected that in particular the use and application of rating based models for credit risk will be increasing further.

On the other hand, it has to be acknowledged that rating agencies are at the center of the subprime mortgage crisis, as they failed to provide adequate ratings for many diverse products in the credit and credit derivative markets like mortgage bonds, asset backed securities, commercial papers, collateralized debt obligations, and derivative products for companies and also for financial institutions. Despite some deficiencies of the current credit rating structure—recommendations for their improvements are thoroughly analyzed in Crouhy et al. (2008) but are beyond the scope of this book—overall, rating based models have evolved as an industry standard. Therefore, credit ratings will remain one of the most important variables when it comes to measurement and management of credit risk.

The literature on modeling and managing credit risk and credit derivatives has been widely extended in recent years; other books in the area include the excellent treatments by Ammann (2002), Arvanitis and Gregory (2001), Bielecki and Rutkowski (2002), Bluhm et al. (2003), Bluhm and Overbeck (2007b), Cossin and Pirotte (2001), Duffie and Singleton (2003), Fabozzi (2006a,b), Lando (2004), Saunders and Allen (2002), and Schönbucher (2003), just to mention a few. However, in our opinion, so far there has been no book on credit risk management mainly focusing on the use of transition matrices, which, while popular in academia, is even more widely used in industry. We hope that this book provides a helpful survey on the theory and application of transition matrices for credit risk management, including most of the central issues like estimation techniques, stability and comparison of rating transitions, VaR simulation, adjustment and forecasting migration matrices, corporate-yield curve dynamics, dependent migrations, and the modeling and pricing of credit derivatives. While the aim is mainly to provide a review of the existing literature and techniques, a variety of very recent results and new work have also been incorporated into the book. We tried to keep the presentation thorough but also accessible, such that most of the chapters do not require a very technical background and should be useful for academics, regulators, risk managers, practitioners, and even students who require an introduction or a more extensive and advanced overview of the topic. The large number of applications and numerical examples should also help the reader to better identify and follow the important implementation issues of the described models.

In the process of writing this book, we received a lot of help from various people in both academia and industry. First of all, we highly appreciated feedback and comments on the manuscript by many colleagues and friends. We would also like to thank various master, research, and PhD students who supplied corrections or contributed their work to several of the chapters. In particular, we are grateful to Arne Benzin, Alexander Breusch, Jens Deidersen, Stefan Harpaintner, Jan Henneke, Matthias Laub, Nicole Lehnert, Andreas Lorenz, Christian Menn, Jingyuan Meng, Emrah Özturkmen, Peter Niebling, Jochen Peppel, Christian Schmieder, Robert Soukup, Martin Sttzel, Stoyan Stoyanov, and Wenju Tian for their contributions. Finally, we would like to thank Roxana Boboc and Stacey Walker at Elsevier for their remarkable help and patience throughout the process of manuscript delivery.

Stefan Trueck *and* Svetlozar T. Rachev

Sydney *and* Karlsruhe, August 2008

1

Introduction: Credit Risk Modeling, Ratings, and Migration Matrices

1.1 Motivation

The aim of this book is to provide a review on theory and application of migration matrices in rating based credit risk models. In the last decade, rating based models in credit risk management have become very popular. These systems use the rating of a company as the decisive variable and not—like the formerly used structural models the value of the firm—when it comes to evaluate the default risk of a bond or loan. The popularity is due to the straightforwardness of the approach but also to the new Capital Accord (Basel II) of the Basel Committee on Banking Supervision (2001), a regulatory body under the Bank of International Settlements (BIS). Basel II allows banks to base their capital requirements on internal as well as external rating systems. Thus, sophisticated credit risk models are being developed or demanded by banks to assess the risk of their credit portfolio better by recognizing the different underlying sources of risk. As a consequence, default probabilities for certain rating categories but also the probabilities for moving from one rating state to another are important issues in such models for risk management and pricing. Systematic changes in migration matrices have substantial effects on credit Value-at-Risk (VaR) of a portfolio but also on prices of credit derivatives like Collaterized Debt Obligations (CDOs). Therefore, rating transition matrices are of particular interest for determining the economic capital or figures like expected loss and VaR for credit portfolios, but can also be helpful as it comes to the pricing of more complex products in the credit industry.

This book is in our opinion the first manuscript with a main focus in particular on issues arising from the use of transition matrices in modeling of credit risk. It aims to provide an up-to-date reference to the central problems of the field like rating based modeling, estimation techniques, stability and comparison of rating transitions, VaR simulation, adjustment and forecasting migration matrices, corporate-yield curve dynamics, dependent defaults and migrations, and finally credit derivatives modeling and pricing. Hereby, most of the techniques and issues discussed will be illustrated by simplified numerical examples that we hope will be helpful to the reader. The following sections provide a quick overview of most of the issues, problems, and applications that will be outlined in more detail in the individual chapters.

1.2   Structural and Reduced Form Models

This book is mainly concerned with the use of rating based models for credit migrations. These models have seen a significant rise in popularity only since the 1990s. In earlier approaches like the classical structural models introduced by Merton (1974), usually a stochastic process is used to describe the asset value V of the issuing firm

$$dV(t) = \mu V(t)dt + \sigma V(t)dW(t)$$

where μ and σ are the drift rate and volatility of the assets, and $W(t)$ is a standard Wiener process. The firm value models then price the bond as contingent claims on the asset. Literature describes the event of default when the asset value drops below a certain barrier. There are several model extensions, e.g., by Longstaff and Schwartz (1995) or Zhou (1997), including stochastic interest rates or jump diffusion processes. However, one feature of all models of this class is that they model credit risk based on assuming a stochastic process for the value of the firm and the term structure of interest rates. Clearly the problem is to determine the value and volatility of the firm's assets and to model the stochastic process driving the value of the firm adequately. Unfortunately using structural models, especially short-term credit spreads, are generally underestimated due to default probabilities close to zero estimated by the models. The fact that both drift rate and volatility of the firm's assets may also be dependent on the future situation of the whole economy is not considered.

The second major class of models—the reduced form models—does not condition default explicitly on the value of the firm. They are more general than structural models and assume that an exogenous random variable drives default and that the probability of default (PD) over any time interval is non-zero. An important input to determine the default probability and the price of a bond is the rating of the company. Thus, to determine the risk of a credit portfolio of rated issuers one generally has to consider historical average defaults and transition probabilities for current rating classes. The reduced form approach was first introduced by Fons (1994) and then extended by several authors, including Jarrow et al. (1997) and Duffie and Singleton (1999). Quite often in reduced form approaches the migration from one rating state to another is modeled using a Markov chain model with a migration matrix governing the changes from one rating state to another. An exemplary transition matrix is given in Table 1.1.

TABLE 1.1. Average One-Year Transition Matrix of Moody's Corporate Bond Ratings for the Period 1982–2001

	Aaa	Aa	A	Baa	Ba	B	C	D
Aaa	0.9276	0.0661	0.0050	0.0009	0.0003	0.0000	0.0000	0.0000
Aa	0.0064	0.9152	0.0700	0.0062	0.0008	0.0011	0.0002	0.0001
A	0.0007	0.0221	0.9137	0.0546	0.0058	0.0024	0.0003	0.0005
Baa	0.0005	0.0029	0.0550	0.8753	0.0506	0.0108	0.0021	0.0029
Ba	0.0002	0.0011	0.0052	0.0712	0.8229	0.0741	0.0111	0.0141
B	0.0000	0.0010	0.0035	0.0047	0.0588	0.8323	0.0385	0.0612
C	0.0012	0.0000	0.0029	0.0053	0.0157	0.1121	0.6238	0.2389
D	0.0000	0.0000	0.0000	0.0000	0.0000	0.0000	0.0000	1.0000

Besides the fact that they allow for realistic short-term credit spreads, reduced form models also give great flexibility in specifying the source of default. We will now give a brief outlook on several issues that arise when migration matrices are applied in rating based credit modeling.

1.3 Basel II, Scoring Techniques, and Internal Rating Systems

As mentioned before, due to the new Basel Capital Accord (Basel II) most of the international operating banks may determine their regulatory capital based on an internal rating system (Basel Committee on Banking Supervision, 2001). As a consequence, a high fraction of these banks will have ratings and default probabilities for all loans and bonds in their credit portfolio. Therefore, Chapters 2 and 3 of this book will be dedicated to the new Basel Capital Accord, rating agencies, and their methods and a review on scoring techniques to derive a rating. Regarding Basel II, the focus will be set on the internal ratings based (IRB) approach where the banks are allowed to use the results of their own internal rating systems. Consequently, it is of importance to provide a summary on the rating process of a bank or the major rating agencies. As will be illustrated in Chapter 6, internal and external rating systems may show quite a different behavior in terms of stability of ratings, rating drifts, and time homogeneity.

While Weber et al. (1998) were the first to provide a comparative study on the rating and migration behavior of four major German banks, recently more focus has been set on analyzing rating and transition behavior also in internal rating systems (Bank of Japan, 2005; Euopean Central Bank, 2004). Recent publications include, for example, Engelmann et al. (2003), Araten et al. (2004), Basel Committee on Banking Supervision (2005), and

Jacobson et al. (2006). Hereby, Engelmann et al. (2003) and the Basel Committee on Banking Supervision (2005) are more concerned with the validation, respectively, classification of internal rating systems. Araten et al. (2004) discuss issues in evaluating banks' internal ratings of borrowers comparing the ex-post discrimination power of an internal and external rating system. Jacobson et al. (2006) investigate internal rating systems and differences between the implied loss distributions of banks with equal regulatory risk profiles. We provide different technologies to compare rating systems and estimated migration matrices in Chapters 2 and 7.

Another problem for internal rating systems arises when a continuous-time approach is chosen for modeling credit migrations. Since for bank loans, balance sheet data or rating changes are reported only once a year, there is no information on the exact time of rating changes available. While discrete migration matrices can be transformed into a continuous-time approach, Israel et al. (2000) show that for several cases of discrete transition matrices there is no "true" or valid generator. In this case, only an approximation of the continuous-time transition matrix can be chosen. Possible approximation techniques can be found in Jarrow et al. (1997), Kreinin and Sidelnikova (2001), or Israel et al. (2000) and will be discussed in Chapter 5.

1.4   Rating Based Modeling and the Pricing of Bonds

A quite important application of migration matrices is also their use for determining the term structure of credit risk. In 1994, Fons (1994) developed a reduced form model to derive credit spreads using historical default rates and a recovery rate estimate. He illustrated that the term structure of credit risk, i.e., the behavior of credit spreads as maturity varies, depends on the issuer's credit quality, i.e., its rating. For bonds rated investment grade, the term structures of credit risk have an upward sloping structure. The spread between the promised yield-to-maturity of a defaultable bond and a default-free bond of the same maturity widens as the maturity increases. On the other hand, speculative grade rated bonds behave in the opposite way: the term structures of the credit risk have a downward-sloping structure. Fons (1994) was able to provide a link between the rating of a company and observed credit spreads in the market.

However, obviously not only the "worst case" event of default has influence on the price of a bond, but also a change in the rating of a company can affect prices of the issued bond. Therefore, with CreditMetrics JP Morgan provides a framework for quantifying credit risk in portfolios using historical transition matrices (Gupton et al., 1997). Further, refining the Fons model, Jarrow et al. (1997) introduced a discrete-time Markovian model to estimate changes in the price of loans and bonds. Both approaches incorporate possible rating upgrades, stable ratings, and rating downgrades in the reduced form approach. Hereby, for determining the price of credit risk, both historical default rates and transition matrices are used. The model of Jarrow et al. (1997) is still considered one of the most important approaches as it comes to the pricing of bonds or credit derivatives and will be described in more detail in Chapter 8.

Both the CreditMetrics framework and Markov chain approach heavily rely on the use of adequate credit migration matrices as will be illustrated in Chapters 4 and 5. Further, the application of migration matrices for deriving cumulative default probabilities and the pricing of credit derivatives will be illustrated in Chapter 11.

1.5   Stability of Transition Matrices, Conditional Migrations, and Dependence

As mentioned before, historical transition matrices can be used as an input for estimating portfolio loss distributions and credit VaR figures. Unfortunately, transition matrices cannot be considered to be constant over a longer time period; see e.g., Allen and Saunders (2003) for an extensive review on cyclical effects in modeling credit risk measurement. Further, migrations of loans in internal bank portfolios may behave differently than the transition matrices provided by major rating agencies like Moody's or Standard & Poor's would suggest (Krüger et al., 2005; Weber et al., 1998). Nickell et al. (2000) show that there is quite a big difference between transition matrices during an expansion of the economy and a recession. The results are confirmed by Bangia et al. (2002) who suggest that for risk management purposes it might be interesting not only to simulate the term structure of defaults but to design stress test scenarios by the observed behavior of default and transition matrices through the cycle. Jafry and Schuermann (2004) investigate the mobility in migration behavior using 20 years of Standard & Poor's transition matrices and find large deviations through time. Kadam and Lenk (2008) report significant heterogeneity in default intensity, migration volatility, and transition probabilities depending on country and industry effects. Finally, Trueck and Rachev (2005) show that the effect of different migration behavior on exemplary credit portfolios may lead to substantial changes in expected losses, credit VaR, or confidence sets for probabilities of default (PDs). During a recession period of the economy the VaR for one and the same credit portfolio can be up to eight times higher than during an expansion of the economy.

As a consequence, following Bangia et al. (2002), it seems necessary to extend transition matrix application to a conditional perspective using additional information on the economy or even forecast transition matrices using revealed dependencies on macroeconomic indices and interest rates. Based on the cyclical behavior of migration, the literature provides some approaches to adjust, re-estimate, or change migration matrices according to some model for macroeconomic variables or observed empirical prices. Different approaches suggest conditioning the matrix based on macroeconomic variables or forecasts that will affect future credit migrations. The first model developed to explicitly link business cycles to rating transitions was in the 1997 CreditPortfolioView (CPV) by Wilson (1997a,b). Kim (1999) develops a univariate model whereby ratings respond to business cycle shifts. The model is extended to a multifactor credit migration model by Wei (2003) while Cowell et al. (2007) extend the model by replacing the normal with an α-stable distribution for modeling the risk factors. Nickell et al. (2000) propose an ordered probit model which permits migration matrices to be conditioned on the industry, the country domicile, and the business cycle. Finally, Bangia et al. (2002) provide a Markov switching model, separating the economy into two regimes. For each state of the economy—expansion and contraction—a transition matrix is estimated such that conditional future migrations can be simulated based on the state of the economy.

To approach these issues, the major concern is to be able to judge whether one has an adequate model or forecast for a conditional or unconditional transition matrix. It raises the question: What can be considered to be a "good" model in terms of evaluating migration behavior or risk for a credit portfolio? Finally, the question of dependent defaults and credit migration has to be investigated. Knowing the factors that lead to changes in migration behavior and quantifying their influence may help a bank improve its estimates about expected losses and Value-at-Risk. These issues will be more thoroughly investigated in Chapters 8, 9, and 10.

1.6   Credit Derivative Pricing

As mentioned before, credit migration matrices also play a substantial role in the modeling and pricing of credit derivatives, in particular collaterized debt obligations (CDOs). The market for credit derivatives can be considered as one of the fastest growing in the financial industry. The importance of transition matrices for modeling credit derivatives has been pointed out in several studies. Jarrow et al. (1997) use historical transition matrices and observed market spreads to determine cumulative default probabilities and credit curves for the pricing of credit derivatives. Bluhm (2003) shows how historical one-year migration matrices can be used to determine cumulative default probabilities. This so-called calibration of the credit curve can then be used for the rating of cash-flow CDO tranches.

In recent publications, the effect of credit migrations on issues like credit derivative pricing and rating is examined by several authors, by Bielecki et al. (2003), Hrvatin et al. (2006), Hurd and Kuznetsov (2005), and Picone (2005), among others. Hrvatin et al. (2006) investigate CDO near-term rating stability of different CDO tranches depending on different factors. Next to the granularity of the portfolio, in particular, credit migrations in the underlying reference portfolio are considered to have impact on the stability of CDO tranche ratings. Pointing out the influence of changes in credit migrations, Picone (2005) develops a time-inhomogeneous intensity model for valuing cash-flow CDOs. His approach explicitly incorporates the credit rating of the firms in the collateral portfolio by applying a set of transition matrices, calibrated to historical default probabilities. Finally, Hurd and Kuznetsov (2005) show that credit basket derivatives can be modeled in a parsimonious and computationally efficient manner within the affine Markov chain framework for multifirm credit migration while Bielecki et al. (2003) concentrate on dependent migrations and defaults in a Markovian market model and the effects on the valuation of basket credit derivatives. Both approaches heavily rely on the choice of an adequate transition matrix as a starting point.

Overall, the importance of credit transition matrices in modeling credit derivatives cannot be denied. Therefore, Chapter 11 is mainly dedicated to the application of migration matrices in the process of calibration, valuation, and pricing of these products.

1.7   Chapter Outline

Chapters 2, 3, and 4 provide a rather broad view and introduction to rating based models in credit risk and the new Basel Capital Accord. Chapter 2 aims to give a brief overview on rating agencies, rating systems, and an exemplary rating process. Then different scoring techniques discriminant analysis, logistic regression, and probit models are described. Further, a section is dedicated to the evaluation of rating systems by using cumulative accuracy profiles and accuracy ratios. Chapter 3 then illustrates the new capital accord of the Basel Committee on Banking Supervision. Since 1988, when the old accord was published, risk management practices, supervisory approaches, and financial markets have undergone significant transformations. Therefore, the new proposal contains innovations that are designed to introduce greater risk sensitivity into the determination of the required economic capital of financial institutions. This is achieved by taking into account the actual riskiness of an obligor by using ratings provided by external rating agencies or internally estimated probabilities of default. In Chapter 4 we review a number of models for credit risk that rely heavily on company ratings as input variables. The models are focused on risk management and give different approaches to the determination of the expected losses, unexpected losses, and Value-at-Risk. We will focus on rating based models including the reduced-form model suggested by Fons (1994) and extensions of the approach with respect to default intensities. Then we will have a look at the industry models CreditMetrics and *CreditRiskPlus*. In particular the former also uses historical transition matrices to determine risk figures for credit portfolios.

Chapters 5, 6, and 7 are dedicated to various issues of rating transitions and the Markov chain approach in credit risk modeling. Chapter 5 introduces the basic ideas of modeling migrations with transition matrices. We further compare discrete and continuous-time modeling of rating migrations and illustrate the advantages of the continuous-time approach. Further, the problems of embeddability and identification of generator matrices are examined and some approximation methods for generator matrices are described. Finally, a section is dedicated to simulations of rating transitions using discrete time, continuous-time, and nonparametric techniques. In Chapter 6 we focus on time-series behavior and stability of migration matrices. Two of the major issues to investigate are time homogeneity and Markov behavior of rating migrations. Generally, both assumptions should be treated with care due to the influence of the business cycle on credit migration behavior. We provide a number of empirical studies examining the issues and further yielding results on rating drifts, changes in Value-at-Risk figures for credit portfolios, and on the stability of probability of default estimated through time. Chapter 7 is dedicated to the study of measures for comparison of rating transition matrices. A review of classical matrix norms is given before indices based on eigenvalues and eigenvectors, including a recently proposed mobility metric, are described. The rest of the chapter then proposes some criteria that should be helpful to compare migration matrices from a risk perspective and suggests new risk-adjusted indices for measuring those differences. A simple simulation study on the adequacy of the different measures concludes the chapter.

Chapters 8 and 9 deal with determining risk-neutral and conditional migration matrices. While the former are used for the pricing of credit derivatives based on observed market probabilities of defaults, the latter focus on transforming average historical transition matrices by taking into account information on macroeconomic variables and the business cycle. In Chapter 8 we start with a review of the seminal paper by Jarrow et al. (1997) and then examine a variety of adjustment techniques for migration matrices. Hereby, methods based on a discrete and continuous-time framework as well as a recently suggested adjustment technique based on economic theory are illustrated. For each of the techniques we give numerical examples illustrating how it can be conducted. Chapter 9 deals with conditioning and forecasting transition matrices based on business cycle indicators. Hereby, we start with the approach suggested in the industry model CreditPortfolioView and then review techniques that are based on factor model representations and other techniques. An empirical study comparing several of the techniques concludes the chapter.

Chapters 10 and 11 deal with more recent issues on modeling dependent migrations and the use of transition matrices for credit derivative pricing. In Chapter 10 we start with an illustration on how dependency between individual loans may substantially affect the risk for a financial institution. Then different models for the dependence structure with a focus on copulas are suggested. We provide a brief review on the underlying ideas for modeling dependent defaults and then show how a framework for modeling dependent credit migrations can be developed. In an empirical study on dependent migrations we show that both the degree of dependence entering the model as well as the choice of the copula significantly affects determined risk figures for credit portfolios. Chapter 11 finally provides an overview on the use of transition matrices for the pricing of credit derivatives. The chapter illustrates how derived credit curves can be used for the pricing of single-named credit derivatives like, e.g., credit default swaps and further shows the use of migration matrices for the pricing of more complex products like collaterized debt obligations. Finally we also have a look at the pricing of step-up bonds that have been popular in particular in the Telecom sector.

2
Rating and Scoring Techniques

This chapter aims to provide an overview on rating agencies, the rating process, scoring techniques, and how rating systems can be evaluated. Hereby, after a brief look at some of the major rating agencies, different qualitative and quantitative techniques for credit scoring will be described. The focus will be set on the classic methods of discriminant analysis and probit and logit models. The former was initially suggested in the seminal paper by Altman (1968) and after four decades is still an often-used tool for determining the default risk of a company. Further we will illustrate how the quality of rating systems can be evaluated by using accuracy ratios.

2.1 Rating Agencies, Rating Processes, and Factors

In this section we will take a brief look at rating agencies, categories, and the rating process. In particular we will provide a rough overview of the rating procedure as it is implemented by Standard & Poor's (S&P)—one of the major credit rating agencies. Rating agencies have a long tradition in the United States. For example, S&P traces its history back to 1860 and began rating the debt of corporate and government issuers more than 75 years ago. The Securities and Exchange Commission (SEC) has currently designated several agencies as "nationally recognized statistical rating organizations" (NRSROs), including, e.g., Moody's KMV, Standard & Poor's, Fitch, or Thomson BankWatch.

Even though methodologies and standards differ from one NRSRO to the other, regulators generally do not make distinctions among the agencies. Although there is a high congruence between the rating systems of Moody's and S&P, different agencies might assign slightly different ratings for the same bond. For studies on split ratings and their effects on bond prices or yields, see, e.g., Cantor et al. (2005); Billingsley et al. (1985); Perry et al. (2008). Today, the S&P's Ratings Services is a business unit of McGraw-Hill Inc., a major publishing company. S&P now rates more than USD 10 trillion in bonds and other financial obligations of obligors in more than

50 countries. Its ratings also serve as input data for several credit risk software models such as CreditMetrics of JP Morgan, a system that evaluates risks individually or across an entire portfolio.

Generally the rating agencies provide two different sorts of ratings:

- Issue-specific credit ratings and

- Issuer credit ratings

Issue-specific credit ratings are current opinions of the creditworthiness of an obligor with respect to a specific financial obligation, a specific class of financial obligations, or specific financial program. Issue-specific ratings also take into account the recovery prospects associated with the specific debt being rated. Issuer credit ratings, on the other hand, give an opinion of the obligor's overall capacity to meet its financial obligations—that is, its fundamental creditworthiness. These so-called corporate credit ratings indicate the likelihood of default regarding all financial obligations of the firm. The practice of differentiating issues in relation to the issuer's overall creditworthiness is known as "notching." Issues are notched up or down from the corporate credit rating level in accordance with established guidelines.

Some of the rating agencies have historically maintained separate rating scales for long-term and short-term instruments. Long-term credit ratings, i.e., obligations with an original maturity of more than one year, are divided into several categories ranging from AAA, reflecting the strongest credit quality, to D, reflecting occurrence of default. Ratings in the four highest categories, AAA, AA, A, and BBB, generally are recognized as being investment grades, whereas debts rated BB or below generally are regarded as having significant speculative characteristics and are also called noninvestment grade. Ratings from AA to CCC may be modified by the addition of a plus or minus sign to show the relative standing within the major rating categories. The symbol R is attached to the ratings of instruments with significant noncredit risks. It highlights risks to principal or volatility of expected returns that are not addressed in the credit rating. Examples include obligations linked or indexed to equities, currencies, or commodities and obligations exposed to severe prepayment risk such as interest-only or principal-only mortgage securities. In case of default, the symbol SD (Selective Default) is assigned when an issuer can be expected to default selectively, that is, continues to pay certain issues or classes of obligations while not paying others. The issue rating definitions are expressed in terms of default risk and the protection afforded by the obligation in the event of bankruptcy. Table 2.1 gives a qualitative description of how the different rating categories should be interpreted.

Of course, in the end the rating of a company or loan should also be transferable to a corresponding default probability. Obviously, as we will see later on in Chapter 6, for example, default probabilities for different

TABLE 2.1. Rating Categories and Explanation of Ratings
Source: S&P's Corporate Ratings Criteria (2000)

Rating	Definition
AAA	The obligor's capacity to meet its financial commitment on the obligation is extremely strong.
AA	An obligation rated AA differs from the highest rated obligations only to a small degree. The obligor's capacity to meet its financial commitment on the obligation is very strong.
A	An obligation rated A is somewhat more susceptible to the adverse effects of changes in circumstances and economic conditions than obligations in higher rated categories.
BBB	An obligation rated BBB exhibits adequate protection parameters. However, adverse economic conditions or changing circumstances are more likely to lead to a weakened capacity of the obligor to meet its financial commitments on the obligation.
BB	An obligation rated BB is less vulnerable to nonpayment than other speculative issues. However, it faces major ongoing uncertainties or exposure to adverse business, financial, or economic conditions that could lead to the obligor's inadequate capacity to meet its financial commitment on the obligation.
B	The obligor currently has the capacity to meet its financial commitment on the obligation. Adverse business, financial, or economic conditions will likely impair the obligor's capacity or willingness to meet financial commitments.
CCC	An obligation rated CCC is currently vulnerable to nonpayment, and is dependent upon favorable business, financial, and economic conditions for the obligor to meet its financial commitment on the obligation.
CC	An obligation rated CC is currently highly vulnerable to nonpayment.
C	The C rating may be used to cover a situation where a bankruptcy petition has been filed or similar action has been taken but payments on this obligation are being continued.
D	The D rating, unlike other ratings, is not prospective. Rather, it is used only where a default has actually occurred and not where a default is only expected.

rating categories vary substantially through time. Therefore, it is difficult to provide a unique or reliable mapping of ratings to default probabilities. A possible mapping, following Dartsch and Weinrich (2002), is provided in Table 2.2 where default probabilities for rating systems with the typical 7 and 18 states (default is not considered a rating state here) are given. Note, however, that due to cyclical effects, these numbers have to be treated very carefully. Further note that other sources, depending on the considered time horizon, might provide quite different default probabilities associated with the corresponding rating categories.

TABLE 2.2. Rating Categories and Corresponding Default Probabilities According to Dartsch and Weinrich (2002)

18 classes	7 classes	Lower PD	Upper PD
AAA	AAA	0.00%	0.025%
AA+		0.025%	0.035%
AA	AA	0.035%	0.045%
AA−		0.045%	0.055%
A+		0.055%	0.07%
A	A	0.07%	0.095%
A−		0.095%	0.135%
BBB+		0.135%	0.205%
BBB	BBB	0.205%	0.325%
BBB−		0.325%	0.5125%
BB+		0.5125%	0.77%
BB	BB	0.77%	1.12%
BB−		1.12%	1.635%
B+		1.635%	2.905%
B	B	2.905%	5.785%
B−		5.785%	11.345%
CCC+		11.345%	17.495%
CCC	CCC	17.495%	−

2.1.1 The Rating Process

Most corporations approach rating agencies to request a rating prior to sale or registration of a debt issue. For example, S&P assigns and publishes ratings for all public corporate debt issues over USD 50 million—with or without a request from the issuer; but in all instances, S&P's analytical staff will contact the issuer to call for cooperation. Generally, rating agency analysts concentrate on one or two industries only, covering the entire spectrum of credits within those areas. Such specialization allows accumulation of expertise and competitive information better than if, e.g., speculative grade issuers were monitored separately from investment-grade issuers. For basic research, analysts expect financial information about the company consisting of five years of audited annual financial statements, the last several interim financial statements, and narrative descriptions of operations and products. The meeting with corporate management can be considered an important part of an agency's rating process. The purpose is to review in detail the company's key operating and financing plans, management policies, and other credit factors that have an impact on the rating. Additionally, facility tours can take place to convey a better understanding of a company's business to a rating analyst. Shortly after the issuer meeting, the industry analyst convenes a rating committee in connection with a presentation. It includes analysis of the nature of the company's business and its operating environment, evaluation of the company's strategic and financial management, financial analysis, and a rating recommendation.

Once the rating is determined, the company is notified of the rating and the major considerations supporting it. It is usually the policy of rating agencies to allow the issuer to respond to the rating decision prior to its publication by presenting new or additional data. In the case of a decision to change an existing rating, any appeal must be conducted as quickly as possible, i.e., within a day or two. The rating committee reconvenes to consider the new information. After the company is notified, the rating is published in the media—or released to the company for publication in the case of corporate credit ratings.

Corporate ratings on publicly distributed issues are monitored for at least one year. For example, the company can then elect to pay the rating agency to continue surveillance. Ratings assigned at the company's request have the option of surveillance, or being on a "point-in-time" basis. Where a major new financing transaction is planned such as, e.g., acquisitions, an update management meeting is appropriate. In any event, meetings are routinely scheduled at least annually to discuss industry outlook, business strategy, and financial forecasts and policies.

As a result of the surveillance process, it sometimes becomes apparent that changing conditions require reconsideration of the outstanding debt rating. After a preliminary review, which may lead to a so-called Credit-Watch listing of the company or outstanding issue, a presentation to the rating committee follows to arrive at a rating decision. Again, the company is notified and afterwards the agency publishes the rating. The process is exactly the same as the rating of a new issue. Reflecting this surveillance, the timing of rating changes depends neither on the sale of new debt issues nor on the agency's internal schedule for reviews.

Ratings with a pi-subscript are usually based on an analysis of an issuer's published financial information. They do not reflect in-depth meetings and therefore consist of less comprehensive information than ratings without a pi-subscript. Ratings with a pi-subscript are reviewed annually based on the new year's financial statements, but may be reviewed on an interim basis if a major event that may affect the issuer's credit quality occurs. They are neither modified with + or − signs nor subject to CreditWatch listings or rating outlooks.

CreditWatch and rating outlooks focus on scenarios that could result in a rating change. Ratings appear on CreditWatch lists when an event or deviation from an expected trend has occurred or is expected and additional information is necessary to take a rating action. For example, an issue is placed under such special surveillance as the result of mergers, recapitalizations, regulatory actions, or unanticipated operating developments. Such rating reviews normally are completed within 90 days, unless the outcome of a specific event is pending. However, a listing does not mean a rating change is inevitable, but in some cases, the rating change is certain and only the magnitude of the change is unclear. In those instances—and generally wherever possible—the range of alternative ratings that could result is shown. A rating outlook also assesses potential for change, but has a longer time frame than CreditWatch listings and incorporates trends or risks with less certain implications for credit quality. Note that, for example, S&P regularly publishes CreditWatch listings with the corresponding designations and rating outlooks to notify both the issuer and the market of recent developments whose rating impact has not yet been determined.

2.1.2 Credit Rating Factors

Table 2.3 exemplarily illustrates possible business risk and financial risk factors that enter the rating process of S&P. All categories mentioned above are scored in the rating process and there are also scores for the overall business and financial risk profile. The company's business risk profile determines the level of financial risk appropriate for any rating category. S&P computes a number of financial ratios and tracks them over time. S&P claims that industry risk—their analysis of the strength and stability of the industry in which the firm operates—probably receives the highest weight in the rating decision, but there are no formulae for combining scores to arrive at a rating conclusion. Generally all of the major rating agencies agree that a rating is, in the end, an opinion and considers both quantitative and qualitative factors.

In the world of emerging markets, rating agencies usually also incorporate country and sovereign risk to their rating analysis. Both business risk factors such as macroeconomic volatility, exchange-rate risk, government regulation, taxes, legal issues, etc., and financial risk factors such as accounting standards, potential price controls, inflation, and access

TABLE 2.3. Corporate Credit Analysis Factors
Source: S&P's Corporate Ratings Criteria (2000)

Business Risk	Financial Risk
Industry Characteristics	Financial Characteristics
Competitive Position	Financial Policy
Marketing	Profitability
Technology	Capital Structure
Efficiency	Cash Flow Protection
Regulation	Financial Flexibility
Management	

to capital are included in the analysis. Additionally, the anticipated ups and downs of business cycles—whether industry-specific or related to the general economy—are factored into the credit rating.

2.1.3 Types of Rating Systems

Recently, there has been quite some literature dealing with the philosophy, dynamics, and classification of different types of rating systems (see, e.g., Altman and Rijken (2006); Basel Committee on Banking Supervision (2005); Varsany (2007)). First of all, we have to decide whether a rating system is an obligor-specific one. Usually, the borrowers who share a similar risk profile are assigned to the same rating grade. Afterwards a probability of default (PD) is assigned. Very often the same PD is assigned to all borrowers of the same rating grade. For such a rating methodology the PDs do not discriminate between better and lower creditworthiness inside one rating grade. Consequently, the probability to migrate to a certain other rating grade is the same for all borrowers having the same rating.

An important classification of rating systems is the decision whether a rating system is point-in-time (PIT) or through-the-cycle (TTC). A PIT-PD describes the actual creditworthiness within a certain time horizon, whereas TTC-PDs also take into account possible changes in the macroeconomic conditions. A TTC-PD will not be affected when the change of the creditworthiness is caused only by a change of macroeconomic variables which more or less describe the state of the economy and which more or less affect the creditworthiness of all borrowers in a similar way. These two types have to be considered as extreme types of possible rating methodologies. Most rating systems are somewhere in between these two methods and are neither PIT nor TTC in a pure fashion. The question whether a rating system is of the type TTC or PIT is quite important. Obviously, we would expect that a TTC-rating method shows fewer rating migrations as the assignment of an upper and lower threshold for the PDs may be adjusted because the state of the economy is taken into consideration. Very often expert judgments override a rating assignment which originally resulted from a rating algorithm. For a further discussion of these issues we refer to Altman and Rijken (2006), Basel Committee on Banking Supervision (2005), or Varsany (2007).

In the following section we will take a closer look at quantitative techniques for determining credit ratings. Note, however, that when quantitative balance sheet data are used as the only input, these techniques should be considered as only a part of the complete rating procedure of an agency.

2.2 Scoring Systems

Credit scoring systems can be found in virtually all types of credit analysis, from consumer credit to commercial loans. The idea is to pre-identify certain key factors that determine the PD and combine or weight them into a quantitative score. This score can be either directly interpreted as a probability of default or used as a classification system.

The first research on bankruptcy prediction goes back to the 1930s (Fitzpatrick, 1932); however, two of the seminal papers in the area were published in the 1960s by Altman (1968) and Beaver (1966). Since then an impressive body of theoretical and especially empirical research concerning this topic has evolved. The most significant reviews can be found in Zavgren (1985), Altman (1983), Jones (1987), Altman and Narayanan (1997), Altman and Saunders (1998), and Balcaena and Oogh (2006). The latter provide a detailed survey of credit risk measurement approaches. Also, the major methodologies for credit scoring should be mentioned: linear probability models, logit models, probit models, discriminant analysis models, and, more recently, neural networks.

The linear probability model is based on a linear regression model, and makes use of a number of accounting variables to try to predict the probability of default. The logit model assumes that the default probability is logistically distributed and was initially suggested in Ohlson (1980). The usefulness of the approach in bankcruptcy predicting is illustrated, for example, in Platt and Platt (1991). Probit models were initially suggested for bankcruptcy prediction by Zmijewski (1984). They are quite similar to logistic regression (logit); however, the assumption of a normal distribution is applied. The multiple discriminant analysis (MDA), initially proposed and advocated by Beaver (1966) and Altman (1968), is based on finding a linear function of both accounting and market-based variables that best discriminate between the groups of firms that actually defaulted and firms that did not default. The models are usually based on empirical procedures: they search out the variables that seem best in predicting bankruptcies.

During the 1990s artificial neural networks also became more popular, since the method often produced very promising results in predicting bankruptcies; see, e.g., Wilson and Sharda (1994), Atiya (1997), and Tucker (1996). However, often no systematic way of identifying the predictive variables for the neural networks has been used in these studies. Genetic algorithms are a new promising method for finding the best set of indicators for neural networks. These algorithms have been applied successfully in several optimization problems, especially in technical fields. Note that a description of neural networks for rating procedures is beyond the scope of this chapter. For further reading we refer, e.g., to Wilson and Sharda (1994), Atiya (1997), Tucker (1996), and the references mentioned there.

Generally, in bankruptcy prediction, two streams of research can be distinguished: the most often investigated research question has been the search for the optimal predictors or financial ratios leading to the lowest misclassification rates. Another stream of literature has been concentrated on the search for statistical methods that would also lead to improved prediction accuracy.

Altman (1968) pioneered the use of a multivariate approach in the context of bankruptcy models. After the Altman study the multivariate approach became dominant in these models and until the 1980s discriminant analysis was the preferred method in failure prediction. However, it suffered from assumptions that were violated very often: the assumption of normality of the financial ratio distributions was problematic, particularly for the failing firms. During the 1980s the method was replaced by logit or probit models, which until recently were still the most popular statistical method for failure prediction purposes.

2.3 Discriminant Analysis

Discriminant analysis (DA) or multiple discriminant analysis (MDA) tries to derive the linear combination of two or more independent variables that will discriminate best between a priori defined groups, which in the most simple case are failing and nonfailing companies. In the two-group case, discriminant function analysis can also be thought of as (and is analogous to) multiple regression. If we code the two groups in the analysis as 1 and 2 and use that variable as the dependent one in a multiple regression analysis, analogous results to using a discriminant analysis could be obtained. This is due to the statistical decision rule of maximizing the between-group variance relative to the within group variance in the discriminant analysis technique. DA derives the linear combinations from an equation that takes the following form:

$$Z = w_0 + w_1 X_1 + w_2 X_2 + \cdots + w_n X_n \tag{2.1}$$

where Z is the discriminant score (Z score), w_0 is a constant, w_i ($i = 1, 2, \ldots, n$) the discriminant coefficients, and $X_i (i = 1, 2, \ldots, n)$ the independent variables, i.e., the financial ratios.

Probably the most famous MDA model goes back to Altman (1968). The Altman Z-score-model can be used as a classificatory model for corporate borrowers, but may also be used to predict default probabilities. In his analysis, based on empirical samples of failed and solvent firms and using linear discriminant analysis, the best fitting scoring model for commercial loans took the form

$$Z = 0.012 X_1 + 0.014 X_2 + 0.033 X_3 + 0.006 X_4 + 0.999 X_5 \tag{2.2}$$

where

$X_1 =$ working capital/total assets

$X_2 =$ retained earnings/total asset

X_3 = earnings before interest and taxes/total asset

X_4 = market value of equity/book value of total liabilities

X_5 = sales/total assets

The weights of the factors were initially based on data from publicly held manufacturers, but the model has since been modified for various other industries. To evaluate the resulting scores, when weighted by the estimated coefficients in the Z-function, results below a critical value (in Altman's initial study this was 1.81) would be classified as "bad" and the loan would be refused. Some basic ideas of Altman's model may be doubtful to still fulfill the needs of a powerful default prediction model: first, the model is based on linear relationships between the X_i's, whereas the path to bankruptcy may be highly nonlinear. Second, the model is based only on backward-looking accounting ratios. It is therefore questionable whether such models can pick up a firm whose condition is rapidly deteriorating. Therefore, during periods with a high number of defaults like, e.g., the Asian crisis in 1998 or the burst of the dot-com bubble in 2001, the model might not have a reliable predictive power.

Overall, the interpretation of the results of a DA or MDA two-group problem is straightforward and closely follows the logic of multiple regression: those variables with the largest standardized regression coefficients are the ones that contribute most to the prediction of group membership. In the end each firm receives a single composite discriminant score, which is then compared to a cut-off value that determines to which group the company belongs. Discriminant analysis does assume that the variables in every group follow a multivariate normal distribution and the covariance matrices for each group are equal. However, empirical experiments have shown that especially failing firms violate the normality condition (Press and Wilson, 1978). In addition, the equal group variances condition often is also violated. Moreover, multicollinearity among independent variables is often a serious problem, especially when stepwise procedures for the variable selection are employed. However, empirical studies have proven that the problems connected with normality assumptions were not weakening its classification capability, but its prediction ability. The two most frequently used methods in deriving the discriminant models have been the simultaneous (direct) method and the stepwise method. The former is based on model construction by, e.g., theoretical grounds, so that the model is ex ante defined and then used in discriminant analysis. When the stepwise method is applied, the procedure selects a subset of variables to produce a good discrimination model using forward selection, backward elimination, or stepwise selection. For further details on discrimant analysis and its application to credit risk modeling, we refer to, e.g., Altman and Saunders (1998).

2.4   Logit and Probit Models

In this section we will have a brief look at logistic regression and probit models that can be considered to be among the most popular approaches in the empirical default-prediction literature; see, e.g., Ohlson (1980), Platt and Platt (1991), and Zmijewski (1984). These models can be fairly easily applied to cases where the dependent variable is either nominal or ordinal and has two or more levels. Further, the independent variables can be any mix of qualitative and quantitative predictors.

The logit and probit regression models regress a function of the probability that a case falls in a certain category of the dependent variable Y, on a linear combination of X_i variables. The general form of both models is

$$Y = f\left(\beta_0 + \sum_{i=1}^{n} \beta_i X_i\right) \tag{2.3}$$

where β_0 has a constant value and the β_i's are the estimated weights of X_i, the transformed raw data. The whole term on the right side is the value that enters into a distribution function, which is either from the logistic (logit) or normal (probit) distribution. The right sides of the logit and probit, then, are the same as they are in the classical normal linear regression model. The slope coefficients tell us about the effect of a unit change in X on a function of the probability of Y, which will be explained later.

The difference between the logit and probit lies on the left side of the equation. In the logit approach the left side is the logit of Y, i.e., the log of the odds that a case falls in one category on Y versus another. For example, if Y denotes whether a child was born to a woman in a given year, the logit model would express the effects of X on the log of the odds of a birth versus a nonbirth. On the other hand, the left side of the probit model can be thought of as being a score similar to the discriminant analysis. In the probit model, a unit change in X_i produces a β_i unit change in the cumulative normal probability, or score, that Y falls in a particular category. For example, the probit model would express the effect of a unit change in X on the cumulative normal probability that a woman had a birth within a year.

Note that generally both the logit and the probit regression models are estimated by maximum likelihood. Consequently, goodness of fit and inferential statistics are based on the log likelihood and chi-square test statistics. One of the main challenges with logit and probit models is the interpretation of the descriptive statistics (the estimated regression function). A number of approaches are commonly used, and these will also be briefly examined below. For further details on logistic regression and probit models we refer, e.g., to Hosmer and Lemeshow (1989), Greene (1993), Maddala (1983), or Mccullagh and Nelder (1989).

2.4.1 Logit Models

Logistic regression analysis has also been used particularly to investigate the relationship between binary or ordinal response probability and explanatory variables. For bankruptcy prediction the binary response probability is usually the default probability, while a high number of explanatory variables can be used. The method usually fits linear logistic regression models for binary or ordinal response data by the method of maximum likelihood (Hosmer and Lemeshow, 1989). One of the first applications of the logit analysis in the context of financial distress can be found in Ohlson (1980) followed, e.g., by Zavgren (1985) to give only a few references. A good treatment on different logistic models, estimation problems, and applications can also be found in Greene (1993) or Maddala (1983). Similar to the discriminant analysis, this technique weights the independent variables and assigns a Y score in a form of failure probability (PD) to each company in a sample.

Let y_i denote the response of company i with respect to the outcome of the explanatory variables $x_{1i}, \ldots, x_{ki}$. For example, let $Y = 1$ denote the default of the firm and $Y = 0$ its survival. Then, using logistic regression, the PD for a company is denoted by

$$P(Y = 1 | x_1, \ldots, x_k) = f(x_1, \ldots, x_k) \tag{2.4}$$

The function f denotes the logistic distribution function such that we get

$$P(Y = 1 | x_1, \ldots, x_k) = \frac{exp(\beta_0 + \beta_1 x_1 + \cdots + \beta_n x_n)}{1 + exp(\beta_0 + \beta_1 x_1 + \cdots + \beta_n x_n)}. \tag{2.5}$$

Obviously, the logistic distribution function transforms the regression into the interval $(0, 1)$. Further defining the $logit(x)$ as

$$logit(x) = log\left(\frac{x}{1 - x}\right) \tag{2.6}$$

the model can be rewritten as

$$logit(P(Y = 1 | x_1, \ldots, x_k)) = \beta_0 + \beta_1 x_1 + \cdots + \beta_n x_n \tag{2.7}$$

with real constants $\beta_0, \beta_1, \ldots, \beta_n$. As mentioned above, the logit model can be estimated via maximum likelihood estimation using numerical methods. The advantage of the approach is that it does not assume multivariate normality and equal covariance matrices as, e.g., discriminant analysis does (Press and Wilson, 1978). In addition, logistic regression is well suited for problems when the predictor variable is binary or has multiple categorical levels, or even when there are multiple independent variables in the problem. For further reading on logit models, we refer to Maddala (1983) and Greene (1993).

2.4.2   Probit Models

Next to the logistic regression approach, probit models also have become quite popular to predict default probabilities of companies. For example, in one of its approaches, the rating agency Moody's KMV uses a probit model. Similar to the idea of logit models, the probability for a company defaulting is modeled based on a nonlinear function f:

$$P(Y = 1|x_1, \ldots, x_k) = f(x_1, \ldots, x_k) \tag{2.8}$$

However, for the probit model the following relationship is assumed:

$$P(Y = 1|x_1, \ldots, x_k) = \Phi(\beta_0 + \beta_1 x_1 + \cdots + \beta_n x_n) \tag{2.9}$$

where Φ denotes the distribution function of the standard normal distribution. Note that similar to the logistic distribution function, Φ also transforms the regression into the interval $(0, 1)$. Generally, the results for the probit model are supposed to be quite similar to the logistic regression model, unless the probabilities being predicted are very small or very large. Figure 2.1 displays the logit and probit distribution function for an exemplary model with only one independent variable and an exemplary choice of the parameters $\beta_0 = 0.1$ and $\beta_1 = 0.5$. Note that the interpretation of the probit coefficients is, in some senses, rather easier than it is for the logit model. The regression coefficients of the probit model are effects on a cumulative normal function of the probabilities that $Y = 1$ (i.e., the probability that a firm defaults). As such, they are already in a metric that can easily be understood: the metric of a standard normal score. Using this, one can interpret the coefficients directly. Note that also probit models are generally estimated using the maximum likelihood technique.

So far we have considered only the binary case, but it is straightforward to extend the logit and probit approach to a framework with ordered values for a higher number of rating categories. Applications of ordered probit models to credit rating can be found in, e.g., Amato and Furfine (2004), Hamerle et al. (2004), and Nickell et al. (2000). Recall that for a binary case we were assuming only two rating categories default: $y_i = 1$ and nondefault $y_i = 0$. Further, the outcome of a latent variable z_i according to the model determines whether company i is in default or not:

$$z_i = \beta_0 + \beta_1 x_{1i} + \cdots + \beta_n x_{ni} + \varepsilon_i \tag{2.10}$$

where ε_i denotes a random variable with a standard normal distribution. We further observe default $y_i = 1$ or nondefault $y_i = 0$ for the company

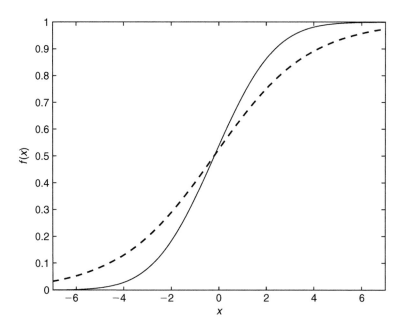

FIGURE 2.1. The logit (*dashed line*) and probit (*solid line*) function for parameters $\beta_0 = 0.1$ and $\beta_1 = 0.5$.

which is related to an unobserved threshold t_1 such that

$$y_i = \begin{cases} 0 & \text{if } z_i \leq t_1, \\ 1 & \text{if } z_i > t_1. \end{cases} \tag{2.11}$$

By introducing $K - 1$ thresholds t_k for the rating classes $k = 1, \ldots, K$, we can extend the approach in a way that, instead of having two rating levels for the binary model, we will then have K levels and $K - 1$ thresholds $t_1, \ldots, t_{K-1}$.

$$y_i = \begin{cases} 1 & \text{if } z_i \leq t_1, \\ 2 & \text{if } t_0 < z_i \leq t_2 \\ 3 & \text{if } t_1 < z_i \leq t_3 \\ \cdots & \cdots \\ K & \text{if } z_i > t_{K-1} \end{cases} \tag{2.12}$$

Note that also the t_k's are unknown parameters which collectively define a series of ranges into which the latent variable z_i may fall. Similar to the β's they will need to be estimated. As mentioned above it is assumed that

ε_i is the standard normally distributed such that the probabilities for y_i taking the values $k = 1, \ldots, K$ can be estimated by

$$P(y_i = 1) = \Phi(t_1 + \beta X_i) - \Phi(\beta X_i) \tag{2.13}$$

$$P(y_i = 2) = \Phi(t_2 + \beta X_i) - \Phi(t_1 + \beta X_i) \tag{2.14}$$

$$\cdots \qquad \cdots \tag{2.15}$$

$$P(y_i = K) = 1 - \Phi((t_{K-1}) + \beta X_i). \tag{2.16}$$

Note that hereby we define $\beta = (\beta_1, \ldots, \beta_n)'$ and $X_i = (x_{1i}, \ldots, x_{ki})$. For further reading, applications, and results on the use of ordered probit models, we refer to Amato and Furfine (2004), Hamerle et al. (2004), or Nickell et al. (2000). Note that with a similar procedure, it is also possible to extend the binary logit model to an ordered one with different categories. Overall, logit and probit are very close and rarely lead to different qualitative conclusions. As a general proposition, the question of the choice between them is unsolved (Greene, 1993).

2.5   Model Evaluation: Methods and Difficulties

The Basel Committee on Banking Supervision highlights the relatively informal nature of the credit model validation approaches at many financial institutions. In particular, the committee emphasized data sufficiency and model sensitivity analysis as significant challenges to validation. Overall, the committee has identified validation as a key issue in the use of quantitative default models and concluded that the area of validation will prove to be a key challenge for banking institutions in the foreseeable future (Basel Committee on Banking Supervision, 2001).

This section briefly describes a number of techniques that can be regarded as valuable for quantitative default model validation and benchmarking. More precisely, we focus on robust segmentation of the data for model validation and testing, and measures of model performance and inter-model comparison that are informative and currently used. These performance measures can be used to complement standard statistical measures.

2.5.1   Model Performance and Benchmarking

Here we will investigate two objective metrics to measure and compare the performance of credit rating risk models to predict default events; see Sobehart et al. (2000) to learn more about the cumulative accuracy profiles, also called power curves. To learn more about other accuracy ratios like Gini coefficients, Somers' D, or Kendall's Tau, see Somers, 1962a, 1938.

The techniques are quite general and can be used to compare a variety of model types.

The cumulative accuracy profiles (CAPs) can be used to make visual qualitative assessments of model performance. While similar tools exist under a variety of different names (lift-curves, dubbed-curves, receiver-operator curves (ROC), power curves, etc.), in the following we use the term "CAP" which refers specifically to the case where the curve represents the cumulative probability of default over the entire population. To plot a CAP, one first orders companies by their model score, from riskiest to safest. For a given fraction x of the total number of companies, a CAP curve is constructed by calculating the percentage $y(x)$ of the defaulters whose risk score is equal to or lower than the one for x.

Obviously, a good model concentrates the defaulters at the riskiest scores and, therefore, the cumulative percentage of all defaulters identified on the y axis increases quickly as the companies with the highest risk score are considered. If the model-assigned risk scores randomly, we would expect to capture a proportional fraction of the defaulters with about $x\%$ of the observations, generating approximately a straight line or random CAP. On the other hand, a perfect model would produce the ideal CAP curve, which is a straight line capturing 100% of the defaults within a fraction of the population equal to the fraction of defaulters in the sample. Because the fraction of defaulters is usually a small number, the ideal CAP is very steep.

Figure 2.2 exemplarily illustrates three CAP curves for a portfolio with a fraction of approximately 10% defaulted firms. Hereby, CAP curves for a random model, an exemplary scoring model, and the perfect model are provided. Obviously, one of the most useful properties of CAPs is that they reveal information about the predictive accuracy of the model over its entire range of risk scores for a particular time horizon. For the exemplary model in the figure, we find that among the 10% of companies with the highest risk score, approximately 35% of the defaulted firms were identified, while approximately 60% of defaulted companies were classified within the group of the 20% with highest risk scores. This kind of information may be particularly helpful to interpret the quality of a rating system with respect to different intervals of the scores.

It is often also convenient to have a single measure that summarizes the predictive accuracy of a model. To calculate one such summary statistic, one generally considers the area that lies above the random power curve and below the model power curve. The greater the area between the model power curve and the random power curve, the better is the overall performance of the model. The maximum area that can be enclosed above the random power curve is identified by the ideal power curve. Therefore, the ratio of the area between a model's power curve and the random power curve to the area between the ideal power curve and the random

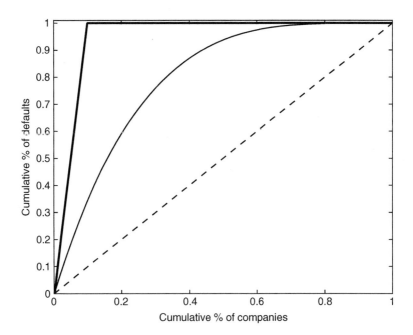

FIGURE 2.2. Illustration of the cumulative accuracy profile (CAP) for a portfolio with a fraction of 10% defaulted firms. The graph provides the CAP curves for a random model (*dashed line*), an exemplary scoring model (*solid line*), and the perfect model (*bold line*).

power curve summarizes the predictive power over the entire range of possible risk values:

$$AR = \frac{A - A_{random}}{A_{perfect} - A_{random}} \qquad (2.17)$$

This measure is called the accuracy ratio (AR), which is a fraction between 0 and 1. Obviously, values of the AR close to 0 display little advantage over a random assignment of risk scores, while those with AR values near 1 display almost perfect predictive power. Mathematically, the AR value can be calculated according to

$$AR = \frac{2 \int_0^1 y(x)dx - 1}{1 - f} \qquad (2.18)$$

Hereby, $y(x)$ is the power curve for a population x of ordered risk scores, and $f = D/(N+D)$ is the fraction of defaults, where D is the total number of defaulting obligors and N is the total number of nondefaulting obligors. The AR is a global measure of the discrepancy between the power curves.

Note, however, that because the comparison of ARs is relative to a database, our definition of the AR is not restricted to having completely independent samples. In fact, AR based on panel databases can provide aggregated information about the time correlation of the risk scores. Generally, most models provide an AR in the range of 50% to 75% for (out-of-sample and out-of-time) validation tests. Additionally, the absolute deviation of the AR due to resampling is generally not significantly different from the original AR (Moody's KMV, 2004).

Next to the AR, the literature also suggests a number of alternative measures to evaluate the performance of a scoring system. In the following, we will briefly describe the following accuracy measures:

- Gini-coefficient

- Somers' D

- Kendall's Tau

The Gini-measure is a very popular measure to quantify the accuracy of a rating system. Let $x_1, x_2, x_3, \ldots, x_n$ be the ordered cumulative percentages of a regarded sample, and thus $0 \leq x_1 \leq x_2 \leq x_3 \leq \cdots \leq x_n \leq 1$. Further, the cumulative relative distribution of the feature (default) is $F_1, F_2, \ldots, F_n$ with the quality that $F_{i+1} - F_i \geq F_i - F_{i-1}$ for $i = 2, 3, \ldots, n-1$. Therefore, the curve through the observations (x_i, F_i) is the called the power curve or CAP. The area under this curve can be calculated according to the following expression:

$$A = \frac{1}{2}x_1 F_1 + \frac{1}{2}\sum_{i=1}^{n-1}(F_i + F_{i+1})(x_{i+1} - x_i). \tag{2.19}$$

Further, let B be the area between the diagonal and the power curve with $B = 0.5 - A$. Then the Gini-coefficient G is calculated based on the following ratio:

$$G = \frac{B}{B + A} \tag{2.20}$$

Note that often an adjusted version of the Gini-coefficient is also used as reference to the perfect model and is able to compare samples with different fractions of the total defaults within a sample. For further reading on the application of the Gini-coefficient in credit scoring models, we refer, e.g., to Servigny and Renault (2004).

The measure Somers' D (Somers, 1962a) is a so-called asymmetric index of association between an independent variable and a dependent variable that can be measured on an ordinal scale. For the application to a rating system, it is based on a pairwise examination of the assigned risk scores and the ordinal-dependent variable default. Assume that two companies with an associated risk score—the independent variable—are examined in terms of their default behavior—the dependent variable. Then they must either be concordant, in the sense that the one ranked higher in terms of the risk score is also ranked higher than the other on the dependent variable. This means that a pair of companies is concordant if company A has a higher risk score than company B and A has defaulted while company B hasn't. The pair would be discordant if, despite the lower risk score, company B defaulted while company A didn't. Note that Somers' D allows for ties such as for the cases when both companies survived or both companies defaulted. The coefficient is defined as the difference between the number of concordant pairs N_c and the number of discordant pairs N_d divided by the total number of pairs that are not tied N:

$$D = \frac{N_c - N_d}{N} \qquad (2.21)$$

Values range from -1.0 (all pairs disagree) to 1.0 (all pairs agree). Two versions exist, a symmetric and asymmetric version, based on the symmetry of the sample. The symmetric version penalizes for tied pairs by averaging both variables, and the asymmetric version penalizes pairs tied on the dependent variable. The symmetric version is equal to Kendall's Tau-b that will be described in the following.

Kendall's Tau is an index of the degree of association between two variables measured on an ordinal scale or based on ranks (Somers, 1938). It is a directional, symmetric measure of association that is generally used for square tables. Similar to Somers' D, its computation involves examining every pair of items. Then the number of pairs that are similarly ranked and the number of pairs that are differently ranked relative to each other on the two variables are calculated. Kendall's coefficient of concordance, or Kendall's Tau, is then the difference between the number of concordant minus the number of discordant pairs divided by the total number of pairs. Again its value ranges from -1.0 (no association) to 1.0 (perfect association).

For further similarities and differences between Somers' D, Kendall's Tau, and alternative measures of association, we refer, e.g., to Somers (1962b), for a review of validation methodologies for default risk models to Sobehart et al. (2000).

2.5.2 Model Accuracy, Type I and II Errors

Measures like the accuracy ratio, Somers' D, or Kendall's Tau may be only one of many dimensions of model quality, as pointed out by Dhar and Stein (1997). Overall, when used as classification tools, default risk models can be mistaken in one of two ways. First, the model can indicate low risk when,

TABLE 2.4. Types of Errors in Assignment of Credit Ratings

Model	Actual	
	Low Credit Quality	High Credit Quality
Low Credit Quality	Correct Prediction	Type II Error
High Credit Quality	Type I Error	Correct Prediction

in fact, the risk is high. This Type I error corresponds to the assignment of high credit quality to issuers who nevertheless default or come close to defaulting in their obligations. The cost to the investor can be the loss of principal and interest, or a loss in the market value of the obligation. Second, the model can assign a low credit quality when, in fact, the quality is high. Potential losses resulting from this Type II error include the loss of return and origination fees when loans are either turned down or lost through noncompetitive bidding. These accuracy and cost scenarios are described schematically in Table 2.4.

Obviously, there are different costs involved with the two types of errors. The Type II error refers mainly to opportunity costs and lost potential profits from lost interest income and origination fees. Further there might be a loss from premature selling of a loan at disadvantageous prices. On the other hand the Type I error refers to lost interest and principal through defaults, recovery costs, and potential loss in market value. Unfortunately, minimizing one type of error usually comes at the expense of increasing the other. The trade-off between these errors is a complex and important issue. It is often the case, for example, that a particular model will outperform another under one set of cost assumptions, but can be disadvantaged under a different set of assumptions. Since different institutions have different cost and pay-off structures, it is difficult to present a single cost function that is appropriate across all firms. Therefore, it is very difficult to provide a general framework for optimal decision making of a financial institution with respect to wrong classification. Overall, this should be kept in mind when rating systems are calibrated or cut-off values are determined based on scoring methodologies.

3

The New Basel Capital Accord

3.1 Overview

This chapter is dedicated to the new Basel Capital Accord with respect to
rating based modeling, probabilities of default, and the required economic
capital of financial institutions. Almost two decades have passed since the
Basel Committee on Banking Supervision[1] (the Committee) introduced its
1988 Capital Accord (the Accord). The major impetus for this Basel I
Accord was the concern of the governors of the central banks that the
capital—as a "cushion" against losses—of the world's major banks had
become dangerously low after persistent erosion through competition.

Since 1988 the business of banking, risk management practices, supervisory approaches, and financial markets have undergone significant transformations. Consequently, the Committee released a proposal in June 1999
to replace the old Accord with a more risk-sensitive framework, the *New
Basel Capital Accord* (Basel II). After the committee received several comments by the industry and research institutions in January 2001, the second
consultative document was published. Again the suggestions were criticized a lot, and according to the committee, some features will be changed
again. Reflecting the comments on the proposal and the results of the
ongoing dialogue with the industry worldwide, the Committee published
a revised version in 2004 with the new corrections (Basel Committee on
Banking Supervision, 2004). In June 1999, the initial consultative proposal contained three fundamental innovations, each designed to introduce
greater risk sensitivity into the accord:

1. The current standard should be supplemented with two additional
   "pillars" dealing with supervisory review and market discipline. They
   should reduce the stress on the quantitative pillar one by providing a
   more balanced approach to the capital assessment process.

2. Banks with advanced risk management capabilities should be permitted to use their own internal systems for evaluating credit risk—known

---

[1]The Basel Committee on Banking Supervision (BCBS) is a committee of central
banks and bank supervisors from the major industrialized countries that meet every
three months at the *Bank for International Settlements* (BIS) in Basel.

as "internal ratings"—instead of standardized risk weights for each class of asset.

3. Banks should be allowed to use gradings provided by approved external credit assessment institutions to classify their sovereign claims into five risk buckets and their claims on corporates and banks into three risk buckets.

In addition, there were a number of other proposals including the refinement of the risk weightings as well as the introduction of a capital charge for other sources of risk. However, the basic definition of capital stayed the same. The comments on the June 1999 paper were numerous and reflected the important impact the old accord had. Nearly all welcomed the intention to refine the accord supported by the three-pillar approach because safety and soundness in today's dynamic and complex financial system can be attained only by the combination of effective bank-level management, market discipline, and supervision. Nevertheless, many details of the proposal were criticized. In particular, the threshold for the use of internal ratings should not be set so high as to prevent well-managed banks from using them.

The 1988 Accord focused on the total amount of bank capital, which is vital in reducing the risk of bank insolvency and the potential cost of a bank's failure for depositors. Building on this, the new framework intends to improve safety and soundness in the financial system by placing more emphasis on banks' own internal control and management, the supervisory review process, and the market discipline. Table 3.1 provides a summary of some of the reasons for a new capital accord. Although the new framework's focus is primarily on internationally active banks, its underlying principles are suitable for application to banks of varying levels of complexity and sophistication, so that the new framework can be adhered to by all significant banks within a certain period of time.

The 1988 Accord provided essentially only one option for measuring the appropriate capital of banks, although the way to measure, manage, and mitigate risks differs from bank to bank. In 1996 an amendment was

TABLE 3.1. Rationale for a New Accord and Differences Between Basel I and Basel II

Basel I Accord	Basel II Accord
Focus on a single risk measure	Emphasis on banks' own internal methodologies, supervisory review, and market discipline
One size fits all	Flexibility, menu of approaches, incentives for better risk management
Broad brush structure	More risk sensitive

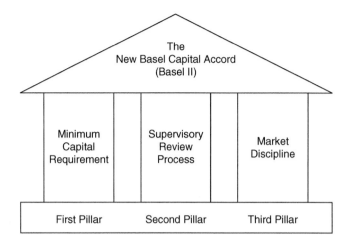

FIGURE 3.1. The three pillars of the new Basel Capital Accord.

introduced focusing on trading risks and allowing some banks for the first time to use their own systems to measure their market risks. The new framework provides a spectrum of approaches from simple to advanced methodologies for the measurement of both credit risk and operational risk in determining capital levels. Therefore, due to the less prescriptive guidelines of the new accord, capital requirements should be more in line with underlying risks and allow banks to manage their businesses more efficiently. Thus, credit ratings and the estimation of probabilities of default are major input variables for the new Accord.

The new Accord consists of three mutually reinforcing pillars, which together contribute to safety and soundness in the financial system. Figure 3.1 displays the three pillars: minimum capital requirements, supervisory review process, and market discipline. The Committee stresses the need for a rigorous application of all three pillars and plans to achieve the effective implementation of all aspects of the Accord.

3.1.1   The First Pillar—Minimum Capital Requirement

The first pillar sets out the minimum capital requirements and defines the minimum ratio of capital to risk-weighted assets. Therefore, it is necessary to know how the total capital is adequately measured by banks. The new framework maintains both the current definition of the total capital and the minimum requirement of at least 8% of the bank's capital to its risk weighted assets (RWA).

$$\text{Capital Ratio} = \frac{\text{Total Capital}}{\text{Credit Risk} + \text{Market Risk} + \text{Operational Risk}} \quad (3.1)$$

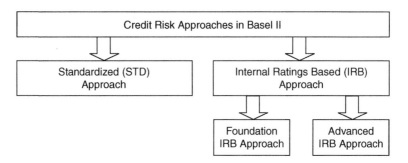

FIGURE 3.2. Different approaches to credit risk measurement in Basel II.

As one can see from formula 3.1, the calculation of the denominator of the capital ratio is dependent on three different forms of risk: credit risk, market risk, and operational risk. In particular the credit risk measurement methods are more elaborate than those in the current accord, whereas the market risk measure remains unchanged. Nevertheless, the new framework proposes for the first time a measure for operational risk.

For the measurement of credit risk two principal options are proposed that will briefly be discussed later. The first option is the *standardized* (STD) approach and the second the *internal ratings based* (IRB) approach. As illustrated in Figure 3.2, the latter offers two different options: a foundation and an advanced IRB approach. The use of the IRB approach is subject to an approval by the supervisors, based on standards established by the Committee.

The STD Approach: This approach is conceptually the same as the present Accord, but it is more risk sensitive. The bank allocates a risk weight to each of its assets and off-balance-sheet positions and produces a sum of RWA values. A risk weight of 100% means that an exposure is included in the calculation of RWA at its full value, which translates into a capital charge equal to 8% of that value. Similarly, a risk weight of 20% results in a capital charge of 1.6% (i.e., 20% of 8%). Individual risk weights currently depend on the broad category of the borrowers, which are sovereigns, banks, and corporates. Under the new Accord, the risk weights are refined by the reference to a rating provided by an *external credit assessment institution* (ECAI), such as rating agencies described in the previous chapter. For example, for corporate lending, the old Accord provided only one risk weight category of 100%, while the new Accord provides four categories: 20%, 50%, 100%, and 150%.

The IRB Approach: Under this approach, banks are allowed to use their internal estimates of borrower creditworthiness to assess credit risk in their portfolios, subject to strict methodological and disclosure standards. Distinct analytical frameworks are provided for different types of loan exposures whose loss characteristics are different. Under the IRB approach, banks estimate each borrower's creditworthiness and translate the results into estimates of a potential future loss amount, which forms the basis of MCR. The framework allows, on the one hand, a foundation method and, on the other hand, more advanced methodologies for corporate, sovereign, and bank exposures. In the foundation methodology, banks estimate the probability of default associated with each borrower, and the supervisors supply the other inputs. In the advanced methodology, a bank with a sufficiently developed internal capital allocation process is permitted to supply other necessary inputs as well. Under both IRB approaches, the range of risk weights is far more diverse than those in the STD approach, resulting in greater risk sensitivity.

Concerning the overall capital, the Committee's goal remains to neither raise nor to lower the aggregate regulatory capital—inclusive of operational risk—for internationally active banks using the STD approach. With regard to the IRB approach, the ultimate goal is to ensure that the regulatory capital requirement is sufficient to address underlying risks and contains incentives for banks to migrate from the STD to the more sophisticated IRB approach.

3.1.2   The Second Pillar—Supervisory Review Process

The supervisory review pillar requires supervisors to undertake a qualitative review of their bank's capital allocation techniques and compliance with relevant standards (Basel Committee on Banking Supervision, 2001). Supervisors have to ensure that each bank has sound internal processes to assess the adequacy of its capital based on a thorough evaluation of its risks. The new framework stresses the importance of bank management developing an internal capital assessment process and setting targets for capital that are commensurate with the bank's particular risk profile and control environment. Thus, supervisors are responsible for evaluating how well banks are assessing their capital adequacy needs relative to their risks. This internal process is—where it is appropriate—subject to supervisory review and intervention.

3.1.3   The Third Pillar—Market Discipline

The third pillar aims to bolster market discipline through enhanced disclosure requirements by banks which facilitate market discipline (Basel Committee on Banking Supervision, 2001). Effective disclosure is essential to ensure that market participants do better understand banks' risk profiles and the adequacy of their capital positions. The new framework sets out disclosure requirements and recommendations in several areas, including the way a bank calculates its capital adequacy and risk assessment methods. The core set of disclosure recommendations applies to all banks with more detailed requirements for supervisory recognition of internal methodologies for credit risk, mitigation techniques, and asset securitization.

3.2   The Standardized Approach

This section describes the STD approach to credit risk in the banking book, which is the simplest of the three broad approaches to credit risk and is not based on banks' internal rating systems like the other two approaches. Instead it assumes the use of external ratings provided by rating agencies. Compared to the old Accord, the STD approach aligns regulatory capital requirements more closely with the key elements of banking risk by introducing a wider differentiation of risk weights and a wider recognition of credit risk mitigation (CRM) techniques, while avoiding excessive complexity. Accordingly, the STD approach produces capital ratios more in line with the actual economic risks that banks are facing. This should improve the incentives for banks to enhance their risk management and measurement capabilities and reduce the incentives for regulatory capital arbitrage. In this review we will concentrate on the most discussed feature— the assignment of risk weights for sovereigns, banks, and, in particular, corporates.

Along the lines of the proposals in the consultative paper to the new capital adequacy framework, the RWA in the STD approach continue to be calculated as the product of the amount of exposures and supervisory determined risk weights:

$$RWA = E \cdot r \qquad (3.2)$$

where: E is the value of the exposure
r is the risk weight of the exposure

As in the old Accord, the risk weights are determined by the category— sovereigns, banks, and corporates—of the borrower. However, there is no distinction on the risk weighting depending on whether the country is a member of the OECD. Instead the risk weights for exposures depend on external credit assessments like rating agencies.

3.2.1   Risk Weights for Sovereigns and for Banks

Despite the concerns regarding the use of external credit assessments— especially credit ratings—the old Accord (with the 0% risk weight for all sovereigns) was replaced by an approach that relies on sovereign assessments of eligible ECAI. Following exemplarily the notation of

Standards & Poor's, the risk weights of sovereigns and their central banks are displayed in Table 3.2.

The assessments used should generally be with respect to the sovereign's long-term rating for domestic and foreign currency obligations. At national discretion, a lower risk weight may be applied to banks' exposures to the sovereign or central bank of incorporation denominated in domestic currency and funded in that currency. To address at least in part the concern expressed over the use of credit ratings and to supplement private sector ratings for sovereign exposures, there is also the possibility of using country risk ratings assigned to sovereigns by export credit agencies (ECAs). The key advantage of using publicly available ECA risk scores for sovereigns is that they are available for a far larger number of sovereigns than private ECAI ratings. Banks may then choose to use the risk scores produced by an ECA recognized by their supervisor. As displayed in Table 3.3, each of these ECA risk scores corresponds to a specific risk weight category.

Further there are also two options for deciding the risk weights on exposures to banks, but national supervisors have to apply one option to all banks in their jurisdiction. As a general rule for both options, no claim on an unrated bank may receive a risk weight less than that applied to its

TABLE 3.2. Risk Weights of Sovereigns—Option 1 in the New Basel Capital Accord

Rating	Risk Weights
AAA to AA−	0%
A+ to A−	20%
BBB+ to BBB−	50%
BB+ to B−	100%
Below B−	150%
Unrated	100%

TABLE 3.3. ECA Risk Score and Risk Weights of Sovereigns—Option 2 in the New Basel Capital Accord

Risk Scores	Risk Weights
1	0%
2	20%
3	50%
4 to 6	100%
7	150%

sovereign of incorporation. Under the first option—as shown in Table 3.4—all banks incorporated in a given country are assigned a risk weight one category less favorable than that assigned to claims on the sovereign of incorporation. Therefore, for banks within countries with a credit rating between AAA to AA−, the Committee remained with the 20% risk weight of the old Accord for all bank claims. However, for claims to banks in sovereigns rated BB+ to B− and unrated countries, the risk weight is capped at 100%. For banks in countries rated below B−, the risk weight is the same as for sovereigns and equals 150%.

The second option bases the risk weighting on the external credit assessment of the bank itself and is provided in Table 3.5. Note that under this option, a preferential risk weight can be applied to short-term claims of three months or less. Hereby, supervisors should ensure that claims with an original maturity under three months which are expected to be rolled over—i.e., where the effective maturity is longer than three months—do not qualify for this preferential treatment. This treatment is available to both rated and unrated bank claims, but not to banks risk weighted at 150%.

TABLE 3.4. Risk Weights for Exposures to Banks—Option 1 in the New Basel Capital Accord

Rating	Sovereign Risk Weights	Bank Risk Weights
AAA to AA−	0%	20%
A+ to A−	20%	50%
BBB+ to BBB−	50%	100%
BB+ to B−	100%	100%
Below B−	150%	150%
Unrated	100%	100%

TABLE 3.5. Risk Weights for Exposures to Banks—Option 1 in the New Basel Capital Accord

Rating	Risk Weights	Short-Term Claim Risk Weights
AAA to AA−	20%	20%
A+ to A−	50%	20%
BBB+ to BBB−	50%	20%
BB+ to B−	100%	50%
Below B−	150%	150%
Unrated	50%	20%

3.2.2 Risk Weights for Corporates

The maybe most-discussed feature of the new Basel Capital Accord is the assignment of different risk weights on corporate claims. Table 3.6 illustrates the risk weighting of rated corporate claims according to the new Accord, including claims on insurance companies. As a general rule, no claim on an unrated corporate may be given a risk weight preferential to that assigned to its sovereign of incorporation and the standard risk weight for unrated claims on corporates is 100%. As with the case of exposures to banks, there is no sovereign floor, recognizing that there are legitimate cases where a corporate can have a higher assessment than the sovereign assessment of its home country.

Note that the assignment of a risk weight of 100% to unrated companies might be questionable in some cases. One might argue that it provides an incentive to companies with lower credit quality to remain unrated and obtain better conditions for loans. However, the fact that a borrower is not rated does not signal low credit quality. In balancing these conflicting considerations, the Committee assigned a 100% risk weight to unrated corporates. This is the same risk weighting that all corporate exposures receive under the present Accord in order to not cause an unwarranted increase in the costs of funding for small and medium-sized businesses, which in most countries are a primary source of job creation and of economic growth. However, in countries with higher default rates, national authorities may increase the standard risk weight for unrated claims where they judge that a higher risk weight is warranted by their overall default experience.

3.2.3 Maturity

Although maturity is a relevant factor in the assessment of credit risk, it is difficult to pursue greater precision in differentiating among the maturities of claims within the STD approach given the rather general nature of the counterparty risk weighting. The STD approach is designed to be suitable for application by banks of varying degrees of size and sophistication. However, the costs of increasing the complexity of the STD approach are relatively high. In general, the benefits of improved risk sensitivity would be outweighed by the costs of greater complexity. Despite its improved risk

TABLE 3.6. Risk Weights of Corporates

Rating	Risk Weights
AAA to AA−	20%
A+ to A−	50%
BBB+ to BB−	100%
Below BB−	150%
Unrated	100%

sensitivity, the new STD approach remains intentionally simple and broad-brush. Therefore, a maturity dimension is not incorporated throughout the STD approach in contrast to the IRB approach. As set out above, the only maturity elements which are included are the distinction between short- and long-term commitments as is discussed below.

3.2.4 Credit Risk Mitigation

Credit risk mitigation (CRM) relates to the reduction of credit risk by, for example, taking collateral, obtaining credit derivatives or guarantees, or taking an offsetting position subject to a netting agreement.

The old Accord recognizes only collateral instruments and guarantees deemed to be identifiably of the very highest quality. This led to an all-or-nothing approach to credit risk mitigants: Some forms were recognized, while others were not. Since 1988, the markets for the transfer of credit risk have become more liquid and complex, and thus, the number of suppliers of credit protection has increased. New products such as credit derivatives have allowed banks to unbundle their credit risks in order to sell those risks that they do not wish to retain. These innovations result in greater liquidity in itself, reduce the transaction costs of intermediating between borrowers and lenders, and also encourage a more efficient allocation of risks in the financial system. In the new framework design for CRM, three main aims were pursued:

- Improving incentives for banks to manage credit risk in an effective manner.

- Offering an approach that may be adopted by a wide range of banks.

- Relating capital treatments to the economic effects of different CRM techniques and greater consistency in the treatment of different forms of CRM.

The revised approach allows a wider range of credit risk mitigants to be recognized for regulatory capital purposes and depart from the all-or-nothing approach. It also offers a choice of approaches that allow different banks to strike different balances between simplicity and risk sensitivity. As a result, there are three broad treatments to CRM depending on which credit risk approach is used by the banks. However, the treatment of CRM in the STD and in the foundation IRB approach is very similar. While CRM techniques generally reduce credit risk, they do not fully eliminate it. In such trans-actions, banks—often for good business reasons—leave some residual risks unhedged. Therefore, three forms of residual risk are explicitly addressed: asset, maturity, and currency mismatch. As a consequence the determi-nation of CRM numbers offers a lot of options and is too manifold to be described in this chapter. For further reading we refer to the original publications by the Bank of International Settlement (Basel Committee on Banking Supervision, 2001, 2004).

3.3   The Internal Ratings Based Approach

In this section we give a brief overview of the main ideas and input parameters of the IRB approach for corporate exposures in the new Basel Capital Accord. We further illustrate the one-factor model that is used for derivation of the so-called benchmark risk weight function in the IRB approach. Interestingly, factor models will also be used in later chapters, as it comes to calculating the impact of business cycle effects on conditional migration matrices. The IRB approach relies—opposite to Basel I or the STD—heavily upon a bank's internal assessment of its counterparties and exposures by rating systems as they were discussed in the previous chapter.

3.3.1   Key Elements and Risk Components

According to the consultative document (Basel Committee on Banking Supervision, 2001), the IRB approach has five key elements:

1. A classification of the exposures by broad exposure type.

2. For each exposure class, certain risk components which a bank must provide, using standardized parameters or its internal estimates.

3. A risk-weight function which provides risk weights (and hence capital requirements) for given sets of these components.

4. A set of minimum requirements that a bank must meet in order to be eligible for IRB treatment for that exposure.

5. Across all exposure classes, supervisory review of compliance with the minimum requirements.

The capital charge for the exposures then depends on a set of four risk components (inputs) which are provided either through the application of standardized supervisory rules (foundation methodology) or internal assessments (advanced methodology), subject to supervisory minimum requirements.

Probability of Default (PD): All banks—whether using the foundation or the advanced methodology—have to provide an internal estimate of the PD associated with the borrowers in each borrower grade. Each estimate of PD has to represent a conservative view of a long-run average PD for the grade in question and has to be grounded in historical experience and empirical evidence. The preparation of the estimates, the risk management processes, and the rating assignments that lie behind them have to reflect full compliance with supervisory minimum requirements to qualify for the IRB recognition.

Loss Given Default (LGD): While the PD—associated with a given borrower—does not depend on the features of the specific transaction, LGD is facility-specific. Losses are generally understood to be influenced by key transaction characteristics such as the presence of collateral and the degree of subordination. The LGD value can be determined in two ways: in the first way—respectively under the foundation methodology—LGD is estimated through the application of standard supervisory rules. The differentiated levels of LGD are based upon the characteristics of the underlying transaction, including the presence and the type of collateral. The starting point is a value of 45% for senior claims, whereas a higher value of 75% is applied to subordinated exposures, but the percentage can be scaled to the degree to which the transaction is secured. If there is a transaction with financial collateral, a so-called haircut methodology is used. Note that a separate set of LGD values is applied to transactions with real estate collateral. In the advanced methodology LGD, which is applied to each exposure, is determined by the banks themselves. Thus, banks using internal LGD estimates for capital purposes are able to differentiate LGD values on the basis of a wider set of transaction and borrower characteristics.

Exposure at Default (EAD): As with LGD, EAD is also facility-specific. Under the foundation methodology, EAD is estimated through the use of standard supervisory rules and is determined by the banks themselves in the advanced methodology. In most cases, EAD is equal to the nominal amount of the exposure but for certain exposures—e.g., those with undrawn commitments—it includes an estimate of future lending prior to default.

Maturity (M): Where maturity is treated as an explicit risk component, as in the advanced approach, banks are expected to provide supervisors with the effective contractual maturity of their exposures. Where there is no explicit adjustment for maturity, a standard supervisory approach is presented for linking effective contractual maturity to capital requirements.

After introducing the input parameters of the IRB approach, we will now briefly describe how the benchmark risk weight function in the new accord can be derived based on a so-called one-factor credit risk model.

3.3.2 Derivation of the Benchmark Risk Weight Function

In credit risk models the discrete event of default is often modeled with a random variable Y which follows a Bernoulli law. This means that Y can take on either 0 or 1 where we assume that $Y = 1$ indicates that the firm defaults. Since the seminal work of Merton in 1972, the so-called structural models using the value of the firm as input variable for determining default probabilities are very popular in credit risk management. In a Merton-style model a firm is said to default if the value of the total assets drops below a certain threshold D, the contractual value of its obligations. The probability of default thus becomes

$$P(Y = 1) = P(V < D) \tag{3.3}$$

The idea of a company defaulting if the value of its assets falls below a threshold c_i is also used in the derivation of the credit Value-at-Risk model of the Basel Committee; see, e.g., Gordy (2002). Let $Z_{i,t}$ therefore be the asset change of company i within a time interval t. In the so-called one-factor models (Belkin et al., 1998a), $Z_{i,t}$ is considered to have a Gaussian distribution with mean 0 and variance 1. This variable can be decomposed in the following way:

$$Z_{i,t} = \sqrt{\rho}\, X_t + \sqrt{1 - \rho}\, \varepsilon_{i,t} \tag{3.4}$$

with $X_t \sim N(0, 1)$ and $\varepsilon_{i,t} \sim N(0, 1)$. The interpretation is that the random effect of the asset value of borrower i is a combination of a systematic risk factor X_t which affects all borrowers, and an idiosyncratic risk factor $\varepsilon_{i,t}$ affecting only borrower i. Hereby, it is assumed that the $\varepsilon_{i,t}$ are independent identically distributed (iid) for all i and t, while the X_t are also iid. The parameter $\sqrt{\rho}$ is often called the factor loading of the systematic risk factor and is interpreted as the sensitivity against systematic risk. Put mathematically, it is simply the square root of the correlation coefficient of the asset value process with the systematic risk factor.

The probability of default can now be formulated as

$$P(Y_{i,t} = 1) = P(Z_{i,t} < c_i) = \Phi(c_i) \tag{3.5}$$

This is the *unconditional* default probability. If the outcome of the systematic risk factor was known, we could calculate the *conditional* probability of default

$$P(Y_{i,t} = 1 | X_t = x) = P(Z_{i,t} \leq c_i | X_t = x) \tag{3.6}$$

$$= P(\sqrt{\rho}\, X_t + \sqrt{1 - \rho}\, \epsilon_{i,t} \leq c_i | X_t = x)$$

$$= P\left(\epsilon_{i,t} < \frac{c_i - \sqrt{\rho} X_t}{\sqrt{1 - \rho}} \Big| X_t = x\right)$$

$$= \Phi\left(\frac{c_i - \sqrt{\rho} x}{\sqrt{1 - \rho}}\right)$$

Hereby, Φ denotes the cumulative standard normal distribution function. Having modeled the probability of default for an individual loan, we now have to establish a model for a whole loan portfolio. Consider a portfolio consisting of n loans to different borrowers where each borrower's probability of default is modeled as described above. We further assume that all borrowers have the same default threshold c. Then, conditional on the state of the economy X, the probability of having k defaults in the portfolio is binomially distributed:

$$P\left(\sum_{i=1}^{n} Y_{i,t} = k \Big| X_t = x\right) = \binom{n}{k} p(x)^k (1 - p(x))^{n-k} \quad (k = 0, \ldots, n) \quad (3.7)$$

with $p(x) = \Phi[(c - \sqrt{\rho}x)/(\sqrt{1-\rho})]$. Using the law of iterated expectations, the probability of k defaults is the expected value of the conditional probability of k defaults:

$$P\left(\sum_{i=1}^{n} Y_{i,t} = k\right) = \int_{-\infty}^{\infty} P\left(\sum_{i=1}^{n} Y_{i,t} = k \Big| X_t = x\right) \phi(x) dx$$

$$= \int_{-\infty}^{\infty} \binom{n}{k} \left(\Phi\left(\frac{c - \sqrt{\rho}x}{\sqrt{1-\rho}}\right)\right)^k \left(1 - \Phi\left(\frac{c - \sqrt{\rho}x}{\sqrt{1-\rho}}\right)\right)^{n-k} \phi(x) dx \quad (3.8)$$

Having described the theoretical model of defaults, we will now investigate how these equations are linked to the IRB framework of Basel II. As it was mentioned above, the IRB functions are based on the VaR measure. With the probability of k defaults in a homogenous portfolio of size n, given in equation (3.8), the cumulative loss distribution function of the portfolio is

$$P\left(\sum_{i=1}^{n} Y_{i,t} \leq m\right) = \sum_{k=0}^{m} \int_{-\infty}^{\infty} \binom{n}{k} (p(x))^k (1 - p(x))^{n-k} \phi(x) dx,$$

$$m = 0, \ldots, n. \quad (3.9)$$

Thus, to determine, for example, the Value-at-Risk at the 99.9% level, one would need to compute $P^{-1}(0.999)$. This is tedious work and will have to be done numerically. Fortunately, VaR can be approximated efficiently in one-factor models. For example, Gordy (2002) provides a portfolio-invariant rule for capital charges at the level of a single loan and thus the foundation of the Basel IRB function.

Let $\alpha_{0.999}$ denote the adverse 99.9% quantile of the state of the economy X_t, meaning that a worse outcome of the systematic risk factor has only a 0.01% chance. Since X_t is standard normally distributed with small values of X_t being unfavorable to a firm, $\text{VaR}(99.9\%) = \Phi^{-1}(0.001)$. Conditional on this bad state of the economy, the probability of default for an individual loan is

$$P(Y_{i,t} = 1 | X_t = \alpha_{0.999}) = \Phi \left(\frac{c_i - \sqrt{\rho}\Phi^{-1}(0.001)}{\sqrt{1-\rho}} \right)$$

and the expected loss on the loan is

$$E[L_i | X_t = \alpha_{0.999}] = LGD \cdot \Phi \left(\frac{c_i - \sqrt{\rho}\Phi^{-1}(0.001)}{\sqrt{1-\rho}} \right) \qquad (3.10)$$

Gordy shows in his work how the sum of these expected conditional losses approaches the true VaR(99.9%) of the whole loan portfolio. Note that for the needed regularity conditions and the exact type of convergence, we refer to Gordy (2002). The threshold c_i can be determined from the PD of the respective loan in the following way:

$$PD_i = P(Y_{i,t} = 1) = P(Z_{i,t} < c_i)$$

Since $Z_{i,t} \sim N(0,1)$ it follows that

$$PD_i = \Phi(c_i) \Leftrightarrow \Phi^{-1}(PD_i) = c_i \qquad (3.11)$$

Taken together (3.10) and (3.11) yield the core of the Basel IRB function to determine the regulatory capital charge on a single loan. With the fact that the standard normal distribution is symmetric around the origin, we get the formula for the so-called worst-case default rate (WCDR) that is used in the Basel II IRB approach:

$$WCDR = \Phi \left(\frac{\Phi^{-1}(PD_i) + \sqrt{\rho}\Phi^{-1}(0.999)}{\sqrt{1-\rho}} \right) \qquad (3.12)$$

This can be considered as the core of the function for calculating the RWA in the Basel II IRB approach. Overall, the formula for RWA suggested in the final version of the new Basel Capital Accord is

$$RWA = 12.5 \times EAD \times LGD \times (WCDR - PD) \times MA \qquad (3.13)$$

Note that the RWA equals 12.5 times the capital required, so that the required capital is 8% of RWA. Obviously next to the probability of default PD, the worst-case default rate WCDR, and the factors exposure at default (EAD), loss given default (LGD), and a maturity adjustment (MA) enter the calculation of RWA. Further, the calculated WCDR is dependent on a correlation parameter ρ. Let us now have a look at these parameters and how they actually enter the calculation of the RWA.

3.3.3 Asset Correlation

The initial version of the new Accord made an implicit assumption that asset correlation for all exposures is equal to 0.2. There has been quite some criticism about this assumption, and the Basel Committee decided to implement a revised formula for RWA where the correlation parameter depends on the estimated PD. Following Lopez (2004), the relationship between PD and correlation can be described by the following expression:

$$\rho(PD) = 0.12 \cdot \left(\frac{1 - e^{-50PD}}{1 - e^{-50}} \right) + 0.24 \cdot \left(1 - \left(\frac{1 - e^{-50PD}}{1 - e^{-50}} \right) \right) \quad (3.14)$$

A very close approximation of this relationship is provided by the more simple expression

$$\rho(PD) = 0.12 \cdot (1 + e^{-50PD}) \quad (3.15)$$

Obviously, according to these expressions, the correlation declines with increasing PD as illustrated by Figure 3.3. Lopez (2004) suggests the following reasons for this relationship: as the PD of a company increases, default becomes more dependent on the idiosyncratic risk of the company and is less affected by overall market conditions. Therefore, the correlation parameter ρ decreases when a company becomes less creditworthy. Note

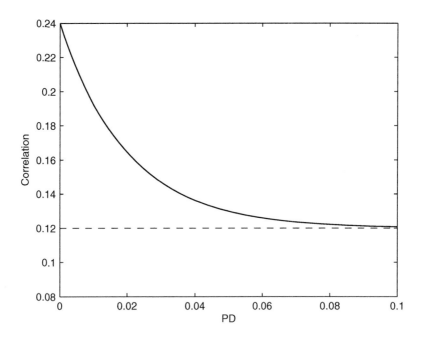

FIGURE 3.3. Relationship between the correlation parameter and the probability of default (PD) in the new Basel Capital Accord.

that results from other studies (Dietsch and Petey, 2004; Düllmann and Scheule, 2003; Rösch, 2002) have not confirmed this relationship; also see, e.g., Henneke and Trueck (2006) for a review on the issue.

However, the assumption of a decrease in correlation with increasing PD also has the effect that WCDR increases not as fast as it would if ρ was assumed to be constant. This was also a reaction to the fact that a lot of criticism was directed towards the initial version of the new Accord, which gave extremely risky weights to companies with higher probability of defaults; see, e.g., Henneke and Trueck (2006). The suggestions of the IRB approach of the second consultative document were subject to extensive discussions. Especially small and medium-sized companies (SMEs) were afraid of higher capital costs for banks that would lead to worse credit conditions for these companies. Also the desired incentive character of the IRB approach for banks was very questionable, since risk weights in many cases were rather higher for the IRB approach than for the STD approach. There was a clear tendency in the IRB approach of assigning lower risk weights to companies with a very good rating and much higher risk weights to such companies with a lower rating. Therefore, the assumption of a decreasing coefficient of correlation in the final version of the Accord keeps the WCDR on a lower level for more risky companies. The relationship between WCDR and PD is illustrated in Figure 3.4.

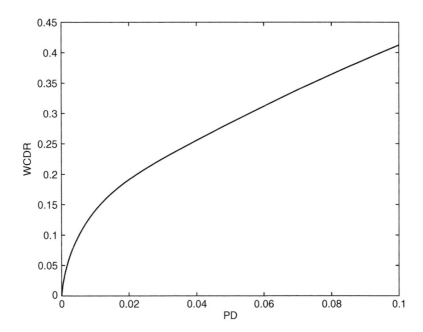

FIGURE 3.4. Relationship between the worst-case default rate (WCDR) and the probability of default (PD) in the new Basel Capital Accord.

3.3.4   The Maturity Adjustment

Especially in the advanced IRB approach, maturity is treated as an explicit risk component. The sensitivity of a loan's end-of-horizon value to a credit quality deterioration short of default is dependent on its maturity. As a consequence, maturity has a substantial influence on economic capital within so-called mark-to-market (MTM) models, with longer-maturity loans requiring greater economic capital. However, also the initially assumed relationship between maturity and the assigned risk weights of the second consultative document was subject to criticism. Figure 3.5 illustrates the extremely high risk weights allocated to companies with a lower rating and long maturities as it was suggested in the initial version of the new Accord.

Comparing the assigned risk weights to actually observed spreads in the market—see, for example, in Chapter 4—one could find that especially for lower rated bonds, market credit spreads do not show a positive correlation with maturity. For Ba rated bonds the spreads are constant, while for single B rated bonds the spreads usually fall as maturity increases. The problems and criticism mentioned above were also confirmed by so-called quantitative impact studies (QIS) conducted by banks for the Basel committee. Therefore, in the final and revised version of the accord for the

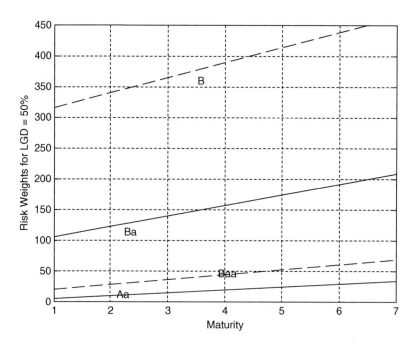

FIGURE 3.5. Assigned risk weights in CP2 as a function of the maturity for different rating classes.

IRB foundation approach, all exposures are assumed to have an average maturity of 2.5 years. Additionally, in the advanced IRB approach in recognition of the unique characteristics of national markets, supervisors will have the option of exempting smaller domestic firms from the maturity framework. In this framework smaller domestic firms are defined as those with consolidated sales and consolidated assets of less than Euro 500 million. If the exemption is applied, those firms will be assumed to have an average maturity of 2.5 years, as under the foundation IRB approach.

For firms with sales greater than Euro 500 million in the advanced IRB approach, the maturity adjustment will be included according to the following factor:

$$MA = \frac{(1 + b(PD) \cdot (M - 2.5)}{1 - 1.5b(PD)} \tag{3.16}$$

with

$$b(PD) = (0.11852 - 0.05478 \log(PD))^2 \tag{3.17}$$

The denominator in the fraction can be interpreted as an adjustment to the average maturity of 2.5 years, while the numerator is the maturity adjustment based on the PD of the exposure and its maturity.

Table 3.7 shows the exemplary maturity adjustments compared to a one-year maturity of an exposure. Obviously for exposures with higher default probabilites the effect of the maturity is much smaller than for higher rated exposures. This points out the intention of the Basel

TABLE 3.7. Maturity Adjustment in the June 2004 Version of the Basel Capital Accord (Factors in Comparison to an Exposure with a One-Year Maturity)

PD	M = 1	M = 2	M = 2.5	M = 3	M = 4	M = 5
0.03%	1.000	1.604	1.906	2.208	2.811	3.415
0.05%	1.000	1.501	1.752	2.002	2.504	3.005
0.10%	1.000	1.392	1.588	1.784	2.177	2.569
0.50%	1.000	1.223	1.334	1.446	1.669	1.892
1.00%	1.000	1.173	1.260	1.346	1.520	1.693
5.00%	1.000	1.091	1.136	1.182	1.272	1.363
10.00%	1.000	1.066	1.099	1.132	1.197	1.263
15.00%	1.000	1.053	1.080	1.107	1.160	1.214
20.00%	1.000	1.046	1.068	1.091	1.137	1.183
25.00%	1.000	1.040	1.060	1.080	1.120	1.160
30.00%	1.000	1.036	1.054	1.072	1.108	1.143

Committee to avoid extremely high benchmark risk weights and, thus, capital requirements for more risky exposures with longer maturities.

3.3.5   Expected, Unexpected Losses and the Required Capital

Finally, a novelty in Basel II is the calibration of the risk weights only to unexpected losses. Therefore, in equation (3.13) the probability of default—corresponding to the expected loss—is subtracted from the worst-case default rate. For illustration, consider the following expression:

$$UL = \underbrace{LGD \cdot \Phi\left(\frac{\Phi^{-1}(PD_i) + \sqrt{\rho}\Phi^{-1}(0.999)}{\sqrt{1 - \rho}} \right)}_{EL+UL} - \underbrace{LGD \cdot PD_i}_{EL}$$

$$= LGD \times (WCDR - PD) \tag{3.18}$$

Thus, for the first time the required capital is based only on unexpected losses, and not the sum of expected plus unexpected losses. This also leads to a reduction of the regulatory capital. One concern that has been identified in the Committee's prior impact surveys has been the potential gap between the capital required under the Basel I approach and the standardized, foundation, and advanced IRB approaches. The overall relationship between the risk-weighted assets (RWA) and the probability of default (PD) for corporate exposures assuming $LGD = 0.45$ for senior claims and $LGD = 0.75$ for subordinated claims is provided in Figure 3.6. Note that for comparison, the comparable risk weight of 100% under the old capital accord is displayed.

We conclude that the capital requirements for the various exposures in the final document have been designed to be consistent with the Committee's goal of neither significantly decreasing nor increasing the aggregate level of regulatory capital in the banking system. The main focus in the final changes of the benchmark risk-weight function of the IRB approach was to reduce the relatively high risk weights for risky exposures as they were allocated in the initial version of the new Accord. From this angle one can conclude that the final version of the Capital Accord gives banks dealing with such companies a much better position than earlier versions.

3.4   Summary

In 1988 when the first Capital Accord was published, there was only one option for measuring the appropriate capital of internationally active banks. Since then the business of banking and the financial markets have undergone significant changes. Therefore, the Committee was obliged to develop a new Accord which should be more comprehensive and more risk sensitive to the default risk of the obligor than the old one. As a consequence,

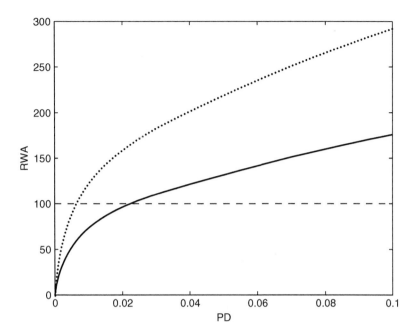

FIGURE 3.6. Relationship between the risk-weighted assets (RWA) and the probability of default (PD) for corporate exposures. The figure provides the RWA for senior claims (LGD = 0.45) (*solid line*), subordinated claims (LGD = 0.75) (*dotted line*), and under the old capital (*dashed line*).

under the new Basel Capital Accord, banks will have the opportunity to choose one of three approaches to credit risk for their portfolios. The choice whether a bank uses the STD, the foundation IRB, or the advanced IRB approach depends critically on the ability of estimating its own risk components and on meeting supervisory requirements. However, in the long run all internationally active banks should use the advanced IRB approach or at least the foundation IRB approach in line with improvements in their risk management practices and in line with the benefit in holding their intrinsic amount of credit risk.

Overall, one can conclude that due to the new Basel Capital Accord the importance of rating based models for credit risk has been enhanced. This might also lead to an extended and more sophisticated use of credit rating systems and migration matrices. Overall, banks will not only be interested in ratings to determine their capital charges, but also in the calculation of the Value-at-Risk, migration behavior, and other related issues for their credit or loan portfolios. Based on internal ratings that have to be provided within the new Basel Capital Accord, the application of a migration matrix approach that also takes into account rating changes and not just the default case will be straightforward.

4
Rating Based Modeling

In the previous chapters we gave a brief overview of the ideas and application of the rating processes to credit risk and how ratings and estimates of
PDs are incorporated into the new Basel Capital Accord. In reduced form or
rating based models, ratings are the decision variable as it comes to determining the loss distribution of portfolios or the credit VaR. The popularity
of these models comes from the straightforwardness of the approach but is
also a consequence of the upcoming new Capital Accord of the Basel Committee on Banking Supervision (2001) that was described in the previous
chapter.

Despite some deficiencies of the current credit rating structure and the
fact that rating agencies failed to provide adequate ratings for several products in the credit and credit derivative markets (Crouhy et al., 2008), the
importance of credit ratings in financial risk management cannot be underestimated. Rating based models of credit risk have evolved as an industry
standard and ratings of a company or product will remain one of the most
important variables when it comes to modeling and measurement of credit
risk.

4.1   Introduction

Note that in this chapter we will not elaborate on structural or firm-value
models, but concentrate only on a number of academic and industry models
that have been suggested in the literature. For further reading on structural
models, we refer, e.g., to Crosbie and Bohn (2002), Lando (2004), or a more
recent review by Elizalde (2006) and the references provided there. Fons
(1994) was the first who developed a so-called reduced form model and
derived credit spreads using historical default rates and recovery rate estimates. In his model he used the rating of a company and historical default
probabilities as decisive variables and not the value of the firm. Although
his approach is rather simple compared to other theoretical models of credit
risk, the predicted credit spreads derived by the model showed strong similarity towards real market data. Since then a variety of intensity models
have been developed using ratings and corresponding default intensities as
a starting point for the evaluation of credit risk. In this chapter we will also
briefly review some of the earlier models in this area. However, these models

generally do not explicitly deal with rating migrations to other states but are rather concerned with transitions to default only. Therefore, we will outline only the basic underlying ideas here and refer to more comprehensive treatments of such models in Duffie and Singleton (2003), Lando (2004), or Schönbucher and Schubert (2001).

Overall, not only the worst case event of default has influence on the price of a bond, but also a change in the rating of a company can affect prices of the issued bond. Clearly, deterioration or improvement in the credit quality of the issuer is highly important. One common way to express changes in the credit quality of market participants is to consider the ratings given by agencies like Standard & Poor's or Moody's, etc. Downgrades or upgrades by the rating agencies are taken very seriously by market players for pricing bonds and loans and, thus, affect the risk premium and the yield spreads. With CreditMetrics JP Morgan provides a framework (Gupton et al., 1997) for quantifying credit risk in portfolios using historical transition matrices. Further, refining Fons model, Jarrow et al. (1997) introduced a discrete-time Markovian model to estimate changes in the price of loans and bonds. Further, Wilson (1997b) and the suggested CreditPortfolioView model (CreditPortfolioView, 1998) take into account the risk arising from credit migrations and suggest use of conditional transition matrices based on a business cycle index. All three approaches incorporate possible rating upgrades, stable ratings, and rating downgrades (with default as a special event) in the reduced-form approach. For determining the price of credit risk, both historical default rates and transition matrices are used. While the CreditMetrics framework will be described in this section for the seminal work of Jarrow et al. (1997), we refer to Chapter 8 where we deal with risk-neutral and real-world migration matrices. The CreditPortfolioView model is described in more detail in Chapter 9 where we deal explicitly with adjusting and forecasting conditional migrations.

Finally, we will also give brief a description of Credit Suisse First Boston's CreditRisk$^+$ model that applies actuarial techniques commonly used for insurance matters to the modeling of credit risk (Credit Suisse Financial Products, 1998). Here, default as the elementary event that drives credit risk is modeled directly by assuming a Bernoullian default game for every firm. Note that while for this model ratings and default probabilities are a substantial input parameter for determination of the risk, generally downgrade risk is not captured as well.

4.2 Reduced Form and Intensity Models

In 1994, Jerome S. Fons developed a reduced form model to derive credit spreads using historical default rates and a recovery rate estimate (Fons, 1994). The approach is based on the results of Moody's corporate bond default studies, which at that time covered 473 defaults of issuers that ever held a Moody's corporate bond rating between January 1, 1970, and

December 31, 1993. He found out that the term structure of credit risk, i.e., the behavior of credit spreads as maturity varies, seems to depend on the issuer's credit quality, i.e., its rating. For bonds rated investment grade, the term structures of credit risk have an upward sloping structure. The spread between the promised yield-to-maturity of a defaultable bond and a default-free bond of the same maturity widens as the maturity increases. On the other hand, speculative grade rated bonds behave in the opposite way: the term structures of the credit risk have a downward sloping structure. Fons's findings are equivalent to the crisis at maturity hypothesis which assumes that highly leveraged firms with near term debt face a great uncertainty with respect to their ability to meet their obligations. Speculative grade rated firms, once past these obstacles and having survived without a default, face a lower risk of default for time horizons of five years or more. Well-established, large, and solid investment grade firms, on the other hand, face a low default risk on the near term, while their credit outlook over longer time horizons, such as 10 or more years, is less certain. In every rating category, Fons compares term structures of credit spreads with weighted-average marginal default rates, using data from Moody's investigations. In his model, Fons assumes that investors are risk neutral. The risky bond price $B(0,T)$ with face value B maturing at time T supplied by Fons can be used to infer the credit spread on that bond by means of a formula which links the price of the bond to its yield to maturity. The price of a risky bond in $t = 0$ can be expressed in terms of its yield, with r being the riskless yield and s being the credit spread:

$$B(0,T) = B \cdot e^{-(r+s) \cdot T}$$

whereas the price of a riskless security is

$$B'(0,T) = B \cdot e^{-r \cdot T}$$

We denote $d_R(t)$ as the probability of default in year t after the bond was assigned rating R, given that the bond has not defaulted before that date. Seen from date $t = 0$, $S_R(t)$ is the survival probability at date t. In the event of default the investor receives a fraction μ of par, the recovery rate. $S_R(t)$ is given by

$$S_R(t) = \prod_{j=1}^{t}(1 - d_R(j))$$

whereas the probability that the bond rated R will default in year t is given by

$$D_R(t) = S_R(t-1) \cdot d_R(t) = \prod_{j=1}^{t-1}(1 - d_r(j)) \cdot d_R(t)$$

The expected value of the random flow X_t received in t is such that

$$E(X_t) = S_R(t-1) \cdot d_R(t) \cdot \mu \cdot B'(0, t)$$

The price of zero-coupon bond with initial rating R maturing at T is then the sum of the expected returns in each year:

$$B_R(0, T) = \underbrace{\sum_{t=1}^{T} E(x_t)} + S_R(T) \cdot B'(0, T)$$

$$= \underbrace{\sum_{t=1}^{T} S_R(t-1) \cdot d_r(t) \cdot \mu \cdot B \cdot e^{-r \cdot t}}_{\text{Bond defaults in } t = 1 \ldots T} + \underbrace{S_R(T) \cdot B \cdot e^{-r \cdot T}}_{\text{No Default}}$$

Thus, with this formula we can compute the spread s of the risky zero bond:

$$s = -\frac{1}{T} \ln \left[\sum_{t=1}^{T} S_R(t-1) \cdot d_r(t) \cdot \mu \cdot e^{-r(t-T)} + S_R(T) \right]$$

Fons determines the term structure of credit risk by calculating the spreads for zero bonds of every maturity T. Obviously, Fons's model also requires an estimate of the recovery rate of a bond, which usually does not depend on the initial rating, but on its seniority and the bankruptcy laws of the issuer's home country. Figures 4.1 and 4.2 show the term structures of credit spreads calculated by Fons's model, using historical probabilities of Moody's default database, assuming a fixed recovery rate of 48.38% of the par value.

The model by Fons (1994) was based on relating the observed term structure of credit spreads to cumulative default rates observed by one of the major rating agencies. Therefore, unlike in structural models using the firm value as the input variable for determining probability of defaults or credit spreads, his approach relates observed market spreads and default probabilities to the rating of company or bond. His model can be considered as one of the first reduced form approaches to the modeling of credit spreads and default risk. Since then various intensity models have been developed using ratings and corresponding default intensities as a starting point for the evaluation of credit risk. In the following we will provide a brief review of earlier models in this area. Note that since these models generally do not explicitly deal with rating migrations to other states but are rather concerned with transitions to default only, we will outline only the basic underlying ideas here. For further reading, we refer to, e.g., the excellent treatments of these models in Duffie and Singleton (2003), Lando (2004), or Schönbucher and Schubert (2001).

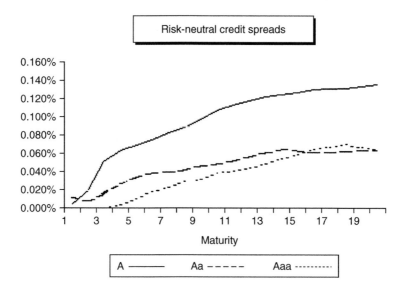

FIGURE 4.1. Term structure of credit spreads for investment grade rating categories Aaa, Aa, and A (Source: Fons, 1994).

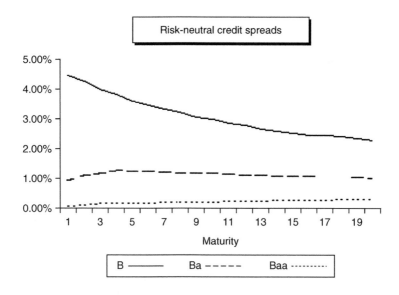

FIGURE 4.2. Term structure of credit spreads for rating categories Baa, Ba, and B (Source: Fons, 1994).

Generally, reduced-form models allow for surprise defaults. They model the time of default as an exogenous process without making assumptions from some underlying asset. Therefore, the default event is modeled as more aggregated than in the structural models where the time of default depends on the firm value that may depend on or be correlated with other variables. At the heart of the reduced-form models lies the instantaneous rate of default, i.e., the default intensity λ. Let $\mathcal{F}_t$ be the information up to time t, τ the default time, Δt a marginally short time interval, and $\lambda(t)$ the default intensity as a function of time. Mathematically expressed is the default intensity (assuming no default up to time t)

$$P(\tau \in (t + \Delta t) \mid \mathcal{F}_t) \approx \lambda(t)\Delta t \qquad (4.1)$$

approximately the proportionality factor between the default probability within a given time interval Δt and the length of this time interval. In other words, λ is the intensity of the process that specifies the default time τ. In the literature, often Poisson processes are used to model the default time as they suit to model rare and discretely countable events such as radioactive decay, number of people in a queue or, in this case, default. In this context, the time of default is interpreted as the first jump of the Poisson process. After default, the intensity is usually set equal to zero. For models with multiple defaults, see, e.g., Schönbucher and Schubert (2001).

TABLE 4.1. Key Assumptions of Different Reduced-Form Models
Source: Uhrig-Homburg (2002)

Model	Default Time	Magnitude of Default	Interest Rate Model	Correlations
Jarrow/ Turnbull (1995)	constant intensity	recovery of face; φ constant	any desired process for r via some spot or forward-rate model	r, τ, and φ mutually independent under Q
Madan/ Ünal (1998)	intensity depends on stock price	recovery of treasury; φ stochastic	any desired process for r via some spot or forward rate	r, τ, and φ mutually independent under Q
Lando (1998)	intensity depends on some state variable Y	recovery-of-face or treasury; φ can depend on Y	any desired process for r via some spot or forward rate; r can depend on Y	correlations allowed
Duffie/ Singleton (1999)	intensity depends on some state variable Y	recovery-of-market; φ can depend on Y	any desired process for r via some spot or forward-rate; r can depend on Y	correlations allowed

One important advantage of reduced-form models is that their framework is capable of reducing the technical difficulties of modeling defaultable claims to modeling the term structure of nondefaultable bonds and related derivatives. Reduced-form models differ in their assumptions about the default time (indirectly the default intensity), the correlations between the risk-free interest rates and the default time, and the way they model the recovery rate φ. Following Uhrig-Homburg (2002), Table 4.1 summarizes the aspects of the reduced-form models we will briefly discuss in the following.

4.2.1   The Model by Jarrow and Turnbull (1995)

Jarrow and Turnbull (1995) were the first ones to develop an intensity-based approach for the valuation of risky debt. The key assumptions in their paper are the following:

- Nonexistence of arbitrage opportunities and the market completeness. This assumption is equivalent to the existence and uniqueness of an equivalent martingale measure Q under which the discounted prices of the default-free and risky zero bonds are martingales.

- A constant recovery-of-face value φ given exogenously.

- The independence of the short-term spot interest rate $r(t)$ and the default process under the martingale measure Q.

Under these assumptions the price of a risky bond can be determined according to

$$v(t,T) = E_t^Q \left(e^{-\int_t^T r(s)ds} \right) E_t^Q \left(1_{(\tau > T)} + \varphi 1_{(\tau < T)} \right) \tag{4.2}$$

$$v(t,T) = p(t,T) E_t^Q \left(1_{(\tau > T)} + \varphi 1_{(\tau < T)} \right) \tag{4.3}$$

Note that hereby it is implicitly assumed that the recovery payment is done at maturity. The equation would not change, however, if we assume a recovery payment at default. In that case, we would roll over the recovery payment φ with the money market account until maturity and then discount it again with the default-free zero bond. The price of the risky zero-coupon bond at time t with maturity T is equal to the expected payoff at maturity T under the martingale measure discounted with the default-free zero-coupon bond with the same maturity. The equation can be further simplified to

$$v(t,T) = p(t,T) \left[\varphi + (1 - \varphi) Q(\tau > T) \right]$$
$$v(t,T) = p(t,T)\varphi + p(t,T)(1 - \varphi) Q(\tau > T) \tag{4.4}$$

with $Q(\tau > T)$ the survival probability until maturity under the martingale measure. The first term on the right side of the equation can be interpreted as the time t value of the recovery rate that will be received surely at maturity. The second term is the time t value of the promised payment if the zero-bond survives beyond the maturity.

4.2.2   The Model Suggested by Madan and Ünal (1998)

Madan and Ünal (1998) decompose the risky debt into the following securities: the *survival security* making the promised payments at maturity in case of survival and paying nothing otherwise, and the *default security* paying the recovery rate in default and nothing otherwise. Thus, different types of risk are addressed by different securities. While the survival security faces only the timing risk of default, the default security faces the recovery risk of default. This simultaneously means that the assumption of constant recovery rates in Jarrow and Turnbull (1995) is relaxed, implying recovery rate uncertainty. Based on this model architecture, the authors state the following assumptions:

- The default payouts are independently and identically distributed across time and interest rate states. This implies the time-homogeneity of recovery rate φ.

- Default timing risks are functions of firm-specific information that are independent of interest rate movements. This is a further relaxation of Jarrow and Turnbull's assumptions. Although the independence between short-term spot interest rate process and the default process remains, the default intensity is not constant anymore, but depends on the stock price of the firm. Thus, Madan and Ünal build a bridge between the structural and the reduced-form models.

- The recovery rate is referenced to an identical default-free zero-bond (recovery-of-treasury).

According to Madan and Ünal (1998), the firm's equity is a sign for the firm's financial strength, and hence, changes in the equity levels will be reflected to the default probabilities. The authors use for their model the (by the money market account $B(t) = e^{-\int_0^t r(s)ds}$ discounted) equity value $s(t)$. The dynamics of the equity value is described by the following stochastic differential equation:

$$ds(t) = \sigma s(t)dW(t)$$

where σ is the constant standard deviation of the equity value and W is a standard Brownian motion.

Based on this assumption, the default intensity equals

$$\lambda(s,t) = \frac{c}{\left(\ln\left(\dfrac{s}{s_{critic}}\right)\right)^2} \qquad (4.5)$$

where s_{critic} is the critical equity value and c is a constant parameter. The choice of such a function is, first, based on the requirement that equity value and default intensity should be inversely related; i.e., an increase in the equity level decreases the probability of default. Second, if the (exogenously given) critical equity level is reached, the default probability goes to infinity; i.e., the firm defaults certainly. This is somewhat equivalent to the default boundary in the structural models. The distance to the critical level determines the default probability.

After having set the foundation for the timing risk of default, which is only relevant for the survival security, Madan and Ünal (1998) model the recovery rate risk. The recovery rate φ is a random variable with a density function $q(\varphi)$. Thus, the expected payout at default equals

$$E(\varphi) = \int_0^1 \varphi q(\varphi) d\varphi \qquad (4.6)$$

Based on the above models and under the assumption of the independence between the default intensity and the risk-free interest rate process, our fundamental equation simplifies to

$$v(t,T) = E_t^Q\left(e^{-\int_t^T r(s)ds}\right) E_t^Q\left(1_{(\tau>T)} + E(\varphi)1_{(\tau<T)}\right)$$

$$v(t,T) = p(t,T) E_t^Q\left(1_{(\tau>T)} + E(\varphi)1_{(\tau<T)}\right)$$

$$v(t,T) = p(t,T)E(\varphi) + p(t,T)(1 - E(\varphi))Q(\tau>T) \qquad (4.7)$$

The main difference between the value of the bond according to Jarrow and Turnbull (1995) and Madan and Ünal (1998) is that the certain payment of $p(t,T)\varphi$ is not certain anymore but depends on the magnitude of recovery. The uncertainty is therefore extended by including the stochastic nature by the recovery rate.

So far, we have concentrated on a model that assumed independence between interest rates and default intensities. Now, we will have a look at two further intensity models where this assumption is relaxed.

4.2.3 The Model Suggested by Lando (1998)

The main feature of the approach suggested in Lando (1998) is to model the default time using a Cox process. Hereby, it is assumed that the default intensity is a function of some state variable, the stochastic process $X(t)$ which may include riskless interest rates, stock prices, growth rate in the economy, or other variables relevant to predict the likelihood of default. Thus, the state variable captures the correlation between the default time process and the interest rates, relaxing the key assumption made in the previous models. In Lando's model, the default time is the first jump time of the Cox process with intensity $\lambda(X(t))$.

Assuming a recovery payment at maturity, Lando models it as

$$\varphi_T 1_{(\tau \leq T)} = \varphi_T - \varphi_T 1_{(\tau > T)} \tag{4.8}$$

Assuming a constant recovery rate, we obtain the following equation for the price of the risky bond:

$$
\begin{aligned}
v(t,T) &= E_t^Q\left(e^{-\int_t^T r(s)ds}1_{(\tau>T)} + e^{-\int_t^T r(s)ds}(\varphi_T - \varphi_T 1_{(\tau>T)})\right) \\
&= E_t^Q\left(e^{-\int_t^T r(s)ds}1_{(\tau>T)}\right) + E_t^Q\left(e^{-\int_t^T r(s)ds}\varphi_T(1 - 1_{(\tau>T)})\right) \\
&= E_t^Q\left(e^{-\int_t^T r(s)ds}1_{(\tau>T)}\right) + \varphi_T E_t^Q\left(e^{-\int_t^T r(s)ds} - e^{-\int_t^T r(s)ds}1_{(\tau>T)}\right) \\
&= E_t^Q\left(e^{-\int_t^T r(s)ds}1_{(\tau>T)}\right) + \varphi_T E_t^Q\left(e^{-\int_t^T r(s)ds}\right) \\
&\quad - \varphi_T E_t^Q\left(e^{-\int_t^T r(s)ds}1_{(\tau>T)}\right) \\
&= p(t,T)\varphi_T + (1 - \varphi_T)E_t^Q\left(e^{-\int_t^T r(s)ds}1_{(\tau>T)}\right) \tag{4.9}
\end{aligned}
$$

Lando further shows that the expectation on the right side of the pricing equation can be expressed as

$$E_t^Q\left(e^{-\int_t^T r(s)ds}1_{(\tau>T)}\right) = E_t^Q\left(e^{-\int_t^T r(s)+\lambda(X(s))ds}\right) \tag{4.10}$$

That is the current value of the promised payment at maturity T, if there has been no default until T.

Overall, similar to the model suggested by Jarrow and Turnbull (1995), the equation can be decomposed into two parts: a certain payment of the recovery rate and a promised payment in case of survival. While the certain payment is still the same, the promised payment additionally depends on the correlation between the interest rate and default processes, for a change in the interest rates will be reflected in the default probabilities. In the model of Jarrow and Turnbull (1995), however, an interest rate change changes only the discounting factor of the promised payment, but not the default probabilities. Besides the value of a promised payment at maturity T, Lando also derives equations for the value of a stream of payments (e.g., swaps), which terminates when default occurs, and for the resettlement payment at the time of default. For further details on the model, we refer to Lando (1998).

4.2.4   The Model of Duffie and Singleton (1999)

Probably one of the most popular intensity-based models goes back to Duffie and Singleton (1999). The special feature of their model is the recovery-of-market value assumption; i.e., the recovery rate is a fraction of the market value of the risky debt prior to default. Under this assumption, the authors construct an adjusted short rate accounting for both the probability and the timing of default and the losses at default:

$$R(t) = r(t) + \lambda(t)(1 - \varphi) \tag{4.11}$$

Given an exogenous default process and a recovery rate, the risky security can be valued as if it were default-free:

$$v(t, T) = E_t^Q \left(e^{- \int_t^T R(s) ds} \right) \tag{4.12}$$

As a special case of their model, Duffie and Singleton (1999) also introduce some state variable Y, of which both the short-term interest rate and the default processes are exogenously given functions. Hereby, the authors consider two cases for the state variable Y. The first one is that Y is a continuous time Markov process under the martingale measure Q. The second approach considers a jump-diffusion process to allow sudden changes of Y. Also the case where the recovery rate and the default intensity depend on the current price of the risky security is discussed. Thus, the model is also able to incorprate the correlation between interest rates and default intensities. For further details on the framework, see Duffie and Singleton (1999), while for further reading on intensity models, we refer, e.g., to Duffie and Singleton (2003), Lando (2004), Schönbucher and Schubert (2001).

4.3   The CreditMetrics Model

The CreditMetrics approach also departs from the assumption that the market value of a bond or its default probability can be derived by using the value of a firm's assets as its main input variable. As a risk management tool, the model must be applicable to all kinds of financial instruments with inherent credit risk. Besides, the valuation procedure must be consistent with actual market prices (Gupton et al., 1997). Therefore, CreditMetrics uses for the valuation the rating of a company, historical transition matrices, and empirically derived bond prices. It is further assumed that all variables, except the current rating state of the issuer,

TABLE 4.2. Average One-year Transition Matrix of Moody's Corporate Bond Ratings for the Period 1982–2001

	Aaa	Aa	A	Baa	Ba	B	C	D
Aaa	0.9276	0.0661	0.0050	0.0009	0.0003	0.0000	0.0000	0.0000
Aa	0.0064	0.9152	0.0700	0.0062	0.0008	0.0011	0.0002	0.0001
A	0.0007	0.0221	0.9137	0.0546	0.0058	0.0024	0.0003	0.0005
Baa	0.0005	0.0029	0.0550	0.8753	0.0506	0.0108	0.0021	0.0029
Ba	0.0002	0.0011	0.0052	0.0712	0.8229	0.0741	0.0111	0.0141
B	0.0000	0.0010	0.0035	0.0047	0.0588	0.8323	0.0385	0.0612
C	0.0012	0.0000	0.0029	0.0053	0.0157	0.1121	0.6238	0.2389
D	0.0000	0.0000	0.0000	0.0000	0.0000	0.0000	0.0000	1.0000

behave deterministically over time. Thus, the value of the bond or loan at the risk time horizon T is essentially dependent on the rating state of the issuer at this point of time, i.

CreditMetrics assumes that if the issuer is not in a state of default at the risk time horizon, the value of the bond or loan is determined by discounting the outstanding cash flows using credit spreads over the riskless interest rate r. The spreads correspond to the rating state i of the issuer in T. The distribution of bond or loan values in T is thus given by the probabilities $P(X = i)$ of the different rating states in T, together with the corresponding values of the bond $V_{i,T}$.

In the first stage of the model, we determine the distribution of ratings of the exposure at the end of a given risk time horizon t. This is done with the help of a transition matrix P; an exemplary transition matrix is provided in Table 4.2.

Suppose that the initial rating of the exposure at time 0 is $i \in \{1, 2, \ldots K\}$. This initial setting can be represented by the vector

$$p_{i.}(0) = \delta_i$$

In the CreditMetrics framework in order to obtain the distribution of possible ratings at t, the initial rating vector is multiplied with a t-step transition matrix. If the risk horizon is more than one year, it is suggested to compute the required vector of transition probabilities $p_{i.}(t)$ either with a multiple of a one-year transition matrix P, thus, $p_{i.}(t) = \delta_i \cdot P^t$ or, if available, with a directly estimated t-year transition matrix $p_{i.}(t) = \delta_i \cdot P(t)$.

Thus, we obtain all possible future ratings at time t and the corresponding transition probabilities:

Rating at t	1	2	...	$K-1$	K
Migration probability	$p_{i1}(t)$	$p_{i2}(t)$	...	$p_{i(K-1)}(t)$	$p_{iK}(t)$

For example, assuming a constant transition matrix for a BB rated bond and a two-year risk time horizon, we obtain the distribution of ratings by

$$
\begin{aligned}
p_{BB.}^{(2)} &= \delta_{BB} \cdot P^2 \\
&= (0,0,0,0,1,0,0,0) \cdot P^2.
\end{aligned}
\tag{4.13}
$$

In a second step a risk-adjusted forward price is derived for each rating state. The cases of default and nondefault states are considered separately. The remaining cash flows from t to T in nondefault categories are discounted with state-specific forward rates. The forward-zero curve for each rating category can be found by calibrating forward rates to observed credit spreads of different maturities.

In the case of nondefault states, agreed payments before t will be fully received and can be added—including the earned interest until t—to the risk-adjusted value of the bond at time t:

$$
\begin{aligned}
B_j(t,T) = \sum_{k=1}^{t} C_k (1 + f^*(k,t))^{t-k} \\
+ \sum_{k=t+1}^{T} \frac{C_k}{(1 + f_j(t,k))^{k-t}} + \frac{B}{(1 + f_j(t,T))^{T-t}}
\end{aligned}
\tag{4.14}
$$

with C_k denoting the nominal coupon in year k, B the nominal principal, f^* being the riskless forward rate, and f_j the forward rate for j-rated bonds. In case the bond defaults before t, a recovery payment is assigned:

$$
B_K(t,T) = R \cdot \left(\sum_{k=1}^{T} C_k + B \right)
\tag{4.15}
$$

where R is the expected fraction of the bond's nominal cash flows that is paid back. The parameter R is estimated as the average return in prior default experience and depends on the seniority class of the bond. Unfortunately, as we will see in Chapter 6, recovery payments are highly uncertain. In CreditMetrics the recovery rate is simulated by a beta distribution whose mean and standard deviation are calibrated in order to fit the parameters of the historically observed recovery rate that corresponds to the seniority of the item.

Regarding the bond price B_j as a random variable, the mass distribution of this random variable is given by the vector $p_{i.}$. Hence, the so-called Distribution of Values (DoV) for a given initial rating and the considered risk time horizon can be obtained by using adequate transition matrices and forward curves. Credit risk measures like the expected or unexpected loss can be derived from the DoV. The DoV gives for each predicted bond price the probability of being assigned to this rating. Due to the shape of the DoV, credit risk cannot be handled with established VaR methods. Most models in finance assume normal distributed returns for changes in stock prices, interest rates, or other variables that are affected by market risk. However, a symmetric distribution is unsuitable for returns subject to credit risk, since there is a large probability of earning a small profit (riskless interest rate plus risk premium) and a very small probability of losing a large amount of investment in the case of default. As a consequence distributions are highly skewed to the right with a "fat tail" on the loss side.

Keeping the new Basel Capital Accord and the required economic capital in mind, one needs to know the average return of a bond and the average loss that a bank may suffer from the default of a bond. This average loss is the minimum amount of capital that should be set aside for compensation. Besides, it is also important to know how much a bank can lose if the outcome is really bad. These issues are treated by the so-called expected and unexpected loss. Figure 4.3 illustrates an exemplary loss distribution for a bond portfolio, the expected loss as the expected value of the loss distribution, the unexpected loss as a more extreme outcome under a worst-case scenario and the corresponding 95% VaR.

The expected return (ER) of an i-rated bond to the risk time horizon t is defined as the expectation of its DoV:

$$ER_i(t) = \sum_{j=1}^{K} p_{ij}(t)B_j(t,T) \qquad (4.16)$$

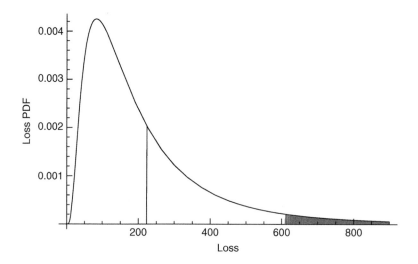

FIGURE 4.3. Exemplary loss distribution, expected loss, and unexpected loss. A worse outcome than the VaR (95%) is a loss in the shaded region.

In risk management tools it is more common to express future values in terms of losses. The expected loss (EL) is defined as the difference between the expected return and the value of a riskless bond with the same cash flows (or simply the expected value of the credit spreads):

$$EL_i(t) = B^*(t, T) - ER_i(t) \tag{4.17}$$

$$= \sum_{j=1}^{K} p_{ij}(t)(B^*(t, T) - B_j(t, T)).$$

The unexpected loss (UL) is an indicator of the amount of money that can be lost in a worst-case scenario. There are two possibilities to measure the UL: calculating the standard deviation or the percentile levels of the DoV.

The UL of an i-rated exposure can be defined as the standard deviation of its DoV:

$$UL_i(t) = \sqrt{\sum_{j=1}^{K} p_{ij}(t)B_j(t, T)^2 - ER_i(t)^2} \tag{4.18}$$

As we mentioned before, recovery rates are always highly uncertain. Therefore, it is recommended that the volatility of the recovery rate also enters into the calculation of the unexpected losses. In this case we obtain

$$UL_i(t) = \sqrt{\sum_{j=1}^{K} p_{ij}(t)(B_j(t, T)^2 + \sigma_j^2) - ER_i(t)^2} \tag{4.19}$$

with

$$\sigma_j^2 = 0; \quad j \neq K$$

For a derivation of this formula, refer to Appendix D of Gupton et al. (1997). As a second measure for the unexpected loss of an exposure with rating i for a given confidence level α, we can define the α-percentile level of the DoV:

$$UL_i^* = Q_\alpha(DoV) \tag{4.20}$$

When one uses these UL definitions, the uncertainty of future bond values comes only from potential rating transitions and from the volatility of recovery rates. One might yield more realistic results by taking into account the volatility of predicted bond values in each rating category.

Obviously, CreditMetrics offers a quite different approach for measuring credit risk than the firm value models or intensity based models. The model provides a rather empirical Value-at-Risk approach for measuring credit risk that should be consistent with actual market prices. Besides, it is rather interested in potential losses during worst-case scenarios. In this framework historical transition matrices and forward prices are more important than the value of the firm. However, we should not forget to mention that, as it comes to deriving joint transition matrices for two or more individual companies, the company's asset value is considered as the key driver of rating changes; see Gupton et al. (1997). For measuring asset return correlations, one uses the issuers' equity returns from publicly available quotations. For more on this, see Chapter 10. Further, the model also provides a method for calculating conditional transition matrices based on an outcome of a business cycle index that will be described in Chapter 9.

Overall, CreditMetrics should not be considered as a reduced-form model only. It is rather a hybrid model that uses both structural and reduced-form approaches in order to measure VaR figures for bond or loan portfolios.

4.4   The CreditRisk$^+$ Model

Credit Suisse First Boston's CreditRisk$^+$ model applies an actuarial approach that has been commonly used for insurance matters. Thus, default as the elementary event that drives credit risk is modeled directly by assuming a Bernoullian default game for every firm. Unlike in other frameworks discussed earlier, generally no assumptions are made about the causes of default, and downgrade risk is not captured. For a better understanding of the CR$^+$ approach, we will initially describe a simplified way of modeling that reveals the basic ideas and analyzes the problems arising. We will introduce an extended version of the CR$^+$ model that overcomes some of the initial deficiencies.

4.4.1   The First Modeling Approach

The derivation of the default loss distribution in the CR$^+$ model comprises the following steps:

- Modeling the frequencies of default for the portfolio.

- Modeling the severities in the case of default.

- Linking these distributions together to obtain the default loss distribution.

Hereby, for every firm, a single stationary default probability for the risk horizon under consideration, p_i, is assigned. Furthermore, default events are assumed to be independent of each other, and the number of defaults is assumed to be independent over periods. Thus, starting with a probability generating function (pgf) for a single obligor i

$$F_i(z) = (1 - p_i) z^0 + p_i z^1 = 1 + p_i(z - 1)$$

the pgf for the portfolio yields

$$F(z) = \prod_i (1 + p_i(z - 1)). \tag{4.21}$$

Using the approximation

$$1 + p_i(z - 1) \simeq e^{p_i(z-1)} \tag{4.22}$$

and setting $\mu = \sum_i p_i$, equation (4.21) becomes

$$F(z) = e^{\sum_i p_i(z-1)} = e^{\mu(z-1)} = e^{-\mu}e^{\mu z} = \sum_{n=0}^{\infty} \frac{e^{-\mu}\mu^n}{n!} z^n \tag{4.23}$$

Hence the probability for n defaults in the portfolio is

$$P(n \text{ defaults}) = \frac{e^{-\mu}\mu^n}{n!} \tag{4.24}$$

which is the well-known Poisson distribution with parameter μ, mean μ, and standard deviation $\sqrt{\mu}$. Note that the approximation in (4.22) is, from a statistical point of view, equivalent to approximating the sum of independent Bernoulli draws by the Poisson distribution.

4.4.2 Modeling Severities

In the case of default, a loss arises that is equal to the (gross) exposure minus the recovery rate. The CR$^+$ model assumes that the recovery rates are exogenously given and for that reason requires adjusted (net) exposures as an input. Thus, talking about exposures here relates to the remaining part of exposure once netted with the recoveries. For computational efficiency, equal exposures are grouped into bands. This is done by assuming some base unit of exposure L and expressing all exposures in rounded multiples of L.

Let

- ν_j be the common exposure in band j in units of L;

- ε_j be the expected loss in band j in units of L;

- μ_j be the expected number of defaults in exposure band j; and

- n_j be the actual number of defaults in exposure band j.

Since default events are assumed to be independent, one can treat every band j as an independent portfolio. The loss in one of those subportfolios expressed in units of L is then $n_j v_j$.

Assume for example $N = 100$ loans in a band with loss exposure of $L = 20.000$ Euro. Let further $p = 0.03$ be the default rate assumed to follow a Poisson distribution.

Then we get for μ_j the expected number of defaults in band j

$$\mu = N \cdot p = 100 \cdot 0.03 = 3 \tag{4.25}$$

and for the probability of k defaults in band j

$$P(k \text{ defaults}) = \frac{e^{-3}3^n}{n!} \tag{4.26}$$

Using the results for frequency and severity of the losses in the portfolio, one can easily derive the distribution of default losses through the following steps:

- Identify the pgf $G_j(z)$ for the default loss distribution of band j.

- Combine the pgfs into a single pgf.

- Find a computationally efficient way of calculating the actual distribution of credit losses on the basis of the combined pgf.

The pgf for a loss of $n_j v_j$ units of L in band j is

$$G_j(z) = \sum_{n_j=0}^{\infty} P(\text{loss of } n_j v_j) \, z^{n_j v_j}$$

$$= \sum_{n_j=0}^{\infty} P(\text{number of defaults is } n_j) \, z^{n_j v_j}$$

and using equation (4.24)

$$G_j(z) = \sum_{n_j=0}^{\infty} \frac{e^{-\mu_j}\mu^{n_j}}{n_j!} \, z^{n_j v_j} \tag{4.27}$$

$$= e^{-\mu_j + \mu_j z^{v_j}} \tag{4.28}$$

gives the pgf for the default loss distribution of band j. Since independence is assumed between the bands, the combined pgf is just the product over the exposure band pgfs.

$$G(z) = \prod_{j=1}^{m} G_j(z)$$

$$= \prod_{j-1}^{m} e^{-\mu_j + \mu_j z^{\nu_j}}$$

$$= e^{-\sum_{j=1}^{m} \mu_j + \sum_{j=1}^{m} \mu_j z^{\nu_j}} \tag{4.29}$$

The final task is now to find a computationally efficient way of calculating the actual distribution of credit losses on the basis of this combined pgf. Since equation (4.29) cannot be transformed into the standard pgf form that offers a closed solution for $P(n)$, the following useful property of a pgf is used.

For an arbitrary pgf $F(z) = \sum_{n=0}^{\infty} P(n) z^n$ holds

$$\frac{\partial^k F(z)}{\partial z^k} = \sum_{n=k}^{\infty} P(n) \frac{n!}{(n-k)!} z^{n-k}$$

$$\left. \frac{\partial^k F(z)}{\partial z^k} \right|_{z=0} = P(k) k!$$

$$\Rightarrow P(n) = \frac{1}{n!} \left. \frac{\partial^k F(z)}{\partial z^k} \right|_{z=0} \tag{4.30}$$

When one uses this property, CSFB[1] derives a recurrence relationship for the probability of an overall portfolio loss of n units of L:

$$P(n) = \sum_{j:\, \nu_j \leq n} \frac{\varepsilon_j}{n} P(n - \nu_j)$$

$$P(0) = e^{-\sum_{j=1}^{m} \frac{\varepsilon_j}{\nu_j}} \tag{4.31}$$

These probabilities can be expressed in closed form and obviously depend only on the parameters ε_j and ν_j.

4.4.3 Shortcomings of the First Modeling Approach

Initially, the distribution of the number of defaults in a portfolio was inferred to be Poisson with parameter μ. This is based on the hypothesis that—in the long term—the average observed volatility should converge towards $\sqrt{\mu}$. However, empirical evidence shows that the observed standard deviation of the number of defaults is significantly larger than $\sqrt{\mu}$. To

---

[1] See CSFB (1997), Section A4.1.

overcome this problem, CR^+ assumes the default rate itself to be stochastic. While the expected number of default events remains the same, the distribution becomes significantly skewed and fat-tailed when introducing default rate volatility.

Another questionable core assumption is the independence of default events. Though there might be no direct dependence between individual events, there is a clear link between the co-movements of default probabilities or default rates, respectively. In an economic recession, for example, one can observe a significantly higher number of defaults than on average. Since the state of the economy is surely not the only explanatory variable for the co-movement of default probabilities, CR^+ introduces a multifactor model that influences the variable default rates of the obligors, and thus induces interdependence among them.

4.4.4   Extensions in the CR^+ Model

As mentioned above, the basic CR^+ model has some limitations. Some of them are overcome by the extensions in the CR^+ model. For example, when stochastic default rates are incorporated, a factor model is introduced that explains the dependence between the variation of the stochastic default rates of the different obligors by attributing their default rate processes to common factors.

For the matter of simplification, we make the assumption that every obligor is driven by exactly one factor. However, a generalization of the model allowing for an arbitrary number of factor affiliations for the different obligors is straightforward.

4.4.5   Allocating Obligors to One of Several Factors

Define a set of n independent background factors that allow the decomposition of the set of obligors into disjoint subsets, each of which is affiliated to exactly one background factor. In CR^+ terminology, the subsets are also called *sectors*. Each background factor influences the expected default rate and the standard deviation of default rate of its sector.

Therefore let X_k be a random variable with mean μ_k and standard deviation σ_k that represents the average default rate of the kth factor. Let every obligor A in sector k have an actual default probabiliy of X_A with mean p_A and standard deviation σ_A and denote the set of obligors that belong to sector k as $\mathbb{K}$.

At this point, the CR^+ model assumes that X_A is modeled proportional to x_k by

$$X_A = p_A \frac{X_k}{\mu_k} \tag{4.32}$$

and sets

$$\mu_k = \sum_{A \in \mathbb{K}} p_A$$

For any proposed relationship between X_k and X_A, we will demand

$$E\left(\sum_{A \in \mathbb{K}} X_A\right) = \mu_k$$

and

$$VAR\left(\sum_{A \in \mathbb{K}} X_A\right) = \sigma_k^2$$

as X_k is supposed to represent the average default rate for sector k.

The actual sector parameters are thus obtained by estimating the parameters p_A and σ_A for every obligor which determines the sector parameters as follows:

$$\mu_k = \sum_{A \in \mathbb{K}} p_A$$

and

$$\sigma_k = \frac{\sigma_k}{\mu_k}\left(\sum_{A \in \mathbb{K}} p_A\right) = \sum_{A \in \mathbb{K}} \frac{p_A}{\mu_k}\sigma_k = \sum_{A \in \mathbb{K}} \sigma_A$$

which shows that the sector standard deviation is just the sum over the standard deviations of all obligors which belong to the sector.

4.4.6 The pgf for the Number of Defaults

Having modeled the background factor dependency, the next step is to develop the pgf for the number of defaults in the kth factor. Overall, the way of proceeding is analogous to the case of a fixed default rate. Recall that, assuming a fixed default rate μ, the pgf as stated in equation (4.23) turned out to be

$$F(z) = e^{\mu(z-1)}$$

Since the random variable X_k represents the average default rate for sector k, it follows that conditional on the value of X_k, the pgf remains the same:

$$F_k(z \mid X_k = x) = e^{x(z-1)}$$

To obtain the unconditional pgf for sector k, we integrate over the density function of X_k which is supposed to be $f_k(x)$:

$$F_k(z) = \sum_{n=0}^{\infty} P(n \text{ defaults in sector } k) z^n$$

$$= \sum_{n=0}^{\infty} z^n \int_{x=0}^{\infty} P(n \text{ defaults in sector } k \mid x) f_k(x) dx$$

$$= \int_{x=0}^{\infty} F_k(z \mid X_k = x) f_k(x) dx = \int_{x=0}^{\infty} e^{x(z-1)} f_k(x) dx \qquad (4.33)$$

To continue solving the integral, one needs a key assumption about the density function $f_k(x)$. Here, the CR$^+$ model assumes a Gamma distribution $\Gamma(\alpha, \beta)$ with mean μ_k and standard deviation σ_k. Therefore, the parameters of the Gamma distribution are

$$\alpha_k = \frac{\mu_k^2}{\sigma_k^2} \quad \text{and} \quad \beta_k = \frac{\sigma_k^2}{\mu_k}$$

After resolving the integral, setting an additional auxiliary variable

$$p_k := \frac{\beta_k}{1 + \beta_k}$$

and expanding the obtained pgf

$$F_k(z) = \left(\frac{1 - p_k}{1 - p_k z} \right)^{\alpha_k}$$

in its Taylor series, we obtain the following explicit formula for the probability of n defaults in sector k:

$$P(n \text{ defaults in sector } k) = (1 - p_k)^{\alpha_k} \binom{n + \alpha_k - 1}{n} p_k^n \qquad (4.34)$$

which is the probability density function of the negative binomial distribution.

To obtain the pgf for the number of defaults in the whole portfolio comprising n sectors, recall that the sectors are assumed to be independent. Thus, the pgf is just the product over the sector pgfs:

$$F(z) = \prod_{k=1}^{n} F_k(z) = \prod_{k=1}^{n} \left(\frac{1 - p_k}{1 - p_k z} \right)^{\alpha_k} \qquad (4.35)$$

Note that the corresponding default event distribution is, accordingly, the sum of the independent negative binomial sector distributions and therefore **not** negative binomial in general.

4.4.7 The pgf for the Default Loss Distribution

Let $G_k(z)$ be the pgf for the default loss distribution of sector k:

$$G_k(z) = \sum_{n=0}^{\infty} P(\text{loss of } nL \text{ in sector } k) z^n$$

$$= \sum_{n=0}^{\infty} z^n \int_{x=0}^{\infty} P(\text{loss of } nL \text{ in sector } k | x_k) f_k(x_k) dx_k \qquad (4.36)$$

This pgf has a similar integral form like the pgf obtained in equation (4.33) and can be solved similarly. The result is[2]

$$G_k(z) = \left(\frac{1 - p_k}{1 - \frac{p_k}{\mu_k} \sum_{A \in \mathbb{K}} p_A z^{\nu_A}} \right)^{\alpha_k} \qquad (4.37)$$

Since the sectors are defined to be independent, the overall pgf for the default loss distribution is just the product over the sector pgfs:

$$G(z) = \prod_{k=1}^{n} G_k(z)$$

Again, a recurrence relation is derived that allows a numerical approximation of the underlying distribution.[3]

4.4.8 Generalization of Obligor Allocation

So far, we have assumed that every obligor can be assigned to one of several mutually independent sectors. Every sector is again driven by one underlying background factor. In another extension (see CSFB, 1997) this assumption can also be relaxed and the default rate of an obligor can now depend on a weighted subset of the set of background factors. The weights $\theta_{A,k}$ are combined to an obligor-specific weight vector θ_A that represents the extent to which the default probability of obligor A is affected by the background factors k. One obligor's weights have to sum up to the unit over all sectors.

---

[2] For detailed calculation, see CSFB (1997), Section A9.
[3] See CSFB (1997), Section A10.1.

4.4.9   The Default Loss Distribution

After estimation of the means and standard deviations of the obligors, and of the weights $\theta_{A,k}$ representing the obligors' sensitivity to the background factors, one can use the above relationships to calculate the mean μ_k and standard deviation σ_k for all factors. The equations developed for a single factor setup are still valid and can be applied directly using the modified parameters. Note that the incorporation of firm-specific factors is directly possible in the factor setup just discussed. Since firm-specific factors are idiosyncratic and uncorrelated to other factors and other firms' idiosyncratic components, it is sufficient to assign them to one common factor with variance zero. This causes the covariance of this specific factor, with all other factors, to be zero.

Overall, CreditRisk$^+$ is an approach derived from an actuarial science framework that is rather easy to implement. Only a few inputs—the probability of default and the exposure for each instrument—are needed. Providing closed-form solutions for the probability of portfolio loan losses and the implementation of marginal risk contributions to obligors makes the model also attractive from the computational point of view. However, there are also some limitations of the approach. CreditRisk$^+$ is a so-called default mode model that does not incorporate migration or market risk of an obligor. Also the exposure for each obligor is fixed and cannot depend on changes on the credit quality of an issuer. This rather unrealistic assumption is not overcome even in the most general form of the model.

5

Migration Matrices and the Markov Chain Approach

Jarrow et al. (1997) (hereafter JLT) were the first to model default and transition probabilities by using a Markov chain on a finite state space $S = \{1, \ldots, K\}$. The model and its relevance for determining risk-neutral migration matrices will be descibed in more detail in Chapter 8. Here we will concentrate on the definition and properties of discrete and continuous-time transition matrices.

5.1 The Markov Chain Approach

The state space S represents the different rating classes. Hereby, state $S = 1$ denotes the best credit rating; state K represents the default case. Hence, in the discrete case, the $(K \times K)$ one-period transition matrix looks as follows:

$$
P = \begin{pmatrix}
p_{11} & p_{12} & \cdots & p_{1K} \\
p_{21} & p_{12} & \cdots & p_{2K} \\
\cdots & \cdots & \cdots & \cdots \\
p_{K-1,1} & p_{K-1,2} & \cdots & p_{K-1,K} \\
0 & 0 & \cdots & 1
\end{pmatrix}
\tag{5.1}
$$

where $p_{ij} \geq 0$ for all $i, j, i \neq j$, and $p_{ii} \equiv 1 - \sum_{\substack{j=1 \\ j \neq i}}^{K} p_{ij}$ for all i. The variable p_{ij} represents the actual probability of going to state j from initial rating state i in one time step.

Thus, rating based models can be seen as a special case of the intensity model framework; see, e.g., Duffie and Singleton, 1999 where randomness in the default arrival is simply modeled via a Markov chain.

Alternatively, credit migration can also be modeled by a continuous-time Markov chain. Therefore, we will also introduce the idea of generator matrices and continuous-time modeling of rating transitions.[1]

---

[1] Some of the results of this section were originally published in Trueck and Özturkmen (2004). The structure of the section follows the original publication.

5.1.1   Generator Matrices

A continuous-time time-homogeneous Markov chain is specified via a $K \times K$ generator matrix of the following form:

$$\Lambda = \begin{pmatrix} \lambda_{11} & \lambda_{12} & \cdots & \lambda_{1K} \\ \lambda_{21} & \lambda_{22} & \cdots & \lambda_{2K} \\ \cdots & \cdots & \cdots & \cdots \\ \lambda_{K-1,1} & \lambda_{K-1,2} & \cdots & \lambda_{K-1,K} \\ 0 & 0 & \cdots & 0 \end{pmatrix} \tag{5.2}$$

where $\lambda_{ij} \geq 0$, for all i, j and $\lambda_{ii} = -\sum_{\substack{j=1 \\ j \neq i}}^{K} \lambda_{ij}$, for $i = 1, \ldots, K$. The off-diagonal elements represent the intensities of jumping from rating i to rating j. The default K is an absorbing state.

Definition 5.1 *Noris (1998): A generator of a time-continuous Markov chain is given by a matrix $\Lambda = (\lambda_{ij})_{1 \leq i, j \leq k}$ satisfying the following properties:*

1. $\sum_{j=1}^{8} \lambda_{ij} = 0$ *for every $i = 1, \ldots, K$;*

2. $0 \leq -\lambda_{ii} \leq \infty$ *for every $i = 1, \ldots, K$;*

3. $\lambda_{ij} \geq 0$ *for all $i, j = 1, \ldots, K$ with $i \neq j$.*

Further, see Noris (1998), the following theorem holds:

Theorem 5.2 *The following two properties are equivalent for matrix $\Lambda \in \mathbb{R}^{k \times k}$ satisfying the following properties:*

1. *Λ satisfies the properties in Definition 5.1.*

2. *$exp(t\Lambda)$ is a transition matrix for every $t \geq 0$.*

Hence, the $K \times K$ t-period transition matrix is then given by

$$P(t) = e^{t\Lambda} = \sum_{k=0}^{\infty} \frac{(t\Lambda)^k}{k!} = \mathcal{J} + (t\Lambda) + \frac{(t\Lambda)^2}{2!} + \frac{(t\Lambda^3)}{3!} + \cdots \tag{5.3}$$

On the other hand, under certain conditions that will be investigated in more detail in the next section, given a discrete-time one-year transition matrix, the corresponding generator matrix can be calculated using the following expression:

$$\Lambda = \sum_{k=1}^{\infty} (-1)^{k+1} \frac{(P - I)^k}{k} \qquad (n \in \mathbb{N} \tag{5.4}$$

For example, consider the transition matrix P

P	A	B	D
A	0.90	0.08	0.02
B	0.1	0.80	0.1
D	0	0	1

where the corresponding generator matrix is of the form

Λ	A	B	D
A	−0.1107	0.0946	0.0162
B	0.1182	−0.2289	0.1107
D	0	0	0

The use of generator matrices in credit risk is manifold. A main issue is, for example, the construction of so-called credit curves, giving information about cumulative default rates; see, e.g., Jarrow et al. (1997). For a given generator matrix Λ the cumulative default rate PD_t^i for rating class i is given by the Kth entry of the vector:

$$p_t^i = exp(t\Lambda)x_i^t \tag{5.5}$$

where x_i^t denotes the row of the corresponding transition matrix to the given rating R. Figure 5.1 shows a chart of the credit curves to the corresponding matrix P on our example.

Similar to the discrete-time framework, JLT transform the empirical generator matrix into a risk-neutral generator matrix by multiplying it with a matrix of risk premiums. This corresponds to an adjustment in order to transform the actual probabilities into the risk-neutral probabilities for valuation purposes:

$$\tilde{\Lambda}(t) \equiv \mathcal{U}(t)\Lambda(t) \tag{5.6}$$

where $\mathcal{U}(t) = diag(\mu_1(t), \ldots, \mu_{K-1}(t), 1)$ is a $K \times K$ diagonal matrix with strictly positive entries $\mu_i(t)$ for $i = 1, \ldots, K-1$ as deterministic functions of t.

The t-period transition matrix under the martingale measure can then be computed by the Kolmogorov forward and backward equations:

$$\frac{\partial \tilde{\mathcal{Q}}(t,T)}{\partial T} = \tilde{\mathcal{Q}}(t,T)\tilde{\Lambda}(T) \tag{5.7}$$

$$\frac{\partial \tilde{\mathcal{Q}}(t,T)}{\partial t} = -\tilde{\Lambda}(t)\tilde{\mathcal{Q}}(t,T) \tag{5.8}$$

Assuming constant risk premiums $(\mu_1, \ldots, \mu_{K-1}, 1)$, the risk-neutral transition matrix under the martingale measure is the solution of

$$\tilde{\mathcal{Q}}(t,T) = e^{\mathcal{U}\Lambda(T-t)}$$

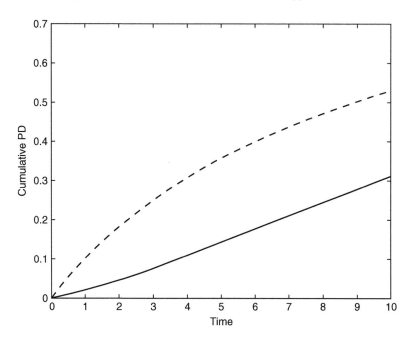

FIGURE 5.1. Credit curves for exemplary transition matrix with three rating states. Cumulative PDs for exemplary rating classes A (*solid line*) and B (*dashed line*).

JLT define a methodology to value risky bonds as well as credit derivatives that is based on ratings that allow for changes in credit quality before default. In the following section we will give a brief outline of the advantages of continuous- versus discrete-time models.

5.2   Discrete Versus Continuous-Time Modeling

Lando and Skødeberg (2002) as well as Christensen et al. (2004) focus on the advantages of the continuous-time modeling over the discrete-time approach used by rating agencies in order to analyze rating transition data. Generally, rating agencies estimate transition probabilities using the multinomial method by computing

$$\hat{p}_{ij} = \frac{N_{ij}}{N_i} \tag{5.9}$$

for $j \neq i$. Where N_i is the number of firms in rating class i at the beginning of the year and N_{ij} is the number of firms that migrated from class i to rating class j.

The authors argue that these transition probabilities do not capture rare events such as a transition from rating AAA to default as they may not be observed. However, it is possible that a firm reaches default through subsequent downgrades from AAA—even within one year and the probability of moving from AAA to default must be non-zero. Following Küchler and Sorensen (1997) a maximum-likelihood estimator for the continuous-time method is proposed:

$$\hat{\lambda}_{ij} = \frac{N_{ij}(T)}{\int_0^T Y_i(s)ds} \tag{5.10}$$

The variable $Y_i(s)$ denotes the number of firms in rating class i at time s and $N_{ij}(T)$ is the total number of transitions over the period from i to j, where $i \neq j$. Under the assumption of time homogeneity over the considered period, the transition matrix for a time interval t can be computed by the formula $P(t) = e^{t\Lambda}$.

Following Lando and Skødeberg (2002), we consider now an example with three rating classes A, B, and D for default. It is assumed that at the beginning of the year there are 10 firms in A, 10 in B, and none in default. Now one A-rated company is downgraded to B after one month and stays there for the rest of the year; a B-rated company is upgraded to A after two months and remains there for the rest of the period, and a B-rated company defaults after six months. The discrete-time multinomial method then estimates the following one-year transition matrix:

P	A	B	D
A	0.90	0.10	0
B	0.1	0.80	0.1
D	0	0	1

The maximum-likelihood estimator for the continuous-time approach computes the following generator matrix:

$\hat{\Lambda}$	A	B	D
A	−0.10084	0.10084	0
B	0.10909	−0.21818	0.10909
D	0	0	0

For instance, the nondiagonal element $\hat{\lambda}_{AB}$ equals

$$\hat{\lambda}_{AB} = \frac{N_{AB}(1)}{\int_0^1 Y_A(s)ds} = \frac{1}{9 + \frac{1}{12} + \frac{10}{12}} = 0.10084$$

The diagonal element $\hat{\lambda}_{AA}$ is computed such that the row sums to zero. Exponentiating the generator gives the following one-year transition matrix:

P	A	B	D
A	0.90887	0.08618	0.00495
B	0.09323	0.80858	0.09819
D	0	0	1

Thus, we have a strictly positive default probability for class A although there have been no observations from A to default in this period. However, this makes sense as the migration probability from A to B and from B to default is non-zero. Hence, it could happen within one year that a company is downgraded from rating state A to B and then defaults from rating state B within one year.

For the time-inhomogeneous case, the Nelson-Aalen estimator [see, e.g., Küchler and Sorensen (1997)] can be used:

$$\hat{\lambda}_{hj}(t) = \sum_{\{k:T_{hjk} \leq t\}} \frac{1}{Y_h(T_{hjk})}$$

where $T_{hj1} < T_{hj2} < \ldots$ are the observed times of transitions from state h to j and $Y_h(t)$ counts the number of firms in rating class h at a time just prior to t. The transition matrix is then computed by

$$\hat{P}(s,t) = \prod_{i=1}^{m} (\mathcal{J} + \Delta\hat{\Lambda}(T)) \tag{5.11}$$

where $\mathcal{J}$ is the identity matrix, T_i is a jump time in the interval $(s,t]$, and

$$\Delta\hat{\Lambda}(T) = \begin{pmatrix} -\frac{\Delta N_1(T_i)}{Y_1(T_i)} & \frac{\Delta N_{12}(T_i)}{Y_1(T_i)} & \cdots & \frac{\Delta N_{1K}(T_i)}{Y_1(T_i)} \\ \frac{\Delta N_{21}(T_i)}{Y_2(T_i)} & -\frac{\Delta N_2(T_i)}{Y_2(T_i)} & \cdots & \frac{\Delta N_{2K}(T_i)}{Y_2(T_i)} \\ \cdots & \cdots & \cdots & \cdots \\ \frac{\Delta N_{K-1,1}(T_i)}{Y_{K-1}(T_i)} & \frac{\Delta N_{K-1,2}(T_i)}{Y_{K-1}(T_i)} & \cdots & -\frac{\Delta N_{K-1,K}(T_i)}{Y_{K-1}(T_i)} \\ 0 & 0 & \cdots & 0 \end{pmatrix}$$

The diagonal elements count the total number of transitions from class i to another rating state divided by the number of exposed firms. The off-diagonal elements count the number of migrations to the corresponding class also divided by the number of exposed firms. This estimator can be interpreted as a cohort method applied to very short time intervals.

Applying this approach to our example, we obtain the following matrices:

$$\Delta\Lambda(T_{\frac{1}{12}}) = \begin{pmatrix} -0.1 & 0.1 & 0 \\ 0 & 0 & 0 \\ 0 & 0 & 0 \end{pmatrix}$$

$$\Delta\Lambda(T_{\frac{2}{12}}) = \begin{pmatrix} 0 & 0 & 0 \\ \frac{1}{11} & -\frac{1}{11} & 0 \\ 0 & 0 & 0 \end{pmatrix}$$

$$\Delta\Lambda(T_{\frac{6}{12}}) = \begin{pmatrix} 0 & 0 & 0 \\ 0 & -0.1 & 0.1 \\ 0 & 0 & 0 \end{pmatrix}$$

Using equation (5.2), we get

$$\hat{P}(0,1) = \begin{pmatrix} 0.90909 & 0.08181 & 0.00909 \\ 0.09091 & 0.81818 & 0.09091 \\ 0 & 0 & 1 \end{pmatrix}$$

As in the time-homogeneous case, we obtain a strictly positive default probability for class A, although the entries in the matrix above are slightly different than in the time-homogeneous case. However, Lando and Skødeberg (2002) indicate that in most cases the results are not dramatically different for large data sets. Compared to the estimator for the transition matrix using the discrete multinomial estimator, we obtain obvious deviations.

Summarizing the key advantages of the continuous-time approach, we find that we get more realistic non-zero estimates for probabilities of rare events, whereas the multinomial method leads to estimates that are zero. Further, using generator matrices, it is also possible to obtain transition matrices for arbitrary time horizons. We will see in later chapters that the continuous time framework also permits us to generate confidence sets for default probabilities in higher rating classes. Finally, in the continous-time approach we do not have to worry which yearly periods we consider. Using a discrete-time approach may lead to quite different results depending on the starting point of our consideration.

However, the last issue is also a critical point for the estimation of generator matrices. In internal rating systems it is often the case that rating changes are reported only once a year and that the exact time of the change is not provided. Then it is not appropriate to use the maximum-likelihood or the Nelson-Aalen estimator for estimation of the transition matrix.

So far we have described the basic ideas of rating based credit risk evaluation methods and the advantages of continuous-time transition modeling over the discrete-time case. Despite these advantages of continuous-time modeling, there are also some problems to deal with, like the existence, uniqueness, or adjustment of the generator matrix to the corresponding discrete transition matrix.

In many cases in the internal rating system of a bank, only discrete-time historical transition matrices are reported. To benefit from the advantages of continuous-time modeling, the bank might still be interested in finding the correspondent generator matrix. In this case an important issue is whether for a given discrete one-year transition matrix a so-called "true" generator exists. For some discrete transition matrices, there is no generator matrix at all, while for some there exists a generator that has negative off-diagonal elements. This would mean that, considering short time intervals, transition probabilities may be negative, which is not acceptable from a practical point of view. Examining the question of existence and suggesting numerical methods for finding true generators, or approximations for true generators, we will follow an approach by Israel et al. (2000).

In their paper they first identify conditions under which a true generator does or does not exist. Then they provide a numerical method for finding the true generator once its existence is proved and show how to obtain an approximate one in case of the absence of a true generator. The authors define two issues concerning transition matrices: *embeddability,* which is to determine if an empirical transition matrix is compatible with a true generator or with a Markov process; and *identification,* which is to search for the true generator once its existence is known.

Given the one-year $N \times N$ transition matrix P, we are interested in finding a generator matrix Λ such that

$$P = e^{\Lambda} = \sum_{k=0}^{\infty} \frac{\Lambda^k}{k!} = \mathcal{J} + \Lambda + \frac{\Lambda^2}{2!} + \frac{\Lambda^3}{3!} + \cdots \qquad (5.12)$$

Dealing with the question if there exists a generator matrix, we can use the following theorem (Noris, 1998):

Theorem 5.3 *If a migration matrix $P = (p_{ij})_{i,j=1,\ldots,k}$ is strictly diagonal dominant, i.e., $p_{ii} > 0.5$ for every i, then the log-expansion*

$$\Lambda_n = \sum_{k=1}^{n} (-1)^{k+1} \frac{(P-I)^k}{k} \qquad (n \in \mathbb{N} \qquad (5.13)$$

converges to a matrix $\Lambda = (\lambda_{ij})i, j = 1, \ldots, k$ satisfying

1. $\sum_{j=1}^{8} \lambda_{ij} = 0$ *for every $i = 1, \ldots, k$;* $\qquad (5.14)$

2. $exp(\Lambda) = P.$ $\qquad (5.15)$

The convergence $\Lambda_n \to \Lambda$ is geometrically fast and denotes an $N \times N$ matrix having row-sums of zero and satisfying $P = e^{\Lambda^*}$ exactly. For the proof, see Israel et al. (2000).

However, it is important to note that even if the series Λ^* does not converge or converges to a matrix that cannot be a true generator, P may still have a true generator.

There is also a simpler way to check if $S < 1$, namely if the transition matrix consists of diagonal elements that are greater than 0.5. In this case we get $S < 1$ and the convergence of (5.3) is guaranteed. In practice, for historical transition matrices of the major rating agencies, this will be true, so we can assume that generators having row-sums of zero and satisfying $P = e^{\Lambda^*}$ can be found.

For the existence of an exact generator matrix, Israel et al. (2000) state the following proposition.

Proposition 5.4 *Let P be a transition matrix. If one of the following three conditions holds*

- $det(P) \leq 0$

- $det(P) > \prod_i p_{ii}$

- *there are states i and j such that j is accessible from i, but $p_{ij} = 0$*

then there does not exist an exact generator matrix for P.

However, often there remains another problem: the main disadvantage of (5.3) is that Λ_n may converge but does not have to be a true generator matrix in economic sense; it is particularly possible that some off-diagonal elements are negative.

We will illustrate this with an example. Consider the one-year transition matrix:

P	A	B	C	D
A	0.9	0.08	0.0199	0.0001
B	0.050	0.850	0.090	0.010
C	0.010	0.090	0.800	0.100
D	0	0	0	1

Calculating the generator that exactly matches $P = e^{\Lambda^*}$ by using (5.3), we get

Λ	A	B	C	D
A	−0.1080	0.0907	0.0185	−0.0013
B	0.0569	−0.1710	0.1091	0.0051
C	0.0087	0.1092	−0.2293	0.1114
D	0	0	0	0

having a negative entry in the off-diagonal element λ_{AD}.

From an economic viewpoint, this is not acceptable because a negative entry in the generator may lead to negative transition probabilities for very short time intervals. Israel et al. (2000) show that it is possible that sometimes there exists more than one generator. They provide conditions for the existence or nonexistence of a valid generator matrix and further a numerical algorithm for finding this matrix.

5.2.1   Some Conditions for the Existence of a Valid Generator

In this section we will examine conditions for the existence and nonexistence of a valid generator matrix. We will first define the conditions to conclude the uniqueness of a generator matrix.

Since a transition matrix P sometimes has more than one valid generator, there is also the problem of its uniqueness. Following Singer and Spilerman (1976), we provide the following theorem.

A theorem for the uniqueness of the generator is as follows:

Theorem 5.5 *Let P be a transition matrix.*

- *If $det(P) > 0.5$, then P has at most one generator.*

- *If $det(P) > 0.5$ and $||P - \mathcal{J}|| < 0.5$, then the only possible generator for P is the one obtained by (5.3).*

- *If P has distinct eigenvalues and $det(P) > e^{-\pi}$, then the only possible generator is the one obtained by (5.3).*

For the proofs of the above conditions and further material, we refer to the original article (Singer and Spilerman, 1976).

If there exists more than one valid generator matrix, the question is which one to choose. Since it is unlikely for a firm to migrate to a "far" rating from its current rating, Israel et al. (2000) suggest to choose among valid generators the one with the lowest value of

$$J = \sum_{i,j} |j - i| |\lambda_{ij}|$$

which ensures that the chance of jumping too far is minimized.

Investigating the existence or nonexistence of a valid generator matrix with only positive off-diagonal elements, we start with another result obtained by Singer and Spilerman (1976):

Proposition 5.6 *Let P be a transition matrix that has real distinct eigenvalues.*

- *If all eigenvalues of P are positive, then the matrix obtained by (5.3) is the only real matrix Λ such that $exp(\Lambda) = P$.*

- *If P has any negative eigenvalues, then there exists no real matrix Λ such that $exp(\Lambda) = P$.*

Using the conditions above, we can conclude for the nonexistence of a valid generator.

Proposition 5.7 *Let P be a transition matrix such that the (5.3) converges to a matrix Λ with negative off-diagonal elements. If at least one of the following three conditions hold*

- $det\,(P) > 1/2$ *and* $|P - I| < 1/2$ *or*
- *P has distinct eigenvalues and $det(P) > e^{-\pi}$ or*
- *P has distinct real eigenvalues*

then there does not exist a valid generator for P.

For the considered example

$$P = \begin{pmatrix} 0.9 & 0.08 & 0.0199 & 0.0001 \\ 0.050 & 0.850 & 0.090 & 0.010 \\ 0.010 & 0.090 & 0.800 & 0.100 \\ 0 & 0 & 0 & 1 \end{pmatrix}$$

we get the following results:

- $det(P) = 0.6015 \geq 1/2$.

- P has the distinct positive eigenvalues 0.9702, 0.8529, 0.7269, and 1.0000 and $det(P) = 0.6015 > 0.0432 \approx e^{-\pi}$.

- P has distinct real eigenvalues.

So we conclude that the conditions in proposition 5.5 for the uniqueness of a generator hold. Since (5.3) converges to

$$\Lambda = \begin{pmatrix} -0.1080 & 0.0907 & 0.0185 & -0.0013 \\ 0.0569 & -0.1710 & 0.1091 & 0.0051 \\ 0.0087 & 0.1092 & -0.2293 & 0.1114 \\ 0 & 0 & 0 & 0 \end{pmatrix}$$

we find with proposition 5.7 that there exists no true generator for the transition matrix P. Israel et al. (2000) also suggest a search algorithm for a valid generator if the series (5.3) fails to converge or converges to a matrix that has some off-diagonal terms but is not unique. For a further description we refer to the original publication. In the following we will provide some approximation methods for generator matrices that are useful in the case of negative off-diagonal elements.

5.3   Approximation of Generator Matrices

In the preceding section we saw that despite the manifold advantages of continuous-time transition modeling there is a chance of the nonexistence of a valid generator matrix to a given discrete-time transition. This may lead to some difficulties in practical implementations. Especially for matrices having rows with several zeros (e.g., no transitions to default states), often no valid generator matrix exists. In this case, some approximation methods can be used to determine an adequate generator matrix that will be discussed in the following.

If we find a generator matrix with negative off-diagonal entries in a row, we will have to correct this. The result may lead to a generator not providing exactly $P = e^{\Lambda^*}$ but only an approximation, though ensuring that from an economic viewpoint the necessary condition that all off-diagonal row entries in the generator are nonnegative is guaranteed. The literature suggests different methods to deal with this problem; see, e.g., Jarrow et al. (1997), Israel et al. (2000), Araten and Angbazo (1997), Kreinin and Sidelnikova (2001). In this section we will describe the approaches suggested in Jarrow et al. (1997) and Israel et al. (2000). For approaches using regularization algorithms that approximate the root of the annual transition matrix, we refer to the original publiations by Araten and Angbazo (1997) and Kreinin and Sidelnikova (2001).

5.3.1   The Method Proposed by Jarrow, Lando, and Turnbull (1997)

The first apporach to deal with off-diagonal row entries in the generator was initially suggested by Jarrow et al. (1997). Note that we will describe this in more detail in Chapter 8, which focuses on risk-neutral migration matrices. In this section we restrict ourselves to a review of their suggestion of how to adjust a generator matrix. In their approach every firm is assumed to have either zero or only one transition throughout the year. Under this hypothesis it can be shown that for $\lambda_i \neq 0$ for $i = 1, \ldots, K - 1$

$$
exp(\Lambda) = \begin{pmatrix}
e^{\lambda_1} & \frac{\lambda_{12}(e^{\lambda_1}-1)}{\lambda_1} & \cdots & \frac{\lambda_{1K}(e^{\lambda_1}-1)}{\lambda_1} \\
\frac{\lambda_{21}(e^{\lambda_2}-1)}{\lambda_2} & e^{\lambda_2} & \cdots & \frac{\lambda_{2K}(e^{\lambda_2}-1)}{\lambda_2} \\
\cdots & \cdots & \cdots & \cdots \\
\frac{\lambda_{K-1,1}(e^{\lambda_{K-1}}-1)}{\lambda_{K-1}} & \frac{\lambda_{K-1,2}(e^{\lambda_{K-1}}-1)}{\lambda_{K-1}} & \cdots & \frac{\lambda_{K-1,K}(e^{\lambda_{K-1}}-1)}{\lambda_{K-1}} \\
0 & 0 & \cdots & 1
\end{pmatrix}
$$

$$(5.16)$$

the estimates of $\hat{\Lambda}$ can be obtained by solving the system

$$\hat{q}_{ii} = e^{\hat{\lambda}_i} \text{ for } i = 1, \ldots, K - 1 \text{ and}$$

$$\hat{q}_{ij} = \hat{\lambda}_{ij}(e^{\hat{\lambda}_i} - 1) \text{ for } i, j = 1, \ldots, K - 1$$

JLT provide the solution to this system as

$$\hat{\lambda}_i = \log(\hat{q}_{ii}) \text{ for } i = 1, \ldots, K - 1 \text{ and}$$

$$\hat{\lambda}_{ij} = \hat{q}_{ij} \cdot \frac{\log(\hat{q}_{ii})}{(\hat{q}_{ii} - 1)} \text{ for } i \neq j \text{ and } i, j \ \ldots, K - 1$$

This leads only to an approximate generator matrix; however, it is guaranteed that the generator will have no nonnegative entries except the diagonal elements.

For our example, the JLT method gives the associated approximate generator

Λ	A	B	C	D
A	−0.1054	0.0843	0.0210	0.0001
B	0.0542	−0.1625	0.0975	0.0108
C	0.0112	0.1004	−0.2231	0.1116
D	0	0	0	0

with nonegative entries; however, $exp(\Lambda)$ is only close to the original transition matrix P:

P_{JLT}	A	B	C	D
A	0.9021	0.0748	0.0213	0.0017
B	0.0480	0.8561	0.0811	0.0148
C	0.0118	0.0834	0.8041	0.1006
D	0	0	0	1

Especially in the last column, high deviations (from 0.0001 to 0.0017 in the first row or 0.0148 instead of 0.010 in the second) for low default probabilities have to be considered as a rather rough approximation. We conclude that the method suggested by JLT in 1997 solves the problem of negative entries in the generator matrix, though we get an approximation that is not really close enough to the "real" transition matrix.

5.3.2 Methods Suggested by Israel, Rosenthal, and Wei (2000)

Due to the deficiencies of the method suggested by JLT, in their paper Israel et al. (2000) suggest a different approach to finding an approximate true generator. They suggest using (5.3) to calculate the associated generator and then adjust this matrix using one of the following methods:

- Replace the negative entries with zero and add the appropriate value back in the corresponding diagonal entry to guarantee that row-sums are zero. Mathematically,

$$\lambda_{ij} = max(\lambda_{ij}, 0), j \neq i; \quad \lambda_{ii} = \lambda_{ii} + \sum_{j \neq i} min(\lambda_{ij}, 0)$$

The new matrix will not exactly satisfy $P = e^{\Lambda^*}$.

- Replace the negative entries with zero and add the appropriate value back into *all* entries of the corresponding row proportional to their absolute values. Let G_i be the sum of the absolute values of the diagonal and nonnegative off-diagonal elements and B_i the sum of the absolute values of the negative off-diagonal elements:

$$G_i = |\lambda_{ii}| + \sum_{j \neq i} max(\lambda_{ij}, 0); \quad B_i = \sum_{j \neq i} max(-\lambda_{ij}, 0)$$

Then set the modified entries

$$\lambda_{ij} = \begin{cases} 0, & i \neq j \text{ and } \lambda_{ij} < 0 \\ \lambda_{ij} - \frac{B_i|\lambda_{ij}|}{G_i} & \text{otherwise if } G_i > 0 \\ \lambda_{ij}, & \text{otherwise if } G_i = 0 \end{cases}$$

In our example where the associated generator was

Λ	A	B	C	D
A	−0.1080	0.0907	0.0185	−0.0013
B	0.0569	−0.1710	0.1091	0.0051
C	0.0087	0.1092	−0.2293	0.1114
D	0	0	0	0

applying the first method and setting λ_{AD} to zero and adding -0.0013 to the diagonal element λ_{AA}, we would get for the adjusted generator matrix Λ^*

Λ^*	A	B	C	D
A	−0.1093	0.0907	0.0185	0
B	0.0569	−0.1710	0.1091	0.0051
C	0.0087	0.1092	−0.2293	0.1114
D	0	0	0	0

which gives us for the approximate one-year transition matrix

P_{IRW1}	A	B	C	D
A	0.8989	0.0799	0.0199	0.0013
B	0.0500	0.8500	0.0900	0.0100
C	0.0100	0.0900	0.8000	0.1000
D	0	0	0	1

Obviously the transition matrix P_{IRW1} is much closer to the "real" one year transition than the result for the method by Jarrow et al. (1997). Especially for the second and third row, we get almost exactly the same transition probabilities than for the "real" transition matrix. Also the deviation for the critical default probability λ_{AD} is clearly reduced compared to the JLT method described above.

Applying the second suggested method and again replacing the negative entries with zero but redistributing the appropriate value to *all* entries of the corresponding row proportional to their absolute values gives us the adjusted generator

Λ^*	A	B	C	D
A	−0.1086	0.0902	0.0184	0
B	0.0569	−0.1710	0.1091	0.0051
C	0.0087	0.1092	−0.2293	0.1114
D	0	0	0	0

and the associated one-year transition matrix

P_{IRW1}	A	B	C	D
A	0.8994	0.0795	0.0198	0.0013
B	0.0500	0.8500	0.0900	0.0100
C	0.0100	0.0900	0.8000	0.1000
D	0	0	0	1

Again we get results that are very similar to the ones using the first method by Israel et al. (2000). The authors state that generally by testing various matrices, they found similar results. To compare the goodness of the approximation, they used different distance matrix norms.

While the approximation of the method suggested by JLT in their 1997 seminal paper is rather rough, the methods suggested by Israel et al. (2000) give better approximations of the true transition matrix. Note, however, that these results are rather qualitative at the moment. For different measures to compare the goodness of the approximation, we refer to Chapter 7.

5.4   Simulating Credit Migrations

In this section we will review some techniques that can be used to simulate credit migration matrices. Simulation results from migration matrices are of particular interest when it comes to calculations of Value-at-Risk or expected shortfall for a credit or loan portfolio. This section provides a quick guide to different simulation techniques and presents algorithms for the time-discrete, time-continuous, and a nonparametric approach.

5.4.1   Time-Discrete Case

In the time-discrete case the simulation procedure is straightforward and can be conducted the following way: depending on the initial rating i of the firm, the interval $[0, 1]$ is divided into subintervals according to the migration probabilities p_{ij} for $j = 1, \ldots, K$. For example, for each rating class i, the intervals can be determined according to the following procedure:

$$
\begin{aligned}
I_{1,i} &= & [0, p_{i,1}) \\
I_{2,i} &= & [p_{i,1}, p_{i,1} + p_{i,2}) \\
\ldots & & \ldots \\
I_{j,i} &= & [\textstyle\sum_{k=1}^{j-1} p_{i,k}, \sum_{k=1}^{j} p_{i,k}) \\
\ldots & & \ldots \\
I_{K,i} &= [\textstyle\sum_{k=1}^{K-1} p_{i,k}, 1]
\end{aligned} \tag{5.17}
$$

Then a uniform distributed random variable u_t between 0 and 1 is drawn. Depending on which subinterval the random variable lies in, the company stays in the same rating class i or migrates to rating class j. The migration process for a company or loan in rating class i is determined by the following function $f : [0, 1] \rightarrow S$:

$$
f_{s_i} = \begin{cases}
S_1, & \text{for } u_t \in I_{1,i} \\
S_2 & \text{for } u_t \in I_{2,i} \\
\ldots & \ldots \\
\ldots & \ldots \\
S_K & \text{for } u_t \in I_{K,i}
\end{cases} \tag{5.18}
$$

If more than one time-period is considered and a migration to rating state j occurs, new subintervals have to be calculated based on the migration probabilities p_{jk} for $k = 1, \ldots, K$ and a new random number u_{t+1} is drawn for the following period. The procedure is either going to be repeated for $t = 1, \ldots, T$ periods or terminated, if the company migrates to the absorbing default state.

5.4.2   Time-Continuous Case

Recall that a continuous-time, time-homogeneous Markov chain is specified via the a $K \times K$ generator matrix of the following form:

$$\Lambda = \begin{pmatrix} \lambda_{11} & \lambda_{12} & \cdots & \lambda_{1K} \\ \lambda_{21} & \lambda_{22} & \cdots & \lambda_{2K} \\ \cdots & \cdots & \cdots & \cdots \\ \lambda_{K-1,1} & \lambda_{K-1,2} & \cdots & \lambda_{K-1,K} \\ 0 & 0 & \cdots & 0 \end{pmatrix} \tag{5.19}$$

where $\lambda_{ij} \geq 0$, for all i,j and $\lambda_{ii} = -\sum_{\substack{j=1 \\ j \neq i}}^{K} \lambda_{ij}$, for $i = 1, \ldots, K$. The off-diagonal elements represent the intensities of jumping from rating i to rating j. The default state K is considered to be absorbing.

In the following we will illustrate two different techniques that might be used to simulate credit migrations from a continuous-time Markov chain. The first one is applied, for example, in Christensen et al. (2004) or Trueck and Rachev (2005).

As the waiting time for leaving state i has an exponential distribution with the mean $\frac{1}{-\lambda_{ii}}$ we draw an exponentially distributed random variable t_1 with the density function

$$f(t_1) = -\lambda_{ii} e^{\lambda_{ii} t_1}$$

for each company with initial rating i. Depending on the considered time horizon T for $t_1 > T$, the company stays in its current class during the entire period T. If we get $t_1 < T$, we have to determine to which rating class the company migrates.

Hence, similar to the discrete-time approach the interval $[0, 1]$ is divided into subintervals according to the migration intensities calculated via $\frac{\lambda_{ij}}{-\lambda_{ii}}$. Then a uniform distributed random variable between 0 and 1 is drawn. Depending on which subinterval the random variable lies in, we determine the new rating class j the company migrates to. Then we draw again from an exponentially distributed random variable t_2—this time with parameter λ_{jj} from the generator matrix. If we find that $t_1 + t_2 > T$, the considered company stays in the new rating class and the simulation is completed for this firm. If $t_1 + t_2 < T$, we have to determine the new rating class. The procedure is repeated until we get $\sum t_k > T$ or the company migrates to the absorbing default state where it will remain for the rest of the considered time period.

An alternative procedure that could be used follows an algorithm that is, e.g., described in Glasserman (1992). Recall that the waiting times for leaving state i to any other rating state j have exponential distributions with mean $1/\lambda_{ij}$. Therefore, we draw for each of the companies with initial rating i_{K-1} exponentially distributed random variables t_{ij} with density functions

$$f(t_{ij}) = \lambda_{ij} exp(\lambda_{ij} t_{ij}) \qquad (5.20)$$

We then determine the minimum of the drawn waiting times $t_{min_1} = min(t_{ij})$ for $j \neq i$. Depending on the time horizon T, if $t_{min_1} > T$, the company stays in its current rating state i for the entire period T. If $t_{min_1} < T$, the company migrates to the rating class j with the smallest drawn waiting time t_{ij}. In the case of migration we again draw seven exponentially distributed random variables t_{jk} with density functions $f(t_{jk}) = \lambda_{jk} exp(\lambda_{jk} t_{jk})$ and determine t_{min_2}. If $t_{min_1} + t_{min_2} > T$, the company stays in the new rating class j and the simulation for this firm is completed. If $t_{min_1} + t_{min_2} < T$, the company migrates to the rating class k with the smallest drawn waiting time t_{jk}. The procedure is repeated until $\sum_i t_{min_i} > T$ or the company migrates to default state.

5.4.3 Nonparametric Approach

Finally, we will describe the underlying idea of nonparametric simulation of credit migrations. For an empirical application, see, e.g., Schuermann and Hanson (2004). The authors use a nonparametric simulation procedure to estimate confidence intervals for probabilities of default. Note that for this approach the estimated discrete or continuous-time migration matrix will not be sufficient. To apply a nonparametric approach, the actual individual migrations of the loans or bonds need to be available. Based on the observed migrations, for each of the rating classes, a data table can be constructed containing the duration times and the rating class the corresponding company migrated to.

The simulation procedure can be described as follows: for each of the companies we draw randomly a row in the corresponding duration time data table. If the duration time t in the drawn row is greater than the considered time horizon T, the company stays in the initial rating class. For $t < T$ we have to differentiate between two cases. If the initial rating and the end rating of the drawn row coincide, the company stays, of course, in the initial rating. We then have to randomly draw another row from the same duration time data table, whereas the considered time horizon T has to be reduced by t. If the end rating j and the initial rating i of the drawn row vary, a migration to rating j occurs. In this case we have to randomly draw a row from the duration time data table of the new rating class j. The procedure is repeated until either a default occurs or the sum of the drawn duration times exceed the simulated time horizon T.

The following example may help to illustrate the procedure. Table 5.1 gives an exemplary representation for hypothetical duration times in rating class AA. Assume that for each of the other rating classes a similar table was

TABLE 5.1. Parts of the Duration Time Table for Rating Class AA

Row	Duration Time t (in months)	Initial Rating i	End Rating j
1	36	AA	AA
2	4	AA	AAA
3	71	AA	AA
4	17	AA	BBB
...	...	...	...

constructed. Hereby, also the duration records of companies which remained in the initial rating class for the considered time period were included. The simulation is then conducted according to the algorithm described above. Depending on the drawn random number, the corresponding row in the table is considered to simulate the duration time in the rating class and the migration.

Note that in this section we assumed that all individual migrations are independent. For approaches that can also be used to simulate dependent credit migrations, we refer to Section 10.5.

6

Stability of Credit Migrations

This chapter is dedicated to the examination of the stability of rating migration with the focus on credit transition matrices. After a first glance at rating behavior through the business cycle, we will provide tests for two major assumptions that are often made about transition matrices: time homogeneity and Markov behavior. Generally, both assumptions should be treated with care. Several studies have shown that migration matrices are not homogeneous through time and that also the assumption of first-order Markov behavior is rather questionable; see, e.g., Bangia et al. (2002), Jafry and Schuermann (2004), Krüger et al. (2005), Nickell et al. (2000), Weber et al. (1998). As a major reason for this, many authors name the influence of macroeconomic variables and their effects on migration behavior (Nickell et al., 2000; Trueck, 2008; Wei, 2003). However, such business cycle effects might have a substantial influence on homogeneity of migration behavior, but they do not implicitly contradict the idea of Markov behavior. For some theoretical explanations of non-Markov behavior in credit migrations, see, e.g., Löffler (2004, 2005). For a framework on stochastic migration matrices and a study on serially correlated rating transitions in the French market, we refer to Gagliardini and Gourieroux (2005a,b). Overall, while the assumption of first-order Markov behavior for credit migrations might be a simplification of the real world, departing from this assumption makes the modeling, estimation, or simulation of rating transitions much more complicated. In this chapter we will review methods that can be used to investigate time homogeneity and Markov behavior of credit migration matrices. They might be helpful to examine deviations from these properties but can also be used to compare different rating systems with respect to their migration behavior. Several of the issues raised will also be illustrated using empirical examples of an internal rating system as well as a history of Moody's yearly credit migration matrices.

6.1 Credit Migrations and the Business Cycle

This section tries to give a first glance at the link between the current state of the economy and default risk or migration behavior of a company.

Intuition gives the following view: when the economy worsens, both downgrades as well as defaults will increase. The contrary should be true when the economy becomes stronger. Figures 6.1 and 6.2 show Moody's historical default frequencies for noninvestment grade bonds of rating class CCC and B for the years 1984 to 2001. Clearly there is a high deviation from the average. For CCC-rated bonds the default frequencies range from 5% in 1996 in high market times to more than 45% in 2001, when there was a deep recession in the American economy. We conclude that taking average default probabilites of a longer time horizon as estimators for future default probabilities might not give correct risk estimates for a portfolio.

Note that also the second major determinant of credit risk, the recovery rate, shows large variations through time. Figure 6.3 illustrates the issuer weighted recovery rates for corporate loans from 1982–2003 according to Moody's KMV investor services. For further results on the investigation of the relation between default and recovery rates, see Altman and Kishore (1996), Altman et al. (2005), Schuermann (2004).

Since our focus is mainly on credit migration matrices, in Tables 6.1 and 6.2 we also provided information on Moody's average one-year transition probabilities for unsecured long-term corporate and sovereign bond

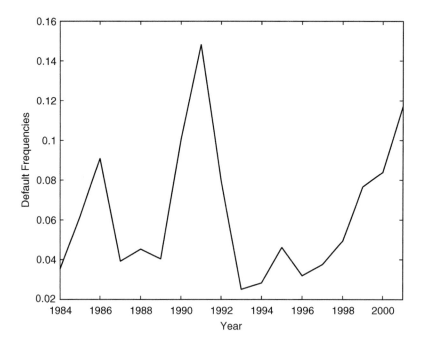

FIGURE 6.1. Moody's historical default rates for rating class B and time horizon 1984–2001.

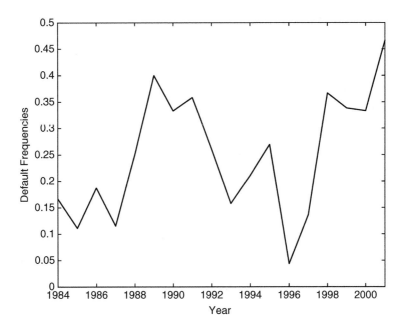

FIGURE 6.2. Moody's historical defaults rates for rating class Caa and time horizon 1984–2001.

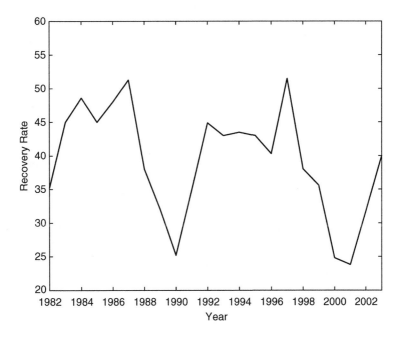

FIGURE 6.3. Issuer weighted recovery rates for corporate loans (1982–2003). Source: Moody's KMV.

TABLE 6.1. Average One-Year Transition Probabilities for Unsecured Moody's Long-Term Corporate and Sovereign Bond Ratings, Business Cycle Recession Source: Nickell et al. (2000)

	Aaa	Aa	A	Baa	Ba	B	Caa	C	D
Aaa	89.60	10.00	0.40	0.00	0.00	0.00	0.00	0.00	0.00
Aa	0.90	88.30	10.70	0.10	0.00	0.00	0.00	0.00	0.00
A	0.10	2.70	91.10	5.60	0.40	0.20	0.00	0.10	0.00
Baa	0.00	0.30	6.60	86.80	5.60	0.40	0.20	0.00	0.10
Ba	0.00	0.10	0.50	5.90	83.10	8.40	0.30	0.00	1.70
B	0.00	0.10	0.20	0.80	6.60	79.60	2.20	1.00	9.40
Caa	0.00	0.00	0.00	0.90	1.90	9.30	63.00	1.90	23.10
C	0.00	0.00	0.00	0.00	0.00	5.90	5.90	64.70	23.50

TABLE 6.2. Average One-Year Transition Probabilities for Unsecured Moody's Long-Term Corporate and Sovereign Bond Ratings, Business Cycle Peak Source: Nickell et al. (2000)

	Aaa	Aa	A	Baa	Ba	B	Caa	C	D
Aaa	92.20	7.40	0.30	0.00	0.10	0.00	0.00	0.00	0.00
Aa	1.50	87.50	10.10	0.70	0.20	0.00	0.00	0.00	0.00
A	0.10	1.80	91.70	5.40	0.80	0.20	0.00	0.10	0.00
Baa	0.10	0.20	5.20	88.10	4.90	1.20	0.00	0.00	0.20
Ba	0.10	0.00	0.30	5.40	85.70	6.70	0.20	0.00	1.50
B	0.10	0.10	0.40	0.80	6.60	83.60	1.60	0.30	6.60
Caa	0.00	0.00	0.00	0.00	2.80	9.30	59.80	8.40	19.60
C	0.00	0.00	0.00	0.00	0.00	8.30	8.30	70.80	12.50

ratings for the case of business cycle trough and peak from 1970–1997. The data are taken from a study by Nickell et al. (2000) and show the clear tendency of higher downgrade probability for investment and speculative grade issues during recessions compared to expansions of the economy. Similar results were obtained by Bangia et al. (2002), who considered Standard & Poor's (S&P) historical transition matrices from 1981 to 1998.

The question arises when two migration matrices or rows of these matrices differ from each other significantly and when they differ from the unconditional average transition matrix. To examine this issue more thoroughly, we will provide tests to detect significant differences between transition matrices in the next section.

Considering assigned new ratings by S&P for the period from 1984–2001 in Table 6.3, we find that in years of economical contraction, as in 1990 or 1991, the lowest percentages of new issuers in speculative grade could be observed. This could be due to the fact that in these times fewer risky

TABLE 6.3. S&P's Assigned Ratings in Investment and Speculative Grade to New Issuers and Downgrade to Upgrade Ratio for all Issuers
Source: Standard & Poor's

Year	% Investment Grade	% Speculative Grade	Downgrade/Upgrade Ratio
1984	54.3	45.7	1.23
1985	60.6	39.4	2.13
1986	40.3	59.7	2.21
1987	43.5	56.5	1.57
1988	59.6	40.4	1.56
1989	55.5	44.5	1.40
1990	77.6	22.4	2.56
1991	86.0	14.0	2.25
1992	62.0	38.0	1.41
1993	50.9	49.1	1.25
1994	65.0	35.0	1.63
1995	54.2	45.8	1.06
1996	53.0	47.0	0.67
1997	43.2	56.8	1.00
1998	37.0	62.5	1.81
1999	39.6	60.4	1.91
2000	49.4	50.6	2.24
2001	56.5	43.5	2.90

businesses emerge and issue debt. Further, in these years as well as during the economic downturn in the year 2001, a very high downgrade to upgrade ratio considering all issuers could be observed. So obviously, ratings themselves but also changes in these ratings, i.e., credit migrations, seem to exhibit different behavior through time and are dependent on the overall macroeconomic situation. Considering the coefficients of variation, a study by Bangia et al. (2002) finds that most of the coefficients of variation during an economic recession are much lower than for all years considered. According to the authors for the expansion matrix, the coefficients of variation are on average reduced by only 2% compared to the unconditional matrix, while the contraction matrix exhibits about 14% less volatility. Furthermore it is striking that many of the largest reductions in variation coefficients for the contraction matrix actually stem from elements on or close to the diagonal supporting the reliability of the results. Overall, these results could be a sign for the fact that migration probabilities are more stable in economic contractions than they are on average, supporting the existence of two distinct economic regimes. The difference in the matrices observed indicates that the historical defaults develop differently during expansions and contractions.

TABLE 6.4. Correlations Between Macroeconomic Variables and Moody's Historical Default Frequencies for Rating Classes Baa-C 1984–2000

Rating Class	Baa	Ba	B	C
Δ GDP	−0.1581	−0.4516	−0.6414	−0.3066
Δ CPI	0.4046	0.5691	0.2271	0.2010
Annual Saving	0.4018	0.5663	0.2258	0.1983
Δ Consumption	−0.0902	−0.0132	−0.3099	−0.1686

Let us finally examine the correlations between yearly default rates in the speculative grade area and macroeconomic variables. Assuming that the variables will have an effect on default rates, we considered the GDP growth, changes in the consumer price index, annual savings, and changes in the personal consumption expenditures for the United States. The correlations were calculated based on an assumed effect of the exogenous variables on rating migrations for the same year (see Table 6.4).

We find that some of the considered variables clearly have a significant impact on the considered migrations. The sign of the correlation in Table 6.4 is in the direction we would expect for all variables. In Chapter 9 we will take a closer look at the relationship between business cycle indicators and credit migration matrices. In this chapter we will mainly focus on the assumptions of Markov behavior and time homogeneity of migration matrices and provide a study on the significant effects changes in migration behavior may have on VaR and estimated probabilities of default for credit portfolios.

6.2 The Markov Assumptions and Rating Drifts

In most rating based models for credit risk management, rating transitions are modeled via a discrete or continuous-time Markov chain. However, in several applications, [see Lando and Skødeberg (2002); Nagpal and Bahar (2000); Frydman and Schuermann (2008)] non-Markov migration behavior also is investigated, and the authors provide methods for detecting higher order Markov behavior or rating drifts in migration models. In this section we summarize tests for Markov behavior or so-called rating drift in credit migrations. The tests will be illustrated using some empirical results for an internal rating system.

The term "Markov behavior" generally denotes Markov behavior of first order. However, later we will also investigate Markov behavior of a higher order. Therefore, we denote that unless it is not explicitly indicated, the term "Markov behavior" refers to first order Markov behavior. We define

Definition 6.1 *A random variable X_t exhibits (first-order) Markov behavior, if its conditional distribution of X_t on past states is a function of X_{t-1} alone, and does not depend on previous states $\{X_{t-2}, X_{t-3}, \ldots\}$:*

$$P(X_t = x_t \mid X_{t-1} = x_{t-1}, X_{t-2} = x_{t-2}, \ldots, X_0 = x_0)$$

$$= P(X_t = x_t \mid X_{t-1} = x_{t-1})$$

As mentioned above, the term "Markov behavior" usually describes a first-order Markov chain. If the probability of moving to a certain state in the next period is not only dependent on the current state X_{t-1} but also on past states $X_{t-2}, \ldots X_{t-n}$ (but not on state $X_{t-(n+1)}, \ldots$), one uses the term "Markov behavior of nth order":

$$P(X_t = x_t \mid X_{t-1} = x_{t-1}, X_{t-2} = x_{t-2}, \ldots, X_0 = x_0)$$

$$= P(X_t = x_t \mid X_{t-1} = x_{t-1}, \ldots, X_{t-n} = x_{t-n})$$

6.2.1 Likelihood Ratio Tests

Following Goodman (1958), we suggest testing the Markov property using a likelihood ratio test. The test is based on comparing two likelihood functions L_B and L_A while one of the models is assumed to show Markov behavior of a higher order. The test statistic

$$LR = 2\ln\left(\frac{L_B}{L_A}\right) = 2\ln(L_B - L_A) \sim \chi^2(b - a) \tag{6.1}$$

is approximately χ^2 distributed; the number of degrees of freedom is the difference between the estimated parameters in model B minus the estimated parameters in model A.

Testing for first-order Markov behavior against independence then is equivalent to testing the hypothesis of an independent identical distribution (iid) against the hypothesis of a first-order Markov chain (MK1). We obtain the likelihood functions

$$L_A(\widehat{P}) = \prod_{j=1}^{n} p_j^{n_j}$$

and

$$L_B(\widehat{P}) = \prod_{i=1}^{n}\prod_{j=1}^{n} p_{ij}^{n_{ij}}$$

Clearly, in order to test on the same data basis, we can include only those records in L_A having at least one period of history. With L_A and L_B the likelihood ratio becomes

$$LR = 2\ln\left(\frac{\prod_{i=1}^{n}\prod_{j=1}^{n}p_{ij}^{n_{ij}}}{\prod_{j=1}^{n}p_j^{n_j}}\right) = 2\left(\sum_{i=1}^{n}\sum_{j=1}^{n}n_{ij}\ln p_{ij} - \sum_{j=1}^{n}n_j\ln p_j\right) \quad (6.2)$$

The likelihood ratio is supposed to be χ^2-distributed with Δm degrees of freedom, where Δm is the difference in the number of estimated parameters in both models.

For higher order Markov behavior, a second test can be deducted on the null-hypothesis of *first-order Markov property* (MK1) against the hypothesis of *second-order Markov property* (MK2). The matter of interest is whether the actual distribution depends only on the last state X_{t-1} or also incorporating the second last state X_{t-2} provides higher likelihoods. The likelihood functions read

$$L_B(\widehat{P}) = \prod_{i=1}^{n}\prod_{j=1}^{n}p_{ij}^{n_{ij}} \quad \text{and} \quad L_C(\widehat{P}) = \prod_{i=1}^{n}\prod_{j=1}^{n}\prod_{k=1}^{n}p_{ijk}^{n_{ijk}}$$

Hence, the likelihood ratio is calculated according to the expression

$$LR = 2\left(\sum_{i=1}^{n}\sum_{j=1}^{n}\sum_{k=1}^{n}n_{ijk}\ln p_{ijk} - \sum_{i=1}^{n}\sum_{j=1}^{n}n_{ij}\ln p_{ij}\right) \quad (6.3)$$

Following Goodman (1958) the expression LR also is χ^2-distributed with Δm degrees of freedom. Again Δm is equal to the difference of the number of estimated parameters in both models. Testing for second-order Markov behavior (MK2) against the hypothesis of third-order Markov behavior (MK3) is straightforward. We therefore exclude the test statistics and simply provide some empirical results on these tests of an empirical study on the internal rating system described above.

6.2.2 Rating Drift

In a number of publications (Altman and Kao, 1992a,b; Bangia et al., 2002; Lando and Skødeberg, 2002), first-order Markov property has been rejected by testing for rating drift or so-called path dependence. Rating changes from the previous period have continued in the actual period in most cases. In a first-order Markov chain, the rating distribution of the next period is dependent only on the present state and not on any developments in the past. If there is a so-called rating drift or path dependence, then it is assumed that loans that have been downgraded before are less frequently upgraded in the next period, while loans that have experienced prior upgrading are prone to further upgrading. Therefore, two-period changes like "Down-Down"[1] or "Up-Up" are generally considered to be more probable than alternating rating changes like "Down-Up" or "Up-Down"—the former is the so-called rating drift.

In order to investigate if such a rating drift exists in our data, we rely on the matrix M, which includes the total number of transitions from one rating grade to another; i.e., $\{M(t)\}_{ij}$ gives the number of transitions from rating grade i at time t to rating grade j at time $t+1$. The matrix M is split into the sum of three matrices, called *Up-Momentum-Matrix*, *Maintain-Momentum-Matrix*, and *Down-Momentum-Matrix*.[2] These three matrices are defined element-by-element in the following way:

$$\{M_{\mathrm{Up}}(t)\}_{ij} := \text{number of transitions from } i \text{ to } j \text{ of companies}$$
$$\text{which were upgraded during the year } t-1 \text{ to } t,$$
$$\{M_{\mathrm{Maintain}}(t)\}_{ij} := \text{number of transitions from } i \text{ to } j \text{ of companies}$$
$$\text{which had no rating change during the year } t-1 \text{ to } t,$$
$$\{M_{\mathrm{Down}}(t)\}_{ij} := \text{number of transitions from } i \text{ to } j \text{ of companies}$$
$$\text{which had no rating change during the year } t-1 \text{ to } t.$$

By construction we have

$$M(t) = M_{\mathrm{Up}}(t) + M_{\mathrm{Maintain}}(t) + M_{\mathrm{Down}}(t).$$

As mentioned above, the issues of Markov bahvior and rating drifts have been studied by various authors (Altman and Kao, 1992a; Bangia et al., 2002; Lando and Skødeberg, 2002). In most of the cases, higher order Markov behavior and rating drift can be detected. However, most of the studies conducted deal with data provided by the major rating agencies. In the following we will illustrate the use of the methods described above to an internal rating system of a financial institution.

6.2.3 An Empirical Study

In the following some empirical results for an internal rating system based on balance sheet data rating process of a German bank are provided.[3] The default probabilities and corresponding ratings were determined based on a logit model (Engelmann et al., 2003) and were used to investigate the time series behavior of the migration matrices for the period from 1988 to 2003. We will start with overview on the observed transitions and average one-year migration matrix for the considered time period; see Krüger et al. (2005).

Hereby, the transition probabilities were calculated by Maximum Likelihood estimation as $\hat{p}_{ij} = \frac{N_{ij}}{N_i}$ where N_{ij} denotes the number of transitions

---

[1] For example, a series of subsequent downgrades like AAA $\longrightarrow$ AA $\longrightarrow$ A.

[2] This procedure is the same as in Bangia et al. (2002).

[3] The results were originally published in Krüger et al. (2005).

TABLE 6.5. Average Rounded One-Year Transitions for the Considered Rating System

	AAA	AA	A	BBB	BB	B	CCC	D	Σ	Portion
AAA	3249	679	479	263	61	13	0	2	4744	14.73%
AA	686	721	744	400	71	12	0	1	2635	8.18%
A	431	744	1805	1648	259	32	0	4	4923	15.29%
BBB	218	368	1552	6609	2288	259	0	31	11325	35.17%
BB	45	56	192	2034	3672	864	1	82	6946	21.57%
B	8	6	22	180	748	762	3	71	1800	5.59%
CCC	0	0	0	0	1	3	0	0	4	0.02%

TABLE 6.6. Average One-Year Transition Probabilities for the Considered Rating System

	AAA	AA	A	BBB	BB	B	CCC	D
AAA	68.48%	14.30%	10.10%	5.54%	1.29%	0.27%	0.00%	0.03%
AA	26.01%	27.37%	28.24%	15.19%	2.69%	0.46%	0.00%	0.04%
A	8.76%	15.12%	36.66%	33.46%	5.26%	0.65%	0.00%	0.08%
BBB	1.93%	3.25%	13.70%	58.36%	20.20%	2.29%	0.00%	0.27%
BB	0.65%	0.80%	2.76%	29.29%	52.86%	12.43%	0.02%	1.18%
B	0.45%	0.35%	1.24%	10.00%	41.54%	42.33%	0.15%	3.94%
CCC	0.00%	2.91%	0.97%	5.83%	19.90%	66.02%	4.37%	0.00%
D	0.00%	0.00%	0.00%	0.00%	0.00%	0.00%	0.00%	100.00%

TABLE 6.7. Results from the LR-Tests for the Considered Internal Rating System

H_0	H_1	# Companies	Likelihood Ratio	f	$\chi^2(f)$
iid	**MK1**	32,380	**26426**	39	54.57
MK1	**MK2**	27,912	**1852**	192	225.33
MK2	MK3	24,575	800	783	**849.21**

from rating i to j and N_i denotes the total number of transitions from rating i. The average rounded one-year number of transitions and transition probabilities for the considered rating system are reported in Tables 6.5 and 6.6. In a next step the estimated yearly migration matrices were investigated by conducting the likelihood ratio tests on Markov behavior and examining rating drifts.

The results for tests on first or higher order Markov behavior are shown in Table 6.7; significant test results are highlighted in bold letters. The first test was on the hypothesis of independent identical distribution (iid) against the hypothesis of a MK1. The results were significant rejecting the iid hypothesis. In a second test the hypothesis of MK1 is tested against second-order Markov property. Based on the results, we also reject MK1 in favor of second-order Markov property. We conclude that for the considered rating system at least a rating history of two periods should be used to estimate the actual state distribution as precisely as possible or make forecasts on future rating distributions. In a third test we examine whether the hypothesis of third-order Markov property (MK3) leads to even better results. Again the number of companies included decreases, because only records with a three-period history could be taken into account. In that case the test is not significant, so we conclude that the hypothesis of MK2 cannot be rejected. We conclude that for the considered internal rating system, the rating state distribution seems to depend on two periods of history.

The average transition probabilities we obtained based on M_{Up}, M_{Maintain}, and M_{Down} for the the years 1990 until 2003 can be found in Table 6.8, Table 6.9, and Table 6.10. Note that due to the very small number of observations in the CCC rating category, we excluded the category from the analysis.

We found an interesting result for our rating system: companies in a rating category that were upgraded in the previous period are more likely to be downgraded than companies in the same rating category that were downgraded in the previous period. Considering transition probabilities obtained from the Up-Momentum-Matrix, we find that upgrades (elements

TABLE 6.8. Average Transition Probabilities Obtained from the Up-Momentum-Matrix

	AAA	AA	A	BBB	BB	B	CCC	D
AAA	49.37%	21.30%	16.67%	9.80%	2.35%	0.47%	0.00%	0.05%
AA	**20.40%**	24.83%	**32.05%**	18.64%	3.43%	0.59%	0.00%	0.06%
A	6.15%	11.15%	33.57%	40.93%	7.13%	0.93%	0.01%	0.12%
BBB	1.27%	1.86%	7.42%	51.81%	32.88%	4.31%	0.00%	0.46%
BB	0.35%	0.74%	1.90%	17.68%	52.76%	24.28%	0.06%	2.24%
B	0.00%	1.96%	0.00%	7.84%	0.00%	78.43%	11.8%	0.00%

TABLE 6.9. Average Transition Probabilities Obtained from the Maintain-Momentum-Matrix

	AAA	AA	A	BBB	BB	B	CCC	D
AAA	75.87%	12.07%	7.42%	3.66%	0.80%	0.15%	0.00%	0.03%
AA	**24.42%**	32.48%	**28.71%**	12.39%	1.80%	0.19%	0.00%	0.01%
A	6.55%	14.98%	41.60%	32.55%	3.95%	0.32%	0.00%	0.06%
BBB	1.12%	2.16%	11.90%	63.58%	19.25%	1.75%	0.00%	0.24%
BB	0.29%	0.47%	1.58%	23.66%	59.54%	13.17%	0.01%	1.27%
B	0.39%	0.26%	0.71%	5.64%	34.22%	54.06%	0.17%	4.54%

TABLE 6.10. Average Transition Probabilities Obtained from the Down-Momentum-Matrix

	AAA	AA	A	BBB	BB	B	CCC	D
AAA	—	—	—	—	—	—	—	—
AA	**34.50%**	26.89%	**23.37%**	12.70%	2.20%	0.28%	0.00%	0.04%
A	13.88%	18.95%	35.23%	27.04%	4.26%	0.55%	0.00%	0.10%
BBB	4.01%	6.44%	22.34%	51.97%	13.35%	1.66%	0.00%	0.21%
BB	0.93%	1.11%	4.10%	38.60%	45.77%	8.57%	0.02%	0.88%
B	0.38%	0.40%	1.45%	12.21%	45.89%	35.69%	0.08%	3.90%

at the left side of the diagonal) have *lower* probabilities than downgrades (elements at the right side of the diagonal). In the Down-Momentum-Matrix we see that upgrades have *higher* probabilities than downgrades. To illustrate this behavior, in Tables 6.8, 6.9, and 6.10 some transition probabilities for upgrades and downgrades of AA rated records have been highlighted in bold. More formally, our observations concerning conditional upgrade and downgrade probabilities of a rating process X can be written as

$$P(X_{t+1} > X_t \mid X_t < X_{t-1}) > P(X_{t+1} > X_t \mid X_t > X_{t-1})$$

$$P(X_{t+1} < X_t \mid X_t > X_{t-1}) > P(X_{t+1} < X_t \mid X_t < X_{t-1})$$

To investigate whether the differences are significant for single states (rows) and for the entire matrices, we used Pearson's χ^2 test. We considered the values of the Maintain-Momentum-Matrix as *expected events* and transitions of the Up-Momentum-Matrix (Down-Momentum-Matrix) as *observed events*. The result both for row-wise comparison and matrix-wise comparison confirms that the matrices are significantly different.

Summarizing the results of this section, we find that for the considered rating system rating transitions tend to compensate previous-period rating changes. These results are quite different to the *rating drift* observed in previous studies—for example, Altman and Kao (1992b), Bangia et al. (2002) or Lando and Skødeberg (2002). The authors found a tendency that companies in a certain rating category which were downgraded in the previous period are more likely to be downgraded in the next period than other companies in the same rating category which were upgraded in the previous period. An analogous statement was found for upgrades. Our results may be a consequence of the fact that, in contrast to other studies, we investigate rating transitions which are based on changes in credit scores only. Personal judgements or so-called soft factors included in the rating procedure by the major rating agencies that might induce effects like a rating drift were not considered.

6.3 Time Homogeneity of Migration Matrices

In the following we will review some techniques that can be used to investigate time homogeneity of migration matrices. While it is well known that generally transition matrices do not exhibit homogeneous migration behavior through time (Bangia et al., 2002; Nickell et al., 2000; Trueck and Rachev, 2005; Weber et al., 1998), for the sake of simplification average historical migration matrices are used as a starting point for evaluating credit risk or also to derive risk-neutral migration matrices as in Jarrow et al. (1997). Nevertheless, this property includes some element of idealization, since different states of the economy will generally result in a different migration behavior of companies in terms of rating upgrades, downgrades, or defaults. Recall, however, that in Section 2.1 it was explained that so-called through-the-cycle ratings should take into account possible changes in the macroeconomic conditions and not be affected when the change of the creditworthiness is caused only by a change of macroeconomic variables.

We will now investigate some methods for detecting time inhomogeneity of transition matrices. The most prominent tests for comparing transition matrices were developed by Anderson and Goodman (1957), Goodman (1958), and Billingsley (1961). They use chi-square and likelihood-ratio tests comparing transition probabilities estimated simultaneously from the entire sample to those estimated from subsamples obtained by dividing the entire sample into at least two mutually independent groups of observations. In our empirical study we will focus on the chi-square test; the LR test statistic is asymptotically equivalent.

For the definition of time homogeneity, let us consider the two years s and u and the corresponding state vectors X_s, X_u. Let us denote the transition matrix which transforms X_s into X_u by $P_t(s)$, where $t := u - s$ denotes the time horizon in years.

Definition 6.2 *A Markov chain is time homogeneous if the property*

$$P(X_s = x_s \mid X_{s-1} = x_{s-1}) = P(X_u = x_u \mid X_{u-1} = x_{u-1})$$

holds for the state vectors X_s and X_u at two different dates s and u, where s and u are arbitrary.

As a consequence of this definition, for $t = v - u = s - r$ we have

$$X_v = P_{v-u}X_r = P_{s-r}X_r = P_t X_r \tag{6.4}$$

where P_t does not depend on the initial date r or u but only on the difference t between the initial date r and s or u and v, respectively.

In the nonhomogeneous case the transition probability matrix would depend on the initial date r or u as well as on the distance t between the dates; i.e., we have $X_v = P_t(u)X_u$ instead of (6.4), whereas in the homogeneous case the transition probability matrix is a function of the distance between dates and not the dates themselves.

For simplicity, let us denote the transition probability matrix for two subsequent years by P. The property time homogeneity offers the nice feature that the state vector x_v at any future date v can be calculated in terms of the initial state vector x_u by $x_v = P^t x_u$, where P^t denotes the tth power of the matrix P.

6.3.1 Tests Using the Chi-Square Distance

In tests using the chi-square distance, time stationarity is simply checked by dividing the entire sample into T periods. Then it is tested whether the transition matrices estimated from each of the T subsamples differ significantly from the matrix estimated from the entire sample.

The test statistic used is

$$Q_t = \sum_{t=1}^{T} \sum_{i=1}^{N} \sum_{j \in V_i} n_i(t) \frac{(\hat{p}_{ij}(t) - p_{ij})^2}{p_{ij}} \sim \chi^2 \left(\sum_{i=1}^{N} (u_i - 1)(v_i - 1) \right) \quad (6.5)$$

Clearly, p_{ij} denotes the average probability of transition from the ith to the jth class estimated from the entire sample, $\hat{p}_{ij}(t)$ the corresponding transition probability estimated from subsample in t. Further we should note that only those transition probabilities are taken into account which are positive in the entire sample; thus, we set $V_i = \{j : \hat{p}_{ij} > 0\}$ and exclude transitions for which no observations are available in the entire sample. Q has an asymptotic chi-square distribution with degrees of freedom equal to the number of summands in T minus the number of estimated transition probabilities $\hat{p}_{ij}$ corrected for the number of restrictions ($\sum_j p_{ij} = 1$ and $\sum_j p_{ij}(t) = 1$ for $t = 1, \ldots, T$). Thus, we get for the degrees of freedom ($\sum_i (u_i - 1)(v_i - 1)$).

6.3.2 Eigenvalues and Eigenvectors

Another possibility to investigate time homogeneity is obtained by considering the eigenvalues and eigenvectors of transition matrices P for different time horizons. For example, Bangia et al. (2002) use this method in an empirical study on the stability of migration matrices of Standard & Poors. Note that a transition matrix P can be decomposed into a diagonal matrix of eigenvalues diag(Θ_1) of P and the basis-transformation matrix $\Phi = \{\phi_1, \ldots, \phi_n\}$

$$P = \Phi \, \text{diag}(\Theta_1) \, \Phi^{-1} \quad (6.6)$$

where the diagonal elements are given by $\theta_1, \theta_2, \ldots, \theta_n$. Without loss of generality, it can be assumed that the column indices are ordered such that

$$|\theta_1| \geq |\theta_2| \geq \cdots \geq |\theta_n|$$

Then the ordered column indices for the average one-period transition matrix P_1 are

$$|\theta_{11}| \geq |\theta_{12}| \geq \cdots \geq |\theta_{1n}|$$

Note that in this notation the first index is used for the time horizon in years in the time-homogeneous case, whereas the second index is the number of the eigenvalue. Let further P_t denote the tth power of the estimated transition matrix for one period P_1. Using the same decomposition as above, we can express the tth power of P_1 as

$$P_t = \Phi \, \text{diag}(\Theta_1)^t \, \Phi^{-1}$$

with

$$(\text{diag}(\Theta_1))^t = \begin{pmatrix} \theta_{11}{}^t & 0 & \cdots & 0 \\ 0 & \ddots & & \vdots \\ \vdots & & \ddots & 0 \\ 0 & \cdots & 0 & \theta_{1n}{}^t \end{pmatrix}$$

Obviously, the eigenvalues of P_t are given by $(\theta_i)^t$. Note that due to the fact that the row sum of a transition matrix must equal one per definition, the largest of the eigenvalues θ_1 must be identically equal to 1. When the matrix is raised to the tth power, the eigenvalue of 1 persists while all the other (nonunity) eigenvalues have magnitudes less than 1. Therefore, when raised to the tth power, they eventually decay away; see Jafry and Schuermann (2004) for further details. Because of $\ln \theta_{1i}{}^t = t \ln \theta_{1i}$ the sequence $\theta_{1i}, \theta_{2i}, \theta_{3i}, \ldots, \theta_{ri}$ of the ith eigenvalues of the matrices $P_1, P_2, P_3, \ldots, P_r$ is a log-linear function of t. For example, we get for the relationship between the second eigenvalue of the matrix P_1 and $P_4 = P_1^4$: $\ln \theta_{42} = 4 \ln \theta_{12}$.

With this in mind, it is straightforward to investigate the property of time homogeneity based on the eigenvalues of estimated k-period migration matrices: consider, for example, the average transition matrices $\bar{P}_1, \bar{P}_2, \bar{P}_3$, and $\bar{P}_4$ for the time horizons of 1, 2, 3, and 4 years from an empirical data set and plot the logarithms $\ln(\bar{\theta}_2(t))$, $\ln(\bar{\theta}_3(t))$, $\ln(\bar{\theta}_4(t))$, and $\ln(\bar{\theta}_5(t))$ of the eigenvalues smaller than 1 of these 4 matrices. Under the assumption of time homogeneity, one could expect that each sequence $\ln \bar{\theta}_j(t)$ $(j \in \{2, \ldots, 5\})$ of eigenvalues can be fit by a straight regression line.

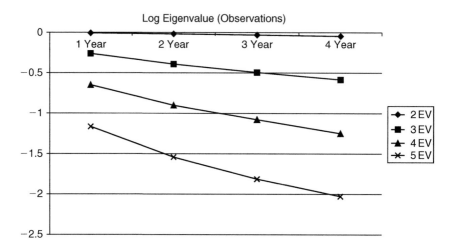

FIGURE 6.4. Relationship between second up to fifth log-eigenvalues of the estimated average transition matrices $\bar{P}_1, \bar{P}_2, \bar{P}_3$, and $\bar{P}_4$.

A plot of the relation between the logarithm of the eigenvalues $\bar{P}_1, \bar{P}_2, \bar{P}_3$, and $\bar{P}_4$ for the considered internal rating system is provided in Figure 6.4. Obviously, the fourth and fifth eigenvalues do not show log-linear behavior, as the plotted lines are not really straight. Further the log-eigenvalues for periods of two or more years are not t-multiples of the log-eigenvalue for one year.

Based on the results in Figure 6.4, we rather assume that the property of time homogeneity should be rejected for the considered rating system. Note, however, that we have not provided a formal test procedure for time homogeneity here, but rather a qualitative way to investigate the issue.

Another way of approaching time homogeneity is analyzing the eigenvectors of a migration matrix P_1. Following Bangia et al. (2002), in the case of time homogeneity the matrices P_1 and any arbitrary power $P_t = P_1^t$ have the same set of eigenvectors. Thus, plotting the ith eigenvectors for different time horizons t should always yield approximately the same result, independently of t. However, when we compute the second eigenvector for $t = 1, \ldots, 4$ years and assign the components to the corresponding rating grades, Figure 6.5 shows that the eigenvectors are far from being equal. The curve is getting less steep as the time horizon increases. Based on Figure 6.5, the hypothesis that the process of rating distributions is a homogeneous one should be rejected. Note, however, that with the eigenvector analysis, a rather qualitative procedure to investigate time homogeneity of transition matrices was considered.

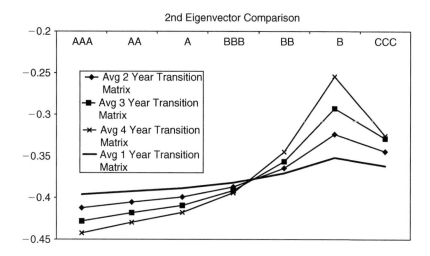

FIGURE 6.5. Second eigenvector for the average migration matrices with time horizon one year, two years, three years, and four years.

Overall, our empirical examination suggests that the considered internal rating system does not exhibit first-order Markov behavior nor time homogeneity. We provided a number of methods investigating these issues and pointed out a particular behavior of the considered internal rating system according to the detected second-order Markov behavior. Opposed to former studies for the considered rating system, downgrade probabilities were higher for companies that were upgraded in the previous period compared to those being downgraded in the period before and vice versa. We conclude that issues like time homogeneity, Markov behavior, and rating drift cannot be assumed to be the same for different rating systems and have to be examined as the case arises. In the following sections we will investigate the consequences of observed business cycle effects and time inhomogeneity in rating migrations on risk capital of credit portfolios and PD estimates through time.

6.4   Migration Behavior and Effects on Credit VaR

This section aims to illustrate how changes in credit migration matrices may have a substantial impact on the associated risk of a credit portfolio.[4] In the previous sections we reviewed methods for investigating the stability of migration matrices and a rating system based on financial ratios and

---

[4] The results of this section were originally provided in Trueck and Rachev (2005).

found that transition matrices showed significant changes over the years. We will now consider the effects of such changes in migration behavior on capital requirements in terms of expected losses and VaR figures for an exemplary credit portfolio. It is well known that the loss distribution for a credit portfolio as well as capital requirements vary between recession and expansion times of the business cycle (Bangia et al., 2002). We will find that for a considered exemplary portfolio these numbers vary substantially and that the effect of different migration behavior through the cycle should not be ignored in credit risk management.

To illustrate the effects, let us consider an exemplary loan portfolio of an international operating major bank consisting of 1120 companies. The average exposure is dependent on its rating class. In the considered portfolio higher exposures could be observed in higher rating classes, while for companies with a non-investment grade rating Baa, B, or Caa, the average exposures were between 5 and 10 million Euro. The distribution of ratings and average exposures in the considered rating classes of the loan portfolio are displayed are Table 6.11.

We further make the following assumptions for the loans. For each of the simulated years, we use the same portfolio and rating distribution to keep the figures comparable. We also assume an average yearly recovery rate of $R = 0.45$ for all companies. This is clearly a simplification of real recovery rates, but since we are mainly interested in the effects of different migration behavior on credit VaR and PDs, it is not a drawback for our investigation. Further, not having enough information on the seniority of the considered loans, it may be considered as an adequate assumption for empirical recovery rates.

For the investigation we use Moody's credit transition histories of a 20-year period from 1982–2001 and a continuous-time simulation approach for determining VaR figures based on $N = 5000$ simulations. Note that the actual reported one-year migration matrices by Moody were in discrete form. However, using the log-expansion 5.4 for Λ and the approximation methods suggested by Israel et al. (2000), we could calculate the corresponding approximate generator matrix. To illustrate the differences in migration behavior, Figures 6.6 and 6.7 show the cumulative default probabilities or credit curves based on years belonging to two different phases of the business cycle. The year 2001 was a year of economic turmoil with high default rates and many downgrades, while in 1997 the macroeconomic situation was stable and the economy was growing. Lower default probabilities and more upgrades than downgrades were the consequences.

TABLE 6.11. Ratings and Exposures for the Considered Credit Portfolio

Rating	Aaa	Aa	A	Baa	Ba	B	Caa
No.	11	106	260	299	241	95	148
Average Exposure (million Euro)	20	15	15	10	10	5	5

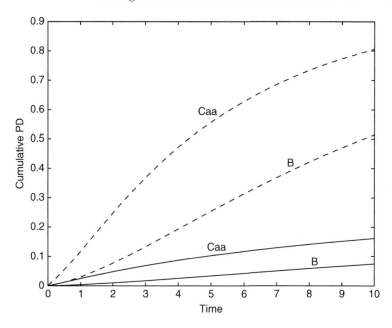

FIGURE 6.6. Credit curves for speculative grade issuers according to Moody's migration matrix 1997 (*solid lines*) and 2001 (*dashed lines*).

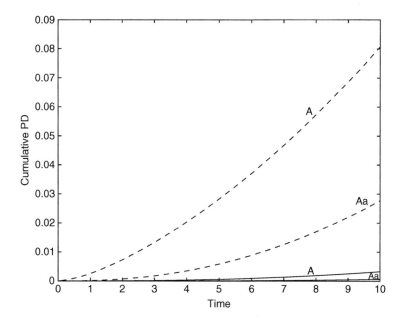

FIGURE 6.7. Credit curves for investment grade issuers according to Moody's migration matrix 1997 (*solid lines*) and 2001 (*dashed lines*).

Both for investment grade issuers and speculative grade issuers, we find completely different credit curves with cumulative default probabilities being substantially higher when the 2001 transition matrix is used as describing the underlying migration behavior. The graphs were plotted for a 10-year time horizon. Clearly, it is rather unrealistic that the macroeconomic situation stays in a recession or expansion state for such a long time. However, in the following we will illustrate that even for a considered shorter time horizon, differences can be quite substantial.

In a second step we investigated the effect of different migration behavior on risk figures for time horizons of six months, one year, and three years. Two typical loss distributions for the years 1998 and 2001 and an assumed one-year time horizon are displayed in Figure 6.8. The distributions have an expected loss of $\mu = 148.55$ million Euro with a standard deviation of $\sigma = 16.67$ million for 1998 and $\mu = 223.15$ million with $\sigma = 21.15$ million for 2001. Both distributions were slightly skewed to the right with $\gamma = 0.1217$ for 1998 and $\gamma = 0.1084$ for 2001. The kurtosis for the loss distributions with $k = 2.99$ for 1998 and $k = 2.97$ for 2001 is very close to the kurtosis of the normal distribution.

Comparing loss distributions for different years, we find that in many cases the distributions do not even coincide. We plotted a comparison of the simulated loss distributions for the years 2000 and 2001 in Figure 6.9 and for the years with minimal (1996) and maximal (2001) portfolio risk in the considered period in Figure 6.10. While for the subsequent years 2000 and 2001 the distributions at least coincide at very low (respectively high) quantiles, we find no intersection at all for the years 1996 and 2001. This points out the substantial effect of migration behavior on risk figures for a credit portfolio.

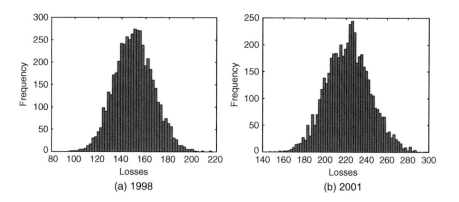

FIGURE 6.8. Typical shape of simulated loss distributions for the years 1998 and 2001.

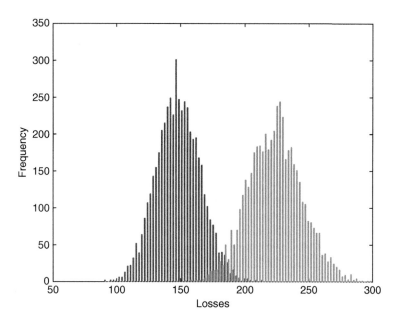

FIGURE 6.9. Simulated loss distributions for the years 2000 (*left side*) and 2001 (*right side*).

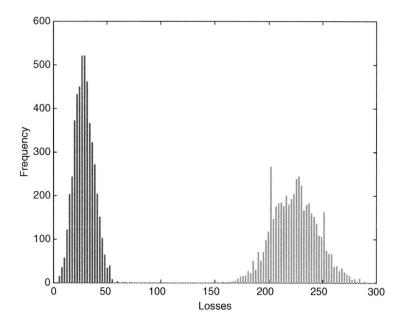

FIGURE 6.10. Simulated loss distributions for the years 1996 (*left side*) and 2001 (*right side*).

A closer picture of the significant changes in the Value-at-Risk for the considered period is provided in Figure 6.11 and in Table 6.12. We find that both expected loss and simulated VaR figures show great variation through the business cycle for all three considered time horizons of six months, one year, and three years. While in the years 1983 and 1996 the average expected loss for the portfolio would be only 31.29 million or 28.84 million Euro in a one-year period, during the recession years 1991 and 2001, the simulated average loss for the portfolio would be 227.25 million or 258.75 million Euro, respectively. The maximum of the simulated average losses for the portfolio is about eight times higher than the minimum amount in the considered period. Similar numbers were obtained considering Value-at-Risk or expected shortfall for the portfolio. The one-year 95%-VaR varies between 45 million and 258.75 million Euro, while the one-year 99%-VaR lies between a minimum of 56.25 million in 1996 and 273.37 million in the year 2001. This illustrates the enormous effect the business cycle might have on migration behavior and, thus, on the risk of a credit portfolio. Ignoring these effects may lead to completely wrong estimates of credit VaR and capital requirements for a loan or bond portfolio. We conclude the necessity to use credit models that include variables measuring the

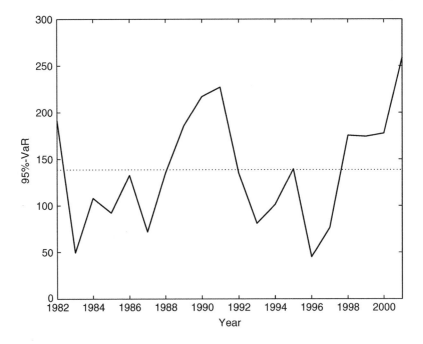

FIGURE 6.11. Simulated one-year VaR alpha = 0.95 for the years 1982–2001 (*solid line*), average one-year VaR for the whole period (*dashed line*).

TABLE 6.12. Simulated Average Loss, 95%-, and 99%-VaR for the Exemplary Portfolio for 1982–2001. Considered was a Six-Month, One-Year and Three-Year Time Horizon

Year	1982	1983	1984	1985	1986	1987	1988	1989	1990	1991
Mean, 6 months	83.48	14.46	44.05	34.66	52.50	27.07	57.42	87.58	97.30	102.21
Mean, 1 year	157.83	31.29	84.67	69.71	105.96	53.03	108.13	158.47	183.59	191.93
Mean, 3 years	343.50	88.95	198.83	178.30	275.23	127.73	233.95	314.05	413.67	411.20

Year	1992	1993	1994	1995	1996	1997	1998	1999	2000	2001
Mean, 6 months	60.05	35.13	42.50	61.57	14.11	30.66	85.91	79.89	79.56	121.17
Mean, 1 year	111.60	61.30	81.54	113.48	28.84	58.05	148.55	146.30	148.84	223.15
Mean, 3 years	240.16	113.84	176.37	235.14	68.33	129.68	280.51	305.39	312.74	477.26

Year	1982	1983	1984	1985	1986	1987	1988	1989	1990	1991
$VaR_{0.95,\,6\,months}$	108.00	27.00	63.00	51.75	72.00	40.50	76.50	110.25	123.75	128.25
$VaR_{0.95,\,1\,year}$	191.25	49.50	108.00	92.25	132.75	72.00	135.00	185.62	217.12	227.25
$VaR_{0.95,\,3\,years}$	393.75	119.25	234.00	216.00	321.75	157.50	272.25	353.25	463.50	461.25

Year	1992	1993	1994	1995	1996	1997	1998	1999	2000	2001
$VaR_{0.95,\,6\,months}$	78.75	50.62	58.50	81.00	24.75	45.00	108.00	101.25	101.25	148.50
$VaR_{0.95,\,1\,year}$	135.00	81.00	101.25	139.50	45.00	76.50	175.50	174.37	177.75	258.75
$VaR_{0.95,\,3\,years}$	274.50	139.50	207.00	270.00	90.00	157.50	317.25	343.12	351.00	531.00

Year	1982	1983	1984	1985	1986	1987	1988	1989	1990	1991
$VaR_{0.99,\,6\,months}$	120.37	33.75	74.25	58.50	83.25	47.25	84.37	119.25	132.75	139.50
$VaR_{0.99,\,1\,year}$	209.25	58.50	120.37	105.75	148.50	79.87	148.50	200.25	231.75	243.00
$VaR_{0.99,\,3\,years}$	421.87	132.75	253.12	236.25	338.62	171.00	285.75	370.12	487.12	482.62

Year	1992	1993	1994	1995	1996	1997	1998	1999	2000	2001
$VaR_{0.99,\,6\,months}$	85.50	56.25	65.25	90.00	31.50	51.75	115.87	112.50	110.25	164.25
$VaR_{0.99,\,1\,year}$	147.37	87.75	112.50	150.75	56.25	87.75	186.75	187.87	190.12	273.37
$VaR_{0.99,\,3\,years}$	288.00	153.00	218.25	283.50	99.00	172.12	333.00	357.75	371.25	553.50

state of the business cycle or the use of conditional migration matrices. In the next section we will further investigate the effect of different migration behavior on confidence sets for PDs.

6.5 Stability of Probability of Default Estimates

Another main issue of credit risk modeling is the modeling of probability of defaults. In the internal rating based approach of the new Basel Capital Accord, PDs are the main input variables for determining the risk and the necessary regulatory capital for a portfolio. Of course, regulators are not the only constituency interested in the properties of PD estimates. PDs are inputs to the pricing of credit assets, from bonds and loans to more sophisticated instruments such as credit derivatives. However, especially for companies with an investment grade rating, default is a rare event. Often high credit quality firms make up the majority of the large corporate segment in a bank's portfolio. But with only little information on actual defaulted companies in an internal credit portfolio, observed PDs for the investment grade categories are likely to be very noisy. The question arises how reliable confidence interval estimates for PDs may be obtained. This is of particular importance, since similar to the VaR or expected shortfall of a credit portfolio, PDs and also PD confidence sets may vary systematically with the business cycle. Thus, investment grade rating PDs are also rather unlikely to be stable over time. Therefore, in this section we tackle the question of obtaining reliable estimates for default probabilities also in the investment grade sector and compare these PDs for the considered time period from 1982–2001.

Christensen et al. (2004) estimate PD confidence intervals for default probabilities for different rating classes by using a continuous-time approach similar to the one suggested in the previous section. They find that a continuous-time bootstrap method can be more appropriate for determining PD distributions than using the estimates based on actual default observations. This is especially true for investment grade ratings where defaults are very rare events.

To illustrate the advantages of the bootstrapping idea, let us first consider a binomial random variable $X \sim B(p_i, n_i)$ where p_i denotes the probability of default for rating class i and n_i the number of companies in the rating class. Now assume that there is an investment grade rating class in the internal rating system where no actual defaults were observed in the considered time period. Clearly, the corresponding estimator for the PD in this rating class is $p_i = 0$. However, for VaR calculations a bank is also interested in confidence intervals for PDs of the investment grade rating classes. Based on the binomial distribution, one could compute the largest default probability not being rejected for a given confidence level α by solving the following equation:

$$(1 - p_i)^{n_i} = \alpha$$

Therefore, the corresponding upper value p_{max} of a confidence interval for a rating class with no observed defaults is

$$\hat{p}_{max}(n_i, \alpha) = 1 - \sqrt[n_i]{\alpha}$$

The disadvantage of this estimation technique becomes obvious in Table 6.13. Let X_i be the number of observed defaults in the two rating classes. Generally, the confidence intervals are dependent on X_i, the number of defaults observed, and n_i, the number of firms in the considered rating class. However, if no defaults are observed for a rating class, the lower n_i, the wider becomes the confidence interval. This is illustrated in Table 6.13 for an exemplary portfolio with 50 companies in the rating class Aaa and 500 companies in rating class Aa. We find that using the binomial distribution, the intervals for rating class Aaa are about ten times wider than those for rating Aa. From an economic point of view, this is rather questionable and simply a consequence of the fact that more companies were assigned with the lower rating.

Of course, the binomial distribution can also be used for calculating two-sided confidence intervals for lower rating classes where transition to defaults also were observed. What is needed is the total number of firms with certain rating i at the beginning of the period and the number of firms among them that defaulted until the end of the considered period. Then, for a given confidence level α, the standard Wald confidence interval is

$$\hat{p}_{i,max/min} = \hat{p}_i \pm q_\alpha \sqrt{\frac{\hat{p}_i(1 - \hat{p}_i)}{n_i}} \tag{6.7}$$

where n_i is the total number of firms in rating class i and q_α is the α-quantile of the standard normal distribution. Unfortunately, as pointed out by Schuermann and Hanson (2004), the estimates for confidence intervals obtained by the Wald estimator are not very tight. Christensen et al. (2004) state that the only advantage in the binomial case is that using this method, one is able to derive genuine confidence sets, i.e., to analyze the

TABLE 6.13. Example for PD Confidence Interval Estimated Based on the Binomial Distribution

	n_i	X_i	$KI_{\alpha = 0.05}$	$KI_{\alpha = 0.01}$
Aaa	50	0	$[0, 0.0582]$	$[0, 0.0880]$
Aa	500	0	$[0, 0.0060]$	$[0, 0.0092]$

set of parameters which an associated test would not reject based on the given observations. The authors point out that obtained confidence sets by a continuous-time bootstrap method are much tighter than those using the standard Wald estimator.

To compare confidence intervals through the business cycle, we therefore used the method described in Christensen et al. (2004). An introduction to bootstrapping can be found in Efron and Tibshirani (1993), so we will only briefly describe the idea of the bootstrap and our simulation algorithm. For our continuous-time simulation, the same procedure as in Section 5.4 is used to obtain histories for each of the considered companies. Note that unlike Schuermann and Hanson (2004) who apply a nonparametric bootstrapping approach, we based our simulations on the parametric assumption of a continuous-time Markov chain with a given migration matrix. For each year we simulate $N = 5000$ times using a fake data set with a number of 1000 issuers in each rating category. Then the issuer's history background Markov process is simulated using the observed historical transition matrix for each year. The simulated rating changes are translated into a history of observed rating transitions. For each replication the generator matrix of the hidden Markov chain model is re-estimated, using the companies' rating history and the maximum-likelihood estimator described above:

$$\hat{\lambda}_{ij} = \frac{N_{ij}(T)}{\int_0^T Y_i(s)ds}$$

From the estimated transition structure, we calculate the one-year default probability for each true state. Exponentiating this matrix gives an estimator of the one-year migration matrix, and the last column of the transition matrix provides the vector of estimated default probabilities for each replication. Thus, for each year or following Christensen et al. (2004)—each true state of the background process—we have $N = 5000$ one-year default probabilities for each rating class.

Another possibility to find confidence sets would have been to develop asymptotic expressions for the distribution of test statistics in the continuous-time formulation and use those for building approximate confidence sets. However, in practice the bootstrap method seems both easier to understand and to implement. The maximum-likelihood estimator does not have a simple closed form expression for its variance-covariance matrix. This makes it difficult to provide information about the confidence sets for estimated parameters. In fact, we would need to use asymptotics twice—first to find the variance of the estimated generator $\hat{\Lambda}$ and additionally to find an expression for the variance of $\exp(\hat{\Lambda})$. The second step again only seems feasible using an asymptotic argument. Unfortunately the asymptotic variance of $\hat{\Lambda}$ is hardly a good estimator, since many types of transitions occur only rarely in the data set. Thus, the bootstrap method provides tighter intervals and is also more understandable.

As mentioned earlier, confidence intervals for PDs can alternatively be obtained by a nonparametric bootstrap as illustrated in Schuermann and Hanson (2004). Here, the resampling is directly based on the observed rating histories and not on the estimated generator matrix. It basically follows the steps described in Section 5.4 for the nonparametric simulation approach. The method can be considered as a recommendable alternative if additional information on rating transitions is available.

Based on the bootstrapped generator matrices, for each year the relevant quantiles and distribution of the PDs can be obtained. The results for investment grade rating classes Aa–Baa can be found in Table 6.14 as well as in Figure 6.12 and 6.13 where boxplots of the PDs for the whole

TABLE 6.14. Descriptive Statistics of the Width of Confidence Intervals for Different Rating Classes

Rating	Aaa	Aa	A	Baa	Ba	B	Caa
mean	0.0001	0.0006	0.0019	0.0049	0.0126	0.0262	0.0473
σ	0.0002	0.0009	0.0017	0.0030	0.0053	0.0065	0.0140
min	0.0000	0.0000	0.0000	0.0002	0.0049	0.0172	0.0021
max	0.0007	0.0040	0.0057	0.0095	0.0246	0.0424	0.0605
$v = \frac{\sigma}{mean}$	1.5994	1.6162	0.9361	0.6125	0.4210	0.2493	0.2955

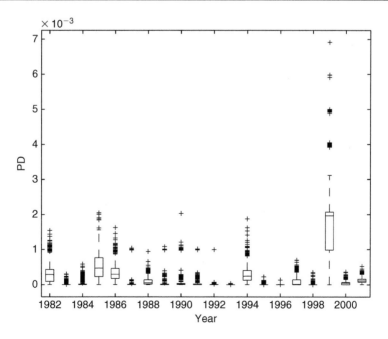

FIGURE 6.12. Boxplot for bootstrapped confidence intervals for rating class Aa from 1982–2001.

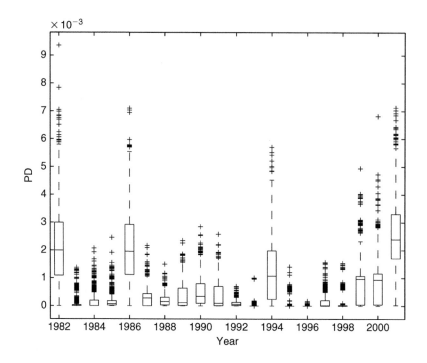

FIGURE 6.13. Boxplot for bootstrapped confidence intervals for rating class A from 1982–2001.

considered period are provided. It becomes obvious that confidence intervals vary substantially through time. This includes not only the level of the mean of the bootstrapped PDs but also the width of the confidence interval. Comparing, for example, the 95% interval for rating class A, we find that the interval in 2001 $KI_{A,2001} = [0.0005, 0.0054]$ compared to the interval in 1993 $KI_{A,1993} = [0.000, 0.0001]$ is about 50 times wider. The variation of the lower and upper boundary of the intervals is illustrated for rating classes Ba and A in Figure 6.14 and 6.15. We also find that with the level the width of an estimated confidence set for the PD increases substantially. Histograms of bootstrapped PD distributions for rating class Ba and different periods—1991 and 1996—can be found in Figure 6.16. Obviously the plotted histograms for the two periods do not coincide. Note that similar results in terms of variation are observed by Schuermann and Hanson (2004) using Standard & Poor's credit rating history.

For noninvestment grade ratings the variations in the level of average PDs is also extreme. However, as one can see in Table 6.15, the width of the intervals does not show the extreme variations as for the investment grade ratings. This is best illustrated by the coefficient of variation $v = \frac{\sigma}{mean}$, comparing the standard deviation of the width of the confidence intervals through time to its mean. We find a decreasing coefficient of variation

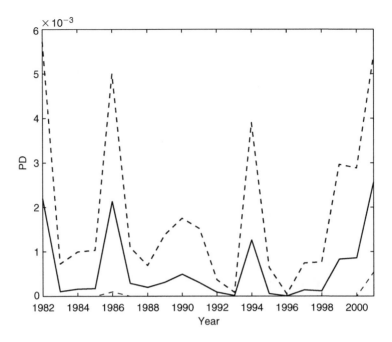

FIGURE 6.14. Mean and 95% PD confidence levels for rating class A from 1982–2001.

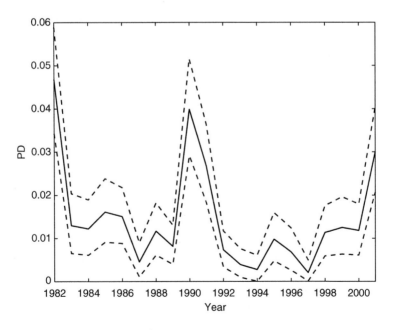

FIGURE 6.15. Mean and 95% PD confidence levels for rating class Ba from 1982–2001.

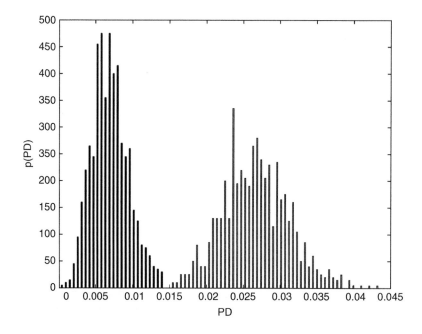

FIGURE 6.16. Histogram of bootstrap PDs for rating class Ba in 1991 (*left*) and 1996 (*right*).

for deteriorating credit quality. Thus, we conclude that the fraction PD volatility divided by average PD decreases with increasing PD.

Overall, the results point out the substantial effects of variations in the economy on the expected loss and VaR for a credit portfolio if a rating based credit risk system is used. The estimated one-year VaR for the considered portfolio was more than twice the average for the period of economic turmoil in 2001 and about eight times higher than VaR in the year 1996. The effect of changes in migration behavior on confidence sets for default probabilities is even more dramatic. Variations in the width and level of confidence intervals for investment grade rating classes were significant. In several cases the intervals did not even coincide in periods of economic expansion or recession. We further found a decreasing coefficient of variation for PD confidence sets with increasing riskiness of the loan. This may also be a useful result for credit derivative modeling, where PD volatilities are also of particular interest. Using average historical transition matrices as input for portfolio risk calculations should be handled with care. The effect of the business cycle on changes of migration behavior and therefore also on Value-at-Risk and PDs might be too imminent to be neglected. To overcome these problems, one could adjust or forecast migration behavior

TABLE   6.15. Bootstrap-95%-Confidence   Intervals   for   Investment   Grade Ratings. Figures Based on Moody's Historical Transition Matrices 1982–2001

Year	Aaa	Aa	A	Baa
1982	[0.0000, 0.0005]	[0.0000, 0.0010]	[0.0000, 0.0057]	[0.0019, 0.0062]
1983	[0.0000, 0.0000]	[0.0000, 0.0001]	[0.0000, 0.0007]	[0.0004, 0.0073]
1984	[0.0000, 0.0001]	[0.0000, 0.0003]	[0.0000, 0.0010]	[0.0026, 0.0121]
1985	[0.0000, 0.0001]	[0.0000, 0.0014]	[0.0000, 0.0010]	[0.0008, 0.0034]
1986	[0.0000, 0.0001]	[0.0000, 0.0010]	[0.0001, 0.0050]	[0.0014, 0.0069]
1987	[0.0000, 0.0000]	[0.0000, 0.0000]	[0.0000, 0.0011]	[0.0001, 0.0015]
1988	[0.0000, 0.0003]	[0.0000, 0.0004]	[0.0000, 0.0007]	[0.0008, 0.0032]
1989	[0.0000, 0.0000]	[0.0000, 0.0001]	[0.0000, 0.0014]	[0.0026, 0.0106]
1990	[0.0000, 0.0000]	[0.0000, 0.0010]	[0.0000, 0.0018]	[0.0023, 0.0101]
1991	[0.0000, 0.0000]	[0.0000, 0.0002]	[0.0000, 0.0015]	[0.0042, 0.0128]
1992	[0.0000, 0.0000]	[0.0000, 0.0000]	[0.0000, 0.0004]	[0.0002, 0.0015]
1993	[0.0000, 0.0000]	[0.0000, 0.0000]	[0.0000, 0.0001]	[0.0001, 0.0010]
1994	[0.0000, 0.0002]	[0.0000, 0.0009]	[0.0000, 0.0039]	[0.0000, 0.0006]
1995	[0.0000, 0.0000]	[0.0000, 0.0001]	[0.0000, 0.0006]	[0.0002, 0.0074]
1996	[0.0000, 0.0000]	[0.0000, 0.0000]	[0.0000, 0.0000]	[0.0000, 0.0002]
1997	[0.0000, 0.0000]	[0.0000, 0.0004]	[0.0000, 0.0007]	[0.0002, 0.0058]
1998	[0.0000, 0.0002]	[0.0000, 0.0001]	[0.0000, 0.0008]	[0.0012, 0.0090]
1999	[0.0000, 0.0007]	[0.0000, 0.0040]	[0.0000, 0.0030]	[0.0002, 0.0052]
2000	[0.0000, 0.0000]	[0.0000, 0.0002]	[0.0000, 0.0029]	[0.0008, 0.0072]
2001	[0.0000, 0.0000]	[0.0000, 0.0003]	[0.0005, 0.0054]	[0.0024, 0.0075]

and PDs in credit risk models with respect to the macroeconomic situation. We will further investigate this issue in Chapter 9, where several approaches for conditioning transition matrices on business cycle effects are reviewed and compared.

7
Measures for Comparison
of Transition Matrices

This chapter reviews the literature on distance measures or indices for credit migration matrices. It summarizes several measures based on cell-by-cell distances, eigenvalues (Geweke et al., 1986), eigenvectors (Arvanitis et al., 1999), or metrics based on singular values (Jafry and Schuermann, 2004). Finally, it derives criteria for risk-adjusted difference indices that can also be used to examine migration matrices with respect to their riskiness (Trueck, 2008) for credit portfolios. Recall from the previous chapter that transition matrices for both of the major rating agencies as well as for internal rating systems show significant variations through time and cannot be considered to be constant through time. In Chapter 5 we also saw that for many discrete time migration matrices there is no corresponding "true" or valid generator (Israel et al., 2000). In this case, following the techniques suggested in Jarrow et al. (1997), Kreinin and Sidelnikova (2001), or Israel et al. (2000), only an approximation of the continous-time transition matrix can be chosen. Again, it might be important to know what can be considered a "good" approximation in a sense that the Value-at-Risk of the portfolio is not significantly under- or overestimated if the approximation is used. In this chapter we will also provide techniques in order to transform real-world transition matrices into risk-neutral ones, while in Chapter 9 we will calculate conditional migration matrices based on macroeconomic conditions. For this purpose it will also be necessary to have a measure of difference or comparison of several migration matrices. In the following we will start with a review of traditional matrix norms and metrics before we provide mobility-based metrics (Jafry and Schuermann, 2004) and risk-adjusted difference indices (Trueck, 2005) for transition matrices.

7.1   Classical Matrix Norms

The first group to be mentioned are the classical cell-by-cell distance measures. Probably the most intuitive and prominent among this class of measures are the L_1, L_2, or L_{max} metrics. These metrics can be denoted as

$$D_{L_1}(P,Q) = \sum_{i=1}^{n} \sum_{j=1}^{n} |p_{ij} - q_{ij}|, \tag{7.1}$$

$$D_{L_2}(P,Q) = \sqrt{\sum_{i=1}^{n} \sum_{j=1}^{n} (p_{ij} - q_{ij})^2}, \qquad \text{and} \tag{7.2}$$

$$D_{L_{max}}(P,Q) = max_{i,j} |p_{ij} - q_{ij}| \tag{7.3}$$

where n is the number of columns and rows, as migration matrices are symmetric. The L_1 metric is used, for example, in Israel et al. (2000) for comparing migration matrices, while Bangia et al. (2002) suggest the L_2 metric as a distance measure. The literature provides several variations and extensions of the L_1 and L_2 metric. Some of them were used in order to solve optimization problems, e.g., in input-output analysis (Jackson and Murray, 2004). Most of them can be represented by a category of distance measures of the form

$$D_{weight}(P,Q) = \sum_{i=1}^{n} \sum_{j=1}^{n} p_{ij}^k |p_{ij} - q_{ij}|^p \tag{7.4}$$

with k varying from -1 to 1 and p varying from 1 to infinity. For k less than 0, the elements p_{ij} cannot be zero, or the fraction will be undefined. Note that obviously (7.4) does not define a metric or distance in the usual sense; see Rachev (1991). That is why we prefer using the term "index," "difference index," or "deviation" to denote a quantity like that in (7.4).

Lahr (2001) suggests a so-called weighted absolute difference (WAD) measure for input-output analysis. The measure is expressed as[1]

$$D_{WAD}(P,Q) = \sum_{i=1}^{n} \sum_{j=1}^{n} p_{ij} |p_{ij} - q_{ij}| \tag{7.5}$$

Matuszewski et al. (1964) suggest a different version of the absolute differences using normalized-absolute differences (NAD). In this formulation, differences in large coefficients will contribute less to the value of distance

---

[1] Note that $D_{WAD}(P,Q) \neq D_{WAD}(Q,P)$, so D_{WAD} does not satisfy the symmetry condition. This could be guaranteed, for example, by defining a distance measure $D_{WAD^{symm}} = 0.5 \cdot (D_{WAD}(P,Q) + D_{WAD}(Q,P))$ or $D_{WAD^{symm}} = max\{(D_{WAD}(P,Q), D_{WAD}(Q,P)\}$.

than will equally sized differences in small coefficients. Clearly, this imposes a greater penalty on changes in small coefficients:

$$D_{NAD}(P,Q) = \sum_{i=1}^{n} \sum_{j=1}^{n} \frac{|p_{ij} - q_{ij}|}{p_{ij}} \qquad (7.6)$$

Again, the elements p_{ij} cannot be zero, or the fraction will be undefined. This makes a straightforward application to transition matrices rather difficult, since it is quite likely that some migration probabilities can be zero. Also, since $D_{NAD}(P,Q) \neq D_{NAD}(Q,P)$, again the symmetry condition is not satisfied, but could be ensured by using the same procedure as was suggested for D_{WAD}. Similar expressions for the L^2 metric are straightforward. The measures obtained are then called weighted squared differences (WSD) and normalized squared differences (NSD).

For application to credit migration matrices, it becomes obvious that the cell-by-cell measures do not distinguish between differences in default or nondefault transitions. Also there is no distinction between differences that appear in cells to the left (upgrades) or right (downgrades) of the diagonal. As we will see later, these difference indices are far from optimal to measure changes in transition matrices in terms of risk.

7.2 Indices Based on Eigenvalues and Eigenvectors

We will now consider difference measures that are based on the eigenvalues or eigenvectors of a transition matrix P. We will first consider some of the indices described in Geweke et al. (1986) that are based on eigenvalues. Let λ_i denote the ith largest eigenvalue of P and $det(P)$ the determinant of the $n \times n$ transition matrix P. Then, Geweke et al. (1986), among others, propose the following metrics to measure the mobility of a transition matrix:

$$M_1(P) = \frac{1}{N-1}(N - \sum_{i=1} N|\lambda_i(P)|, \qquad (7.7)$$

$$M_2(P) = 1 - |\lambda_2(P)|, \qquad \text{and} \qquad (7.8)$$

$$M_3(P) = 1 - det(P). \qquad (7.9)$$

To compare the similarity of two matrices in terms of these mobility metrics, we then need to take the difference between the values of a metric M_i for two different migration matrices:

$$D_{EVAL}(P,Q) = M_i(P) - M_i(Q) \quad (i = 1, 2) \qquad (7.10)$$

Arvanitis et al. (1999) provide a metric that is based on the eigenvectors of a transition matrix. Note that most credit migration matrices derived from actual market data incorporate an absorbing default state. Thus, the first eigenvector of the transpose of the migration matrix that is equivalent to the the steady-state solution is ineffective as a basis for comparing matrices. However, it makes sense to consider the information that is contained in the remaining eigenvectors. Therefore, Arvanitis et al. (1999) propose to assess the similarity of all eigenvectors between two matrices by computing a ratio of matrix norms. They define a distance metric between two matrices P and Q according to

$$D_{AGL}(P,Q) = \frac{\|PQ - QP\|}{\|PQ\|} \qquad (7.11)$$

with $0 \leq D_{AGL}(P,Q) \leq 2$. If P and Q have exactly the same eigenvectors (regardless of their eigenvalues), the distance metric takes the value of zero. In Arvanitis et al. (1999) it is concluded that values for the difference measure of around 0.08 for two matrices at an annual frequency are assumed to be similar, since in this case the eigenvectors vary by only a small amount. Unfortunately, the authors neither give an explanation why they chose a value of 0.08 nor a decision rule when similarity can be rejected.

A more appealing approach in terms of interpretation is provided by Jafry and Schuermann (2004). They developed a scalar metric that captures the overall dynamic size of given matrices and contains sufficient information to facilitate meaningful comparisons between different credit migration matrices. Primarily, a so-called mobility matrix $\tilde{P}$ is calculated by subtraction of the identity matrix I from the original transition matrix P. Obviously, the identity matrix can be considered as a static migration matrix. The authors conclude that by subtracting the identity matrix, only the dynamic part of the originial matrix remains. Following Strang (1988) the mobility of a matrix can be captured by its so-called amplifying power on a state vector x. In Strang (1988), therefore, it is suggested to use the largest singular value of a matrix as a mobility norm. However, Jafry and Schuermann (2004) conclude that the maximally amplified vector x is not representative of a feasible state vector. Thus, it is proposed to use the average of all singular values of P to capture the general characteristics of P.[2] The metric is defined as the average of the singular values of the mobility matrix:

$$M_{SVD}(P) = \frac{\sum_{i=1}^{n} \sqrt{\lambda_i(\tilde{P}'\tilde{P})}}{n} \qquad (7.12)$$

---

[2] The singular values of $\tilde{P}$ are equal to the eigenvalues λ_i of $\tilde{P}'\tilde{P}$.

The authors show that this metric captures the so-called amplification factor or the dynamic part of the migration matrix. Therefore, it approximates the average probability of migration which can be considered as a meaningful magnitude calibration for a metric. Similar to equation (7.10), to measure the difference between two migration matrices in terms of mobility, one has to calculate

$$D_{SVD}(P,Q) = M_{SVD}(P) - M_{SVD}(Q) \qquad (7.13)$$

Expression (7.13) gives a directional deviation between two matrices in terms of the mobility or approximate average probability of migration. Due to its advantages in terms of interpretation, in our empirical analysis we will choose the SVD metric as representative of the distance measures based on eigenvectors or eigenvalues. In the following, we will investigate the derivation of risk-sensitive difference indices for comparison of migration matrices.

7.3   Risk-Adjusted Difference Indices

We will now analyze differences in migration behavior as they affect risk measurement or VaR calculations for credit portfolios.[3] Clearly, there are several issues that contribute to different risk estimates based on transition matrices. We will illustrate the issues with some examples based on simplified matrices and then devise risk-sensitive distance measures for migration matrices. For illustration purposes we consider exemplary transition matrices $P_1, \ldots, P_9$ with four rating categories $\{A, B, C, D\}$. Hereby, state A denotes the highest rating, B a rating state with a higher probability of default, state C a speculative grade rating, and D the absorbing default state. Starting from the matrix P_1, we will illustrate how shifts in the probability mass may affect the associated risk for a credit portfolio.

P_1	A	B	C	D
A	0.80	0.10	0.08	0.02
B	0.05	0.85	0.05	0.05
C	0.05	0.1	0.7	0.15
D	0	0	0	1

7.3.1   The Direction of the Transition (DIR)

An important issue for effects on the estimated risk for a credit portfolio based on changes in migration behavior is whether the probability mass is shifted to an upgrade or downgrade transition. Thus, a risk-sensitive

---

[3] Results of this section were originally published in Trueck and Rachev (2007).

criterion may consider whether the probability is shifted to the left or to the right side of the diagonal. Assume that the change in migration behavior for a portfolio could be denoted by a change from P_1 to P_2, respectively, from P_1 to P_3. In the following, the cells where actual deviations from the initial migration matrix P_1 took place are highlighted in bold:

P_2	A	B	C	D
A	0.80	0.10	0.08	0.02
B	**0.08**	**0.82**	0.05	0.05
C	0.05	0.1	0.7	0.15
D	0	0	0	1

P_3	A	B	C	D
A	0.80	0.10	0.08	0.02
B	0.05	**0.82**	**0.08**	0.05
C	0.05	0.1	0.7	0.15
D	0	0	0	1

We are interested in the difference between matrix P_1 and P_2, and between P_1 and P_3. In both cases the probability mass 0.03 for rating category B is shifted from the diagonal element—in P_2 to the first columns, in P_3 to rating category C. Obviously, the distance according to most of the considered cell-by-cell distance measures would be the same between matrix P_1 and P_2 or P_3, respectively. However, from a risk perspective for a hypothetical credit portfolio, there is a difference between a shift of the probability mass as in matrix P_2 or in matrix P_3. In the first case we would expect the risk to be reduced, while in the second case due to a higher downgrade probability for companies with a rating B, a higher risk will be associated with the changes in migration behavior. We conclude that to examine whether probability mass is shifted to the left or right side of the diagonal elements will be a necessary criterion for devising a risk-sensitive distance measure. In the following we will call this the direction of the change (DIR) in migration behavior.

7.3.2   Transition to a Default or Nondefault State (TD)

Examining the related risk for a portfolio, it is also important to consider if the difference between two migration matrices refers to a cell that denotes a transition to a default or nondefault state. For illustration, consider the migration matrices P_4 and P_5:

P_4	A	B	C	D
A	0.80	0.10	0.08	0.02
B	0.05	**0.88**	0.05	**0.02**
C	0.05	0.1	0.7	0.15
D	0	0	0	1

P_5	A	B	C	D
A	0.80	0.10	0.08	0.02
B	0.05	**0.88**	**0.02**	0.05
C	0.05	0.1	0.7	0.15
D	0	0	0	1

In comparison to P_1, for both matrices the probability mass 0.03 is shifted to the diagonal element of rating category B: in P_4 the mass is shifted from a transition to default, in P_5 from rating category C. Again, the difference $D(P_1, P_4)$ and $D(P_1, P_5)$ between P_1 and each of the two matrices would be the same according to most of the considered cell-by-cell measures. However, from a risk perspective, for a hypothetical credit portfolio there is a significant difference between a migration behavior according to P_4 or P_5. Deviations in the default column will make a substantial difference, while for transitions to other categories the difference may not change the risk that much.

We conclude that a distance measure allowing for the inclusion of a risk perspective should be able to distinguish between transitions to the default column from other columns. In the following, we will call this the transition-to-default (TD) criterion that should also be included when devising a risk-sensitive distance measure.

7.3.3   The Probability Mass of the Cell (PM)

It will make sense to set the change in a cell of a migration matrix in relation to the usual transition probability. For illustration consider the matrices P_6 and P_7: comparing the matrices with P_1, for P_6 the probability mass 0.03 is shifted from the diagonal element of rating category A to the default column. For P_7 the mass is shifted from transition $C \to A$ to the default column.

P_6	A	B	C	D
A	**0.77**	0.10	0.08	**0.05**
B	0.05	0.85	0.05	0.05
C	0.05	0.1	0.7	0.15
D	0	0	0	1

P_7	A	B	C	D
A	0.80	0.10	0.08	0.02
B	0.05	0.85	0.05	0.05
C	**0.02**	0.1	0.7	**0.18**
D	0	0	0	1

While the absolute change in both default columns is 0.03, the default probabilites for A rated bonds or loans in the portfolio has more than

doubled for P_6 from 0.02 to 0.05. In P_7, however, the default probability
increased by only 20%. Hence, the former change in migration behavior may
be more grave than the latter in terms of risk measurement. We conclude
that a risk-sensitive difference index should also include the probability
mass of the cell (PM) where the change took place.

7.3.4   Migration Distance (MD)

From a risk perspective, far migrations have a different effect on a portfolio
than near migrations. As the most obvious example, we discussed migrations to the default state in comparison to migrations to a nondefault state.
Let us now consider the transition matrices P_8 and P_9:

P_8	A	B	C	D
A	**0.77**	**0.13**	0.08	0.02
B	0.05	0.85	0.05	0.05
C	0.05	0.1	0.7	0.15
D	0	0	0	1

P_9	A	B	C	D
A	**0.77**	0.10	**0.11**	0.02
B	0.05	0.85	0.05	0.05
C	0.05	0.1	0.7	0.15
D	0	0	0	1

In both examples, the probability mass 0.03 is shifted from the diagonal
element of rating category A to downgrades. When we examine the differences $D(P_1, P_8)$, respectively, $D(P_1, P_9)$ and further take into account
longer time horizons, the change in the first row of P_9 is more severe: when
more companies migrate to a C rating within the next period, they will
have a significantly higher default probability in later periods in comparison
to companies migrating to rating state B.

We conclude that a risk-sensitive difference index should also take into
account whether changes in migration matrices take place in near or far
migrations. We will refer to this criterion as migration distance (MD).

7.3.5   Devising a Distance Measure

Based on the criteria introduced, we will now devise indices for measuring
the distance between two migration matrices. Clearly the idea is to take
into account as many of the criteria DIR, TD, PM, and MD as possible. The
suggested criteria will also be based on a weighted cell-by-cell comparison
of the matrices. However, the weighting will be more specific and complex
than the difference measures suggested in equations (7.1) to (7.6). Hence,

as a starting point we suggest a generalization of the representation in equation (7.4):

$$D_*(P,Q) = \sum_{i=1}^{n} \sum_{j=1}^{n} w_{ij}(p_{ij} - q_{ij})^p \qquad (7.14)$$

where w_{ij} is a function dependent on the derived criteria suggested above. The question is how to define adequate functions for the weights w_{ij} and the order p. For the order p we will follow the classical cell-by-cell matrix norm approach. Therefore, we suggest measuring the difference between p_{ij} and q_{ij} either by using the actual difference $(p_{ij} - q_{ij})$ or squared difference $(p_{ij} - q_{ij})^2$. Note that since our measures should also provide the idea of direction of the difference, namely $(p_{ij} > q_{ij})$ or $(p_{ij} < q_{ij})$, for the squared differences the sign of $(p_{ij} - q_{ij})$ will also be included. More effort will be dedicated to deriving an adequate choice of the function w_{ij}. In the following we will provide some straightforward functional relations to capture the introduced criteria.

As illustrated, a risk-sensitive difference index for migration matrices should incorporate the direction of the shift in probability mass that has been denoted by the criterion DIR. If more mass is shifted to upgrades, there will be fewer defaults to expect, and a shift of the probability mass to downgrades will end in a higher risk for the credit portfolio. To capture this circumstance in a weighted cell-by-cell comparison of two matrices, we define the direction coefficient for each cell as

$$dir(i,j) = \begin{cases} -1 & \text{for } i < j \\ 0 & \text{for } i = j \\ 1 & \text{for } i > j \end{cases} \qquad (7.15)$$

According to the criterion TD, devising a risk-sensitive difference index, we would also like to seperate deviations in the default columns from the other columns. Therefore, we suggest multiplying differences between two matrices in cells of the default column, depending on the dimension n of the transition matrix P. Possible multipliers, for example, may be

- n
- $2n$
- n^2
- $exp(n)$

Of course, other multipliers may be chosen depending on needs. However, as we will see later, choosing a multiplier to be n and n^2 gave quite promising results.

To capture the criterion probability mass (PM) in an individual cell, we will use the normalized weights NAD or NSD for the differences as they are suggested, e.g., in Matuszewski et al. (1964). It is reasonable to assume that differences in large coefficients will contribute less to the value of distance than will equally sized differences in small coefficients. Thus, when we are incorporating MD, in the following, the difference between individual cells of two migration matrices will be given a weight of $1/p_{ij}$.

Finally, to capture the difference between close and far migrations (MD), we simply define a coefficient for measuring a cell's distance from the diagonal:

$$md(i, j) = |i - j| \tag{7.16}$$

Obviously, the increase in weight will be a linear function of the distance of a cell from the diagonal. Note that both upgrades and downgrades are treated in a similar way according to the chosen MD criterion. However, recall that the default column will get an additionally higher weight due to the TD criterion.

Based on the developed criteria, we suggest the following functions for the weights of an individual cell (i, j) when calculating a difference index for two transition matrices P and Q. We will start with the following simple weighting functions d_1 and d_2:

$$d_1(i, j) = (i - j) \cdot (p_{ij} - q_{ij}) \tag{7.17}$$

$$d_2(i, j) = \frac{(i - j)}{p_{ij}} \cdot (p_{ij} - q_{ij}), \quad p_{ij} \neq 0 \tag{7.18}$$

Obviously, the weights d_1 and d_2 include the mentioned criteria DIR and MD. Far transitions get a higher weight than near transitions. Further, the sign multiplied by the difference between the cells leads to a higher value of the measure when more probability mass is shifted to the right side of the diagonal. Note that d_2 is simply an extension of d_1 including normalized weights and, therefore, taking into account the original transition probability PM where the deviation occurred. Since d_2 requires that $p_{ij} \neq 0$, the weight can only be calculated for cells with a non-zero entry.

Alternatively, one may also want to consider the squared differences $(p_{ij} - q_{ij})^2$ in a cell. As mentioned above, in this case it will also be necessary to include the sign of $(p_{ij} - q_{ij})$. Therefore, we suggest the following weighting functions d_3 and d_4:

$$d_3(i, j) = (i - j) \cdot sign(p_{ij} - q_{ij}) \cdot (p_{ij} - q_{ij})^2 \tag{7.19}$$

$$d_4(i, j) = \frac{(i - j)}{p_{ij}} sign(p_{ij} - q_{ij}) \cdot (p_{ij} - q_{ij})^2, \quad p_{ij} \neq 0 \tag{7.20}$$

We are well aware of the fact that measuring the cell-by-cell differences of two migration matrices with d_1, d_2, d_3, d_4 will give us difference indices that cannot satisfy the required conditions for a metric. This seems to be critical from a mathematical point of view at first sight. However, we will show that the advantages over standard deviation measures for matrices or norms are so clearcut that we are willing to accept this. From the perspective of application for risk management purposes, we will show the superior properties of the weighting functions in our empirical study.

Based on the weights for individual cells of two migration matrices, we define the following indices measuring the difference between migration matrices in terms of risk:

$$D_k(P,Q) = \sum_{i=1}^{n} \sum_{j=1}^{n} d_k(i,j), \quad k = 1,2,3,4 \tag{7.21}$$

Note that the criterion TD has not been considered yet. However, transition to defaults is clearly the credit event with the most influence on the loss in the portfolio. Therefore, following the suggestions of a multiplier for the default column, we additionally suggest the following indices:

$$D_5(P,Q) = \sum_{i=1}^{n} \sum_{j=1}^{n-1} d_3(i,j) + \sum_{i=1}^{n} n \cdot d_3(i,n) \tag{7.22}$$

and

$$D_6(P,Q) = \sum_{i=1}^{n} \sum_{j=1}^{n-1} d_3(i,j) + \sum_{i=1}^{n} n^2 \cdot d_3(i,n) \tag{7.23}$$

Note that D_5 and D_6 use squared differences $(p_{ij} - q_{ij})^2$ between the cells of two migration matrices. Alternatively, we will also suggest a multiplier for the default column in combination with a measure that uses absolute differences between the cells. Therefore, we define the difference indices D_7 and D_8 according to

$$D_7(P,Q) = \sum_{i=1}^{n} \sum_{j=1}^{n-1} d_1(i,j) + \sum_{i=1}^{n} n \cdot d_1(i,n) \tag{7.24}$$

and

$$D_8(P,Q) = \sum_{i=1}^{n} \sum_{j=1}^{n-1} d_1(i,j) + \sum_{i=1}^{n} n^2 \cdot d_1(i,n) \tag{7.25}$$

We will now investigate how the introduced indices will measure the difference between the exemplary transition matrices $P_1 - P_9$.

7.3.6   Difference Indices for the Exemplary Matrices

We will now examine the adequacy of the reviewed and newly introduced indices to measure the changes and differences in transition matrices from a risk perspective. We will take a look at the distances of the exemplary matrices $P_2 - P_9$ from matrix P_1 to show the deficiencies of most of the distance measures suggested in the literature so far. To begin with, recall the expected effect of changes in the matrix P_1 to $P_2 - P_9$ in terms of risk for a credit portfolio. The expected directions are displayed in Table 7.1. Hereby, the second column of the table indicates whether the migration behavior according to the matrix $P_i, i = 2, \ldots, 9$ involves a higher $(+)$ or lower $(-)$ risk in comparison to P_1 for a credit portfolio. Therefore, we would expect a higher risk for the migration matrices P_6, P_7, P_8, P_9 and a lower risk for the matrices P_2, P_4, P_5.

In a first step we consider the classical cell-by-cell distance measures L_1, L_2, and L_{max}, since they are suggested in the literature to measure the difference between two migration matrices (Israel et al., 2000; Bangia et al., 2002). The results are displayed in the upper part of Table 7.2. We find that for the simplified exemplary transition matrices according to the norms L_1, L_2, and L_{max}, the differences between P_1 and all other matrices $P_2 - P_9$ are the same. The distance for L_1 is constantly $D(P_1, P_i) = 0.0600$ for $i = 2, \ldots, 9$ while for L_2 and L_{max} we obtain $D(P_1, P_i) = 0.0424$ and $D(P_1, P_i) = 0.0300$, respectively, for $i = 2, \ldots, 9$. However, as illustrated earlier, from an economic point of view there is quite a big difference between the considered changes in the matrices $P_1 - P_9$. Recall, for example, the substantial effect on a credit portfolio the change from P_1 to P_4 has in comparison to the change from P_1 to P_6. While in the first case we should expect a clear reduction of risk capital for a credit portfolio, in the second case there will be a substantial increase in terms of risk. From a first glance at the results, we conclude that the distance measures L_1, L_2, and L_{max} are not able to capture changes in migration matrices from a risk calculation angle.

The next step is to analyze the results for weighted cell-by-cell distance measures WAD, NAD, WSD, and NSD. Again the results are not really promising. For the weighted absolute and squared differences, the distance between P_1 and $P_2 - P_9$ is approximately the same for all matrices. There is no distinction between differences on the right side of the diagonal or on

TABLE 7.1. Expected Effect on Risk Capital When Changing the Matrix P_1 to $P_2 - P_9$

Matrix	P_2	P_3	P_4	P_5	P_6	P_7	P_8	P_9
$\delta(P_1, P_i)$	$-$	$+$	$-$	$-$	$+$	$+$	$+$	$+$

TABLE 7.2. Distances for Exemplary Migration Matrices $D(P_1, P_i)$ for $i = 2, \ldots, 8$ According to Weighted Cell-by-cell Distance Indices L_1, L_2, L_{max} WAD, NAD, WSD, NSD, the SVD Metric, and for the Risk-Sensitive Indices $D_1 - D_8$

Classical Distance Measures

Measure	Expected	L_1	L_2	L_{max}	WAD	NAD	WSD	NSD	SVD
$D(P_1, P_1)$	0	0	0	0	0	0	0	0	0
$D(P_1, P_2)$	−	0.0600	0.0424	0.0300	0.0270	0.5234	0.0008	0.1246	−0.0064
$D(P_1, P_3)$	+	0.0600	0.0424	0.0300	0.0270	0.5234	0.0008	0.1246	−0.0075
$D(P_1, P_4)$	−	0.0600	0.0424	0.0300	0.0270	1.0847	0.0008	0.1763	0.0103
$D(P_1, P_5)$	−	0.0600	0.0424	0.0300	0.0270	1.0847	0.0008	0.1763	0.0070
$D(P_1, P_6)$	+	0.0600	0.0424	0.0300	0.0246	1.0882	0.0008	0.1766	−0.0091
$D(P_1, P_7)$	+	0.0600	0.0424	0.0300	0.0060	1.2333	0.0008	0.1893	−0.0041
$D(P_1, P_8)$	+	0.0600	0.0424	0.0300	0.0270	0.3036	0.0002	0.0953	−0.0088
$D(P_1, P_9)$	+	0.0600	0.0424	0.0300	0.0264	0.3621	0.0008	0.1040	−0.0085

Risk-Sensitive Distance Indices

Measure	Expected	D_1	D_2	D_3	D_4	D_5	D_6	D_7	D_8
$D(P_1, P_1)$	0	0	0	0	0	0	0	0	0
$D(P_1, P_2)$	−	−0.0300	−0.6000	−0.0009	−0.0180	−0.0009	−0.0009	−0.0300	−0.0300
$D(P_1, P_3)$	+	0.0300	0.6000	0.0009	0.0180	0.0009	0.0009	0.0300	0.0300
$D(P_1, P_4)$	−	−0.0600	−1.2000	−0.0018	−0.0360	−0.0072	−0.0288	−0.2400	−0.9600
$D(P_1, P_5)$	−	−0.0300	−0.6000	−0.0009	−0.0180	−0.0009	−0.0009	−0.0300	−0.0300
$D(P_1, P_6)$	+	0.0900	4.5000	0.0027	0.1350	0.0108	0.0432	0.3600	1.4400
$D(P_1, P_7)$	+	0.0700	1.0000	0.0017	0.0220	0.0044	0.0152	0.1600	0.5200
$D(P_1, P_8)$	+	0.0300	0.3000	0.0009	0.0090	0.0009	0.0009	0.0300	0.0300
$D(P_1, P_9)$	+	0.0600	0.7500	0.0018	0.0225	0.0018	0.0018	0.0600	0.0600

the left side. Also the results for the distance measures using the normalized absolute and squared differences do not suggest that the differences capture the changes according to the direction displayed in Table 7.1. We conclude that the classic cell-by-cell distance measures that are generally used in the literature to compare migration matrices are not capable of giving information that could be interpreted in terms of risk for a credit portfolio.

Examining the SVD metric, we obtain clearly better results. Recall that the value of the SVD metric can be interpreted as a proxy for the average probability of migration. We are calculating the distance between the matrix P_1 and P_i by $D_{SVD}(P_1, P_i) = M_{SVD}(P_1) - M_{SVD}(P_i)$. Since migration matrices with a higher probability mass outside the diagonal elements are more risky, we would expect $D_{SVD}(P_1, P_i)$ to be negative if P_i involves more risk and to be positive for P_i being less risky. As Table 7.2 indicates, for $P_3 - P_9$ the sign shows the expected direction. Only for the matrix P_2 we find a negative sign despite a lower risk which can be explained by the fact that probability mass was shifted from the diagonal to the left side of the diagonal. So in this case, for P_2, despite a higher mobility the matrix is actually less risky. In general, measuring differences between migration matrices using the SVD metric will provide good results, assuming that in periods of higher risk there will also be a higher mobility in migration behavior.

Overall, the most promising results are obtained for the introduced directed difference indices $D_1 - D_8$. All of the indices show a strong tendency to vary with the changes in the considered migration matrices. For each of the suggested difference indices $D_1 - D_8$, we observe the changes in a direction we would expect from a risk perspective: a positive value for the index, if P_i involves a higher risk than the original matrix and vice versa. Note that we will not give an interpretation of the actual magnitude of the changes for each of the indices yet. However, we observe that for all risk-sensitive indices the increase in risk seems to be the highest for $D(P_1, P_6)$ where the default probability for the rating category A is more than doubled. On the other hand the magnitude of risk reduction is the highest for $D(P_1, P_6)$ when the default probability for rating category B is reduced substantially.

7.4   Summary

Overall the results of this chapter point out that further research on adequate difference measures for credit migration matrices will be needed. Most of the distance measures for matrices as they have been suggested in the literature so far are not really capable of measuring the difference between two migration matrices from a risk perspective. Based on some exemplary transition matrices, in this chapter it was illustrated that the metric suggested by Jafry and Schuermann (2004) as well as so-called risk-adjusted difference indices provide promising results for comparing migration matrices from a risk perspective. For further application of the Jafry-Schuermann metric or risk-adjusted difference indices, we refer to Bank of Japan (2005), Frydman and Schuermann (2008), Kadam and Lenk (2008), Trueck and Rachev (2007), Trueck (2008) and Chapter 9.

8

Real-World and Risk-Neutral Transition Matrices

In this chapter we will investigate how real-world or historical transition matrices can be transformed into risk-neutral ones. As we have seen in the previous chapters, the former are rather used to determine Economic Capital or Value-at-Risk for credit portfolios. On the other hand, the use of the latter is rather to construct risk-neutral credit curves for different time horizons and adequately price credit derivatives. Using credit spreads from empirically observed bond prices, in their seminal paper Jarrow et al. (JLT 1997) were the first to suggest methods for transforming real-world transition and default probabilties into risk-neutral ones. Due to some difficulties with the initially suggested approach in practice, alternative techniques have been suggested by different authors (see Lando (2000); Kijima and Komoribayashi (1998); Lando and Mortensen (2005)). In the following we will review techniques for deriving risk-neutral transition matrices out of historical migration matrices and empirically observed credit spreads. The methods will be illustrated by numerical examples using a simplified transition matrix with only three rating states.

Note that an alternative approach on deriving implied migration rates from barrier models is suggested by Albanese and Chen (2006). Their model is characterized by an underlying stochastic process representing credit quality and default events associated with barrier crossings. For further description of their approach on deriving risk-neutral migration rates, we refer to the original publication.

8.1 The JLT Model

The model by Fons (1994) concentrates on the default event, its timing, and magnitude and does not consider any changes in the credit quality up to the default event. However, deterioration or improvement in the credit quality of the issuer is highly important if someone wants to value credit derivatives like credit spread options whose payouts depend on the yield spreads that are influenced by such changes. One common way to express these changes to market participants is the ratings given by agencies like Standard & Poor's and Moody's. Downgrades or upgrades by the rating agencies are taken very seriously by market players to price bonds and loans, thus effecting the risk premium and the yield spreads.

Jarrow et al. (1997) model default and transition probabilities by using a discrete, time-homogeneous Markov chain on a finite state space $S = \{1, \ldots, K\}$. The state space S represents the different rating classes. While state $S = 1$ denotes the best credit rating, state K represents the default case. Hence, the $(K \times K)$ one-period transition matrix looks as follows:

$$P = \begin{pmatrix} p_{11} & p_{12} & \cdots & p_{1K} \\ p_{21} & p_{12} & \cdots & p_{2K} \\ \cdots & \cdots & \cdots & \cdots \\ p_{K-1,1} & p_{K-1,2} & \cdots & p_{K-1,K} \\ 0 & 0 & \cdots & 1 \end{pmatrix} \tag{8.1}$$

where $p_{ij} \geq 0$ for all $i, j, i \neq j$, and $p_{ii} \equiv 1 - \sum_{\substack{j=1 \\ j \neq i}}^{K} p_{ij}$ for all i. The variable p_{ij} represents the actual probability of going to state j from initial rating state i in one time step.

Thus, rating based models can be seen as a special case of the so-called intensity model framework (Duffie and Singleton, 1999) where randomness in the default arrival is simply modeled via a Markov chain. A key issue of the JLT model is the assumption of complete markets with no arbitrage opportunities. Thus, JLT assume the existence and uniqueness of the martingale measure $\tilde{Q}$. Further it is assumed that the interest rates and the default process are independent under the martingale measure $\tilde{Q}$ and that the transition matrix is time homogeneous. The default state is an absorbing state, represented by $p_{Ki} = 0$ for $i = 1, \ldots, K - 1$ and $p_{KK} = 1$.

Under the assumption of time homogeneity, the multiperiod transition matrix equals

$$P_{0,n} = P^n$$

while under the martingale measure the one-period transition matrix equals

$$\tilde{Q}_{t,t+1} = \begin{pmatrix} \tilde{q}_{11}(t,t+1) & \tilde{q}_{12}(t,t+1) & \cdots & \tilde{q}_{1K}(t,t+1) \\ \tilde{q}_{21}(t,t+1) & \tilde{q}_{22}(t,t+1) & \cdots & \tilde{q}_{2K}(t,t+1) \\ \cdots & \cdots & \cdots & \cdots \\ \tilde{q}_{K-1,1}(t,t+1) & \tilde{q}_{K-1,2}(t,t+1) & \cdots & \tilde{q}_{K-1,K}(t,t+1) \\ 0 & 0 & \cdots & 1 \end{pmatrix} \tag{8.2}$$

where $\tilde{q}_{ij}(t,t+1) \geq 0$, for all $i, j, i \neq j$, $\tilde{q}_{ij}(t,t+1) \equiv 1 - \sum_{\substack{j=1 \\ j \neq i}}^{K} \tilde{q}_{ij}$, and $\tilde{q}_{ij}(t,t+1) > 0$ if and only if $q_{ij} > 0$.

JLT argue that, without additional restrictions, the martingale probabilities $\tilde{q}_{ij}(t,t+1)$ can depend on the entire history up to time t, i.e., the

Markov property is not satisfied anymore. Therefore, they assume that the martingale probabilities $\tilde{q}_{ij}(t, t+1)$ satisfy the following equation:

$$\tilde{q}_{ij}(t, t+1) = \pi_i(t)p_{ij} \tag{8.3}$$

for all $i, j, i \neq j$ where $\pi_i(t)$ denotes a deterministic function of time.

In other words, given a current state i, the martingale probabilities of moving from state i to j are proportional to the actual probabilities, and the proportionality factor depends on time t and the current rating state i but not on the next state j. JLT call this factor the risk premium.

Equation (8.3) can also be written in matrix notation:

$$\tilde{Q}_{t,t+1} - \mathcal{J} = \Pi(t)[P - \mathcal{J}] \tag{8.4}$$

where $\mathcal{J}$ is the $(K \times K)$ identity matrix and $\Pi(t) = \operatorname{diag}(\pi_1(t), \ldots, \pi_{K-1}(t), 1)$ is a $(K \times K)$ diagonal matrix. Given the time dependence of the risk premium, one gets a time-inhomogeneous Markov chain under the martingale measure $\tilde{Q}$. In the theoretical framework constructed so far, JLT define the survival probability given the current rating state i under the martingale measure as

$$\tilde{Q}_t^i(\tau > T) = \sum_{j \neq K} \tilde{q}_{ij}(t, T) = 1 - \tilde{q}_{iK}(t, T) \tag{8.5}$$

where τ denotes the default time of the bond.

Given the current state i, JLT rewrite the valuation formula for risky zero-coupon debt with recovery rate φ in Jarrow and Turnbull (1995) as follows:

$$v^i(t, T) = p(t, T)\varphi + p(t, T)(1 - \varphi)\tilde{Q}_t^i(\tau > T) \tag{8.6}$$

In order to compute the theoretical prices for risky zero-coupon bonds, one needs the risk premium for all rating classes. However, they cannot be observed directly on the market; therefore, the risk premium is chosen such that the theoretical prices equal the market prices of the risky bonds. Given the market prices of the default-free and defaultable bonds with maturity of one year, at initial time $(t = 0)$, given initial rating i and a constant recovery rate φ, equation (8.4) can be rewritten as

$$\tilde{Q}_0^i(\tau \leq 1) = \left(\frac{p(0, 1) - vi(0, 1)}{p(0, 1)(1 - \varphi)} \right) \tag{8.7}$$

for $i = 1, \cdots, K - 1$. This is the one-period default probability of an issuer with rating i under the martingale measure $\tilde{Q}$. Given the empirical transition matrix P and equation (8.6), we get

$$\pi_i(0) = \left(\frac{p(0, 1) - v^i(0, 1)}{p(0, 1)(1 - \varphi)p_{iK}} \right) \tag{8.8}$$

Thus, we can calculate the risk premium for all rating classes and then compute the one-period risk-neutral transition matrix $\tilde{\mathcal{Q}}_{0,1}$.

Finally, we have the time-homogeneous empirical transition matrix P and the one-period time-inhomogeneous risk-neutral transition matrix $\tilde{\mathcal{Q}}_{0,1}$. Calculating $\tilde{\mathcal{Q}}_{0,2}$, $\tilde{\mathcal{Q}}_{0,3}$, etc., can then be conducted by an iterative procedure using equation (8.3). In practical applications the nonnegativeness and some additional conditions of the risk premium have to be checked in order to ensure that the resulting matrices are indeed probability matrices.

Overall, JLT define a methodology that can be used to value risky bonds as well as credit derivatives based on ratings allowing changes in credit quality before default. Before we go to extensions of this model, let us have a quick look at some disadvantages of JLT; see Uhrig-Homburg (2002). The term structures of interest rates for all rating classes are rarely available. This is especially the case for low rated bonds. Hence, it might be difficult to find the necessary information of risk-neutral default probabilities for all rating classes and time horizons. The second critical assumption is that all bonds are driven by the same Markov chain. Thus, in a real-world application, one has to make the unrealistic assumption that all debtors of a rating class are subject to the same rating transitions. Another critical point refers to the adjustment of the migration matrices. In practice market prices of defaultable claims often do not reflect historical default or transition probabilities. Therefore, using the method described here, quite extreme adjustments have to be conducted to transform a historical transition matrix into the transition matrix $\tilde{Q}$ under the martingale measure. Under certain circumstances this can even lead to nonvalid transition matrices.

8.2   Adjustments Based on the Discrete-Time Transition Matrix

Obviously, there is not a unique way, based on a historical transition matrix (8.1) and the calculated risk premiums (8.1), a risk-neutral transition matrix (8.2) can be obtained. In this chapter we will provide a variety of possible techniques that can be used to achive this goal.[1]

To illustrate the suggested methods, we will always give an example based on a hypothetical one-year transition matrix P with three possible rating categories $\{A, B, C\}$ and a default state $\{D\}$ of the following form:

---

[1] The following sections provide results originally published in Prokopczuk and Trueck (2008).

P	A	B	C	D
A	0.900	0.080	0.017	0.003
B	0.050	0.850	0.090	0.010
C	0.010	0.090	0.800	0.100
D	0	0	0	1

Let us further assume that based on empirically observed credit spreads, we have calculated the risk-neutral one-year default probabilities $\tilde{q}_{iK}$ for the three rating classes.

	A	B	C
$\tilde{q}_{iK}$	0.006	0.030	0.200

To start with, we will describe the technique that was initially suggested in Jarrow et al. (1997). The approach is quite simple and uses the following procedure to transform the real-world transition matrix into a risk-neutral one:

$$\tilde{q}_{ij}(t,T) = \begin{cases} \pi_i(t,T)p_{ij}(t,T) & \text{for } j \neq i \\ 1 - \pi_i(t,T)(1 - p_{ii}(t,T)) & \text{for } j = i \end{cases}$$

for $i = 1, \ldots, K - 1$, and $j = 1, \ldots, K$.

Obviously for this approach, the relationship between the risk premium, historical, and risk-neutral transition probability is the following:

$$\pi_i(0,1) = \frac{\tilde{q}_{iK}(0,1)}{p_{iK}(0,1)} \tag{8.9}$$

Thus, for our numerical example we get the risk premiums $\pi_A = 2$, $\pi_B = 3$, and $\pi_C = 2$. The adjustment procedure then yields the risk-neutral migration matrix:

$$\tilde{\mathcal{Q}}(0,1) = \begin{pmatrix} 0.8000 & 0.1600 & 0.0340 & 0.0060 \\ 0.1500 & 0.5500 & 0.2700 & 0.0300 \\ 0.0200 & 0.1800 & 0.6000 & 0.2000 \\ 0.0000 & 0.0000 & 0.0000 & 1.0000 \end{pmatrix} \tag{8.10}$$

Obviously, this method effectively speeds up the rating process or slows it down, depending on whether the calculated risk premium π_i is greater (up) or less (down) than one. It implies that in each row the upgrade and default entries are adjusted in the same direction. Unfortunately, in real-world applications often extremely high π_i's may be needed, since the empirical default probabilities are very low for high credit ratings.

Since each entry—apart from the diagonal element—in a row of the historical transition matrix P is multiplied by the calculated risk premium, this may even make the method infeasible, as we shall see in the following example.

Assume that the risk-neutral default probability for rating class B derived from bond prices is $\tilde{q}_{BD} = 0.1$ instead of $\tilde{q}_{BD} = 0.03$. Then we obtain a risk premium $\pi_B = 10$ and the algorithm yields the following (infeasible) risk-neutral transition matrix:

$$\tilde{\mathcal{Q}}(0,1) = \begin{pmatrix} 0.8000 & 0.1600 & 0.0340 & 0.0060 \\ 0.5000 & -0.5000 & 0.9000 & 0.1000 \\ 0.0200 & 0.1800 & 0.6000 & 0.2000 \\ 0.0000 & 0.0000 & 0.0000 & 1.0000 \end{pmatrix} \qquad (8.11)$$

Obviously in matrix $\tilde{\mathcal{Q}}(0,1)$ the diagonal element $\tilde{q}_{BB} = -0.5$ is negative such that the matrix is not valid.

As pointed out by Lando (2004), even small changes in the uncertain empirical estimates of high-grade default probabilities may lead to extremely high changes in risk adjustments with this method.

The numerical problems of the method are investigated and addressed by Kijima and Komoribayashi (1998). To overcome these difficulties, the authors propose an alternative procedure that equally multiplies all elements in a row—excluding the default element but including the diagonal element—such that the change in the default entry is distributed over the row. The algorithm that needs to be followed for each row is

$$\tilde{q}_{ij}(t,T) = \begin{cases} \pi_i(t,T)p_{ij}(t,T) & \text{for } j \neq K \\ 1 - \pi_i(t,T)(1 - p_{iK}(t,T)) & \text{for } j = K \end{cases}$$

Note that for the method suggested by Kijima and Komoribayashi (1998), the relationship between the risk premium, historical, and risk-neutral transition probability is

$$\pi_i(0,1) = \frac{1 - \tilde{q}_{iK}(0,1)}{1 - p_{iK}(0,1)} \qquad (8.12)$$

For our numerical example, the π's will then be estimated to be $\pi_A = 0.9970$, $\pi_B = 0.9798$, and $\pi_C = 0.8889$. Further, the adjusted risk-neutral transition matrix will be of the form

$$\tilde{\mathcal{Q}}(0,1) = \begin{pmatrix} 0.8973 & 0.0798 & 0.0169 & 0.0060 \\ 0.0490 & 0.8328 & 0.0882 & 0.0300 \\ 0.0089 & 0.0800 & 0.7111 & 0.2000 \\ 0.0000 & 0.0000 & 0.0000 & 1.0000 \end{pmatrix} \qquad (8.13)$$

The procedure suggested by Kijima and Komoribayashi (1998) guarantees numerical stability, but adjusts the default and all other entries in opposite directions. This may be counterintuitive, since one might assume that when for a certain rating state the risk-neutral default probability is higher than the real-world one, the same should hold for the probabilities for a downgrade.

8.3   Adjustments Based on the Generator Matrix

In this section[2] we will provide some numerical adjustment methods suggested by Lando (2000). Similar to the methods described in the previous section, the methods were designed to match historical transition matrices with default probabilities implied in bond prices observed in the market. The difference, however, is that the methods conduct a numerical adjustment procedure that is based on the continuous-time generator matrix and not the discrete-time transition matrix. Let us therefore consider the continuous-time case where the time-homogeneous Markov chain is specified via the $(K \times K)$ generator matrix such that the series

$$P(t) = exp(t\Lambda) = \sum_{k=0}^{\infty} \frac{(t\Lambda)^k}{k!} \qquad (8.14)$$

gives the $K \times K$ t-period transition matrix. Lando (2000) extends the JLT approach and describes three different methods to modify the transition matrices such that default probabilities implied in bond prices are matched. Again, using (8.7) the risk-neutral default probabilities are calculated and the aim is to create a family of transition matrices $(\tilde{Q}(0,t))_{t>1}$ in a way that the default probabilities implied in bond prices for each maturity match the corresponding entries in the last column of $\tilde{Q}(0,t)$.

In the suggested procedure the generator matrix Λ is modified such that

$$\tilde{Q} = e^{\tilde{\Lambda}}$$

and the default column of the risk-neutral transition matrix equals the risk-neutral default probabilities derived from bond prices $\tilde{q}_{iK}(0,1)$ for all rating classes i.

Note that the generator matrix has to be checked to see if it still fulfills the criteria, namely nonnegative off-diagonal elements and row sums of zero for each row. To illustrate the suggested methods, we will stick to the numerical example of the previous section of our hypothetical transition matrix P with three possible rating categories $\{A, B, C\}$ and a default state $\{D\}$.

---

[2] Some of the results of this section were originally published in Trueck and Özturkmen (2004). The structure of the section follows the original publication.

The associated generator Λ to the real-world transition matrix P is

$$\Lambda = \begin{pmatrix} -0.1080 & 0.0909 & 0.0151 & 0.0020 \\ 0.0569 & -0.1710 & 0.1092 & 0.0050 \\ 0.0087 & 0.1092 & -0.2293 & 0.1114 \\ 0.0000 & 0.0000 & 0.0000 & 0.0000 \end{pmatrix} \qquad (8.15)$$

Now the unconditional migration matrix should be adjusted in a way that it fits the risk-neutral default probabilities with $\widetilde{q}_{AD} = 0.006, \widetilde{q}_{BD} = 0.030$, and $\widetilde{q}_{CD} = 0.200$. Lando (2000) suggests three different adjustment methods that will be outlined in the following.

8.3.1 Modifying Default Intensities

The first method we describe modifies the default column of the generator matrix and simultaneously modifies the diagonal element of the generator according to

$$\begin{aligned} \widetilde{\lambda}_{1K} = \pi_1 \cdot \lambda_{1K} \quad &\text{and} \quad \widetilde{\lambda}_{11} = \lambda_{11} - (\pi_1 - 1) \cdot \lambda_{1K} \\ \widetilde{\lambda}_{2K} = \pi_2 \cdot \lambda_{2K} \quad &\text{and} \quad \widetilde{\lambda}_{22} = \lambda_{22} - (\pi_2 - 1) \cdot \lambda_{2K} \\ \cdots \quad & \qquad\qquad \cdots \end{aligned}$$

and for row $K-1$:

$$\widetilde{\lambda}_{K-1,K} = \pi_{K-1} \cdot \lambda_{K-1,K} \quad \text{and}$$

$$\widetilde{\lambda}_{K-1,K-1} = \lambda_{K-1,K-1} - (\pi_{K-1} - 1) \cdot \lambda_{K-1,K}$$

such that for the new transition matrix $\tilde{Q}$ with

$$\tilde{Q} = exp(t\widetilde{\Lambda}) = \sum_{k=0}^{\infty} \frac{(t\widetilde{\Lambda})^k}{k!} \qquad (8.16)$$

the last column equals the risk-neutral PDs. Obviously, after the modifications $\widetilde{\Lambda}$ will also be a generator matrix with rows summing to zero. The modifications are done numerically such that all conditions are matched simultaneously.

Using a numerical solution algorithm, we get $\pi_1 = 1.7443, \pi_2 = 4.1823$, $\pi_3 = 2.1170$ and thus, for the modified generator matrix

$$\widetilde{\Lambda} = \begin{pmatrix} -0.1095 & 0.0909 & 0.0151 & 0.0034 \\ 0.0569 & -0.1869 & 0.1092 & 0.0209 \\ 0.0087 & 0.1092 & -0.3537 & 0.2358 \\ 0 & 0 & 0 & 0 \end{pmatrix} \qquad (8.17)$$

and the associated risk-neutral migration matrix:

$$\tilde{\mathcal{Q}}(0,1) = \begin{pmatrix} 0.8987 & 0.0793 & 0.0161 & 0.0060 \\ 0.0496 & 0.8365 & 0.0840 & 0.0300 \\ 0.0094 & 0.0840 & 0.7066 & 0.2000 \\ 0 & 0 & 0 & 1.0 \end{pmatrix} \tag{8.18}$$

We find that due to the fact that the changes in the generator take place only in the last column and in the diagonal elements, for the new probability transition matrix most of the probability mass is shifted from the default probability to the diagonal element—especially when the new (calculated) default probability is significantly higher. Still, if a jump occurs, interpreting $-\frac{\lambda_{ij}}{\lambda_{ii}}$ as the probability for a jump into the new rating class j also, these probabilities slightly change since λ_{ii} is modified. In our case we find that, for example, for rating class A, the conditional probability for a jump to default has increased from 1.8% to more than 3% while the other conditional probabilities slightly decrease from 84% to 83% and from 14% to 13.8%. These results are confirmed by taking a look at the other rows and also by the associated new one-year risk-neutral transition matrix. Overall, we conclude that for this method the main adjustments take place in the diagonal element and in the default entry of the transition matrix.

8.3.2 Modifying the Rows of the Generator Matrix

This method is very similar to the adjustment suggestd in Jarrow et al. (1997); however, the multiplication of the row is conducted using the corresponding generator and not the discrete-time migration matrix. The idea is not only to adjust the last column and the diagonal elements of the generator matrix but multiply each row by a factor such that the calculated or forecasted default probabilities are matched.

Thus, we get

$$\tilde{\Lambda} = \begin{pmatrix} \pi_1 \cdot \lambda_{11} & \pi_1 \cdot \lambda_{12} & \cdots & \pi_1 \cdot \lambda_{1K} \\ \pi_2 \cdot \lambda_{21} & \pi_2 \cdot \lambda_{22} & \cdots & \pi_2 \cdot \lambda_{2K} \\ \cdots & \cdots & \cdots & \cdots \\ \pi_{K-1} \cdot \lambda_{K-1,1} & \pi_{K-1} \cdot \lambda_{K-1,2} & \cdots & \pi_{K-1} \cdot \lambda_{K-1,K} \\ 0 & 0 & \cdots & 0 \end{pmatrix} \tag{8.19}$$

Applying this method, then

$$\tilde{\mathcal{Q}}(t) = exp(t\tilde{\Lambda}) = \sum_{k=0}^{\infty} \frac{(t\tilde{\Lambda})^k}{k!} \tag{8.20}$$

needs to be solved subject to the condition that the last column of the new transition matrix equals the risk-neutral default probabilities: $\tilde{q} = (\tilde{q}_{1K}, \tilde{q}_{2K}, \ldots, \tilde{q}_{K-1,K}, 1)$.

For our numerical example we get

$$
\tilde{\Lambda} = \begin{pmatrix}
-0.1455 & 0.1225 & 0.0204 & 0.0027 \\
0.1149 & -0.3457 & 0.2207 & 0.0101 \\
0.0198 & 0.2482 & -0.5212 & 0.2532 \\
0 & 0 & 0 & 0
\end{pmatrix} \tag{8.21}
$$

and for the associated risk-neutral transition matrix:

$$
\tilde{Q}(0,1) = \begin{pmatrix}
0.8706 & 0.0988 & 0.0246 & 0.0060 \\
0.0926 & 0.7316 & 0.1458 & 0.0300 \\
0.0247 & 0.1639 & 0.6114 & 0.2000 \\
0 & 0 & 0 & 1
\end{pmatrix} \tag{8.22}
$$

In this case due to the different adjustment procedure, more probability mass is shifted from the diagonal element of the transition matrix to the other row entries. Considering, for example, the new transition matrix, we find that for rating state B the probability for staying in the same rating category decreases from 0.85 to approximately 0.73, while for all the other row entries the probability significantly increases—e.g., from 0.05 to 0.09 for moving from rating state B to rating state A. These results were confirmed by applying the method to different transition matrices, so we conclude that the method that modifies the complete row of the generator spreads clearly more probability mass from the diagonal element to the other elements than the first method does. It could be used when the transition matrix should be adjusted to an economy in a rather unstable situation.

8.3.3   Modifying Eigenvalues of the Transition Probability Matrix

The third method described here adjusts the real-world migration matrix by modifying the eigenvalues of the generator matrix. To do this, one has to assume that the transition matrix and, thus, also the generator are diagonalizable. Let M be a matrix of eigenvectors of the transition matrix P and D a diagonal matrix of eigenvalues of P. Then the generator matrix is changed by numerically modifying the eigenvalues by multiplying the matrix D with a diagonal matrix $\Pi(t)$ with diagonal elements $(\pi_{11}, \pi_{12}, \ldots, \pi_{1K}, 0)$. Therefore, the new generator matrix $\tilde{\Lambda}$ will be

$$
\tilde{\Lambda} = M \, \Pi(t) D \, M^{-1} \tag{8.23}
$$

Again, (8.23) needs to be solved subject to the condition that the last column of the new transition matrix equals the risk-neutral default probabilities: $\widetilde{q} = (\widetilde{q}_{1K}, \widetilde{q}_{2K}, \ldots, \widetilde{q}_{K-1,K}, 1)$.

For our empirical example, the numerical solution yields for the diagonal matrix

$$\Pi = \begin{pmatrix} 2.1747 & 0.0000 & 0.0000 & 0.0000 \\ 0.0000 & 2.2893 & 0.0000 & 0.0000 \\ 0.0000 & 0.0000 & 2.3081 & 0.0000 \\ 0.0000 & 0.0000 & 0.0000 & 0.0000 \end{pmatrix} \qquad (8.24)$$

Therefore, the adjusted generator matrix is

$$\widetilde{\Lambda} = \begin{pmatrix} -0.2459 & 0.2108 & 0.0347 & 0.0003 \\ 0.1319 & -0.3925 & 0.2537 & 0.0069 \\ 0.0200 & 0.2538 & -0.5278 & 0.2540 \\ 0.0000 & 0.0000 & 0.0000 & 0.0000 \end{pmatrix} \qquad (8.25)$$

and the corresponding risk-neutral transition matrix is

$$\widetilde{\mathcal{Q}}(0,1) = \begin{pmatrix} 0.7930 & 0.1587 & 0.0423 & 0.0060 \\ 0.0991 & 0.7065 & 0.1644 & 0.0300 \\ 0.0253 & 0.1643 & 0.6104 & 0.2000 \\ 0.0000 & 0.0000 & 0.0000 & 1.0000 \end{pmatrix} \qquad (8.26)$$

Obviously, for our empirical example, the third method shifts most of the probability mass from the diagonal elements to the other elements of the row. The results are more similar to those when we modified the complete row of the generator than to those where only the default intensities were modified. For other transition matrices that were examined, we found similar results. It seems that the methods modifying the eigenvalues and the complete rows of the generator should be used if rather grave changes in transition probabilities are expected, while the method that modifies the default intensities changes the transition probabilities more cautiously.

Unfortunately Lando doesn't give any information on the size of the change. However, it should be pointed out that in adjusting transition matrices the degree of the changes could be very important. Recall the strong impact of changes in migration matrices on the risk for a portfolio as it was illustrated in Section 6.4. To tackle this task, in the next section we will suggest some methods to measure the difference between two migration matrices in portions of risk.

8.4   An Adjustment Technique Based on Economic Theory

Alternatively, Lando and Mortensen (2005) suggest that the adjustment might be conducted based on another approach that is inspired by economic theory. Let us consider a one-period model from t to $t+1$ with discrete state space given by the usual K rating classes. The authors further assume that in a stylized economic setting all agents allocate their utility according to a power utility function $u(w)$ of the form

$$u(w) = \frac{w^{1-\theta}}{1-\theta} \tag{8.27}$$

Note that this assumption implies a constant relative risk aversion of θ. Now it is further assumed that traded assets are the riskless bank account and a risky zero-coupon bond with maturity T, rating i priced at $V_i(t)$. Further, the riskless interest rate r is assumed to be constant and so are the credit spreads s_j for each of the rating classes. Therefore, the price of the risky bond with rating state j is $V_j(t) = e^{(r+s_j)T}$. Further, the real-world transition probabilities are denoted by a transition matrix $P = (p_{ij})$. Then by the end of one period the new rating state of the zero-coupon bond will be j with probability p_{ij} for $j = 1, \ldots, K$.

Further using the first-order condition for utility-maximizing agents implying that the state price density is proportional to the marginal utility given optimal investment (Lando and Mortensen, 2005), the authors derive the following relationship between real-world and risk-neutral transition probabilities:

$$\frac{p_{ij}}{\widetilde{q}_{ij}} = \frac{(1 - a_i(1 - e^{s_j+(s_i-s_j)T})^{-\theta_i}}{\sum_{k=1}^{K} p_{ik}(1 - a_i((1 - e^{s_k+(s_i-s_k)T})^{-\theta_i}} \tag{8.28}$$

From this expression, in a first step using real-world transition probabilities p_{ij}, risk-neutral default probabilities $\widetilde{q}_{iK}$, credit spreads s_j, maturity T, and a value of a_i, the parameter θ_i can be determined. Then in a second step, the other risk-neutral transition probabilities are calculated based on the estimated θ_i. Note that a_i actually denotes the optimal fraction of wealth that should be invested in the risky asset. Ensuring internal consistency in the stylized setting of the economy, the parameters a_i would have to be determined in agreement with the price of the bond using risk-neutral transition probabilities $\widetilde{q}_{ij}$: $V_i(t) = \sum_{j=1}^{K} \widetilde{q}_{ij} e^{-r} V_j(t+1)$. However, as stated by the authors, the risk adjustments θ_i are rather insensitive to the value of a_i such that the condition of internal consistency is not applied in the calculation of $\widetilde{q}_{ij}$. The authors further point out that, in a more realistic setting, one had to allow for more states of nature, heterogenous agents, multiple risky assets, and time periods as well as stochastic interest rates and credit spreads (Lando and Mortensen, 2005). However, it is argued by Lando and Mortensen (2005) that even without considering these aspects, the functional form of the risk adjustments still provides a good approximation. Overall, it seems that the results for adjustments of the real-world transition matrix based on economic theory are more reasonable than for the methods that were discussed in Section 8.2. For example, the method overcomes the infeasibility of the Jarrow et al. (1997) method and the deficiency of the Kijima and Komoribayashi (1998) method to counterintuitively adjust the default probability and all other entries in opposite directions.

Let us now have a look at a numerical example. We assume the following credit spreads (in bp) for the four rating categories:

Rating Class	A	B	C	D
Credit Spreads (bp)	80	200	800	1800

We further set the values for $a_i = 0.5$ for all rating categories and assume that $T = 2$ for the bonds. Then, when we plug in the transition matrix

$$P = \begin{pmatrix} 0.900 & 0.080 & 0.017 & 0.003 \\ 0.050 & 0.850 & 0.090 & 0.010 \\ 0.010 & 0.090 & 0.800 & 0.100 \\ 0.000 & 0.000 & 0.000 & 1.000 \end{pmatrix} \tag{8.29}$$

and the risk-neutral default probabilities $\widetilde{q}_{AD} = 0.006$, $\widetilde{q}_{BD} = 0.030$, $\widetilde{q}_{CD} = 0.200$ into (8.28), the optimization procedure yields $\theta_A = 8.5243$, $\theta_B = 14.7619$, and $\theta_C = 13.0577$.

Based on these estimates, we then calculate the elements $\widetilde{q}_{ij}$, for $j = 1, \ldots, K - 1$ of the risk-neutral transition matrix by using expression (8.28) and obtain

$$\widetilde{\mathcal{Q}} = \begin{pmatrix} 0.8898 & 0.0832 & 0.0209 & 0.0060 \\ 0.0436 & 0.8110 & 0.1154 & 0.0300 \\ 0.0064 & 0.0627 & 0.7309 & 0.2000 \\ 0.0000 & 0.0000 & 0.0000 & 1.0000 \end{pmatrix} \tag{8.30}$$

8.5   Risk-Neutral Migration Matrices and Pricing

In this chapter we have reviewed several techniques that can be used to transform real-world transition matrices into risk-neutral ones. Some of them were applied using discrete time migration matrices (Jarrow et al., 1997; Kijima and Komoribayashi, 1998), while others used the corresponding continuous-time generator matrix for the adjustment (Lando, 2004).

Finally, following Lando and Mortensen (2005), an approach was described where the adjustment is inspired by economic theory.

Overall, so far there has been no extensive empirical study comparing the different adjustment techniques in terms of which method works best for pricing credit derivatives. The few exceptions on comparing the methods rather deal with the feasibility of the approaches. Lando and Mortensen (2005) find that the method intially suggested by Jarrow et al. (1997) yields infeasible results in a real-world application for pricing step-up bonds, while the adjustments using the utility-based method inspired by economic theory provide more intuitive results than the method by Kijima and Komoribayashi (1998). However, they also point out that the utility-based method is very sensitive to the values of real-world default probabilities. To overcome this problem by using a smoothed version of the empirical rating transition matrix, see Lando and Mortensen (2005). On the other hand, Trueck (2008) finds that in particular the numerical adjustment method that modifies the whole row of the generator by multiplying with a factor π_i spreads too much of the probability mass and yields rather bad results for forecasting future migration matrices. Note, however, that in this analysis the focus is not on pricing of credit derivatives, but conditioning migration matrices on business cycle effects. For a further discussion on the different adjustment techniques and their results, we also refer to Prokopczuk and Trueck (2008). As mentioned above, an alternative approach on deriving implied migration rates from barrier models is suggested by Albanese and Chen (2006).

Another problem in practical applications is the assumption that each rating state is associated with a risk-adjusted default intensity that determines the price of the bond. However, as pointed out in Lando (2004), the rating process is to some extent disconnected from the default intensity process. This is also illustrated by the fact that default intensities implied by a Merton-type or the KMV model that are based on the value of the firm are much more volatile than the actual rating process. If a rating change happens every time the expected default frequency passes a certain threshold, then the rating process was much more volatile than can be observed in the real world.

Finally, one has to keep in mind that important information related to a single company might be ignored when transition matrices are used to price credit derivatives. By using the rating of the company and the corresponding migration probabilities as input variables, one measures the dynamics of the rating class but not those of the individual firm. Unfortunately, many characteristics of a company affecting the default process or rating changes may not be captured by the rating class. As we will see in Chapter 11, one usually tries to overcome this problem by only considering the bond of the particular issuer and conducting the adjustment based on the observed spread and implied default probability. However, in real-world applications, often there are too few bonds available to conduct a proper adjustment.

9

Conditional Credit Migrations: Adjustments and Forecasts

9.1 Overview

In Chapter 6 we illustrated methods for detecting significant differences between transition matrices. While Bangia et al. (2002) examined the stability of migration matrices of a major agency, we found that transition matrices of an internal rating system also could not be considered as being time homogeneous or a first-order Markov chain. We further investigated the substantial effects of changes in migration behavior on expected loss, VaR, and especially on confidence intervals for PDs. One finding was that, especially in times of an economic downturn, the risk of a credit portfolio can be several times higher than during an expansion of the economy. The findings are similar to some other studies in the field. Helwege and Kleiman (1997) as well as Alessandrini (1999) have shown, respectively, that default rates and credit spreads clearly depend on the stage of the business cycle. Belkin et al. (1998b) developed a simple model for adjustment of transition matrices to the economy, while Nickell et al. (2000) have shown that probability transition matrices of bond ratings depend on business cycles. By separating the economy into two states or regimes, expansion and contraction, and conditioning the migration matrix on these states, Bangia et al. (2002) showed significant differences in the loss distribution of credit portfolios.

Still, despite the obvious importance of recognizing the impact of business cycles on rating transitions, the literature is rather sparse on this issue. The first model developed to explicitly link business cycles to rating transitions was in the 1997 CreditPortfolioView (CPV) by Wilson (1997a,b) and McKinsey & Company. Belkin et al. (1998b) developed a univariate model whereby ratings respond to business cycle shifts. Nickell et al. (2000) proposed an ordered probit model which permits migration matrices to be conditioned on the industry, the country domicile, and the business cycle. In this chapter we will first review some of the approaches on adjusting migration matrices to the business cycle mentioned above. Then we will illustate the adjustment methods suggested in Lando (2000), as we will use them later for our own adjustment procedure. The methods suggested there were actually not introduced for linking transition matrices to the business cycle but to obtain risk-neutral migration matrices being in line with market credit spreads. However we will show that they can also be used for the purpose of linking macroeconomic variables to changes in migration matrices.

9.2   The CreditPortfolioView Approach

In the so-called macro simulation approach by Wilson (1997b), a time series model for the macroeconomic situation is used to forecast an index $Y_{j,t}$ for each rating class j at time t. This index is then used in a logit model to determine the conditional default probability $p_{j,t}$ in period t:

$$p_{j,t} = \frac{1}{1 + e^{-Y_{j,t}}} \tag{9.1}$$

The index $Y_{j,t}$ is derived from a multifactor time-series model of the form

$$Y_{j,t} = \beta_{j,0} + \beta_{j,1} X_{j,1,t} + \beta_{j,2} X_{j,2,t} + \ldots + \beta_{j,m} X_{j,m,t} + v_{j,t} \tag{9.2}$$

According to the model the index $Y_{j,t}$ is dependent on economic variables $X_{j,k}$ with $k = 1, \ldots, m$ using the coefficients β_j. Further, $v_{j,t}$ represents an error term. In the CPV model the error term $v_{j,t}$ is interpreted as the index innovation vector and assumed to be independent of the $X_{j,k}$ and identically normally distributed. Thus, we get $v_{j,t} \sim N(0, \sigma_j)$ and $v_j \sim N(0, \Sigma_v)$. Hence, Σ_v denotes the variance/covariance matrix of the index innovations.

The macroeconomic factors $X_{j,k}$ are assumed to follow an autoregressive process of order 2 AR(2):

$$X_{j,k,t} = \gamma_{j,k,0} + \gamma_{j,k,1} X_{j,k,t-1} + \gamma_{j,k,2} X_{j,k,t-2} + e_{j,k,t} \tag{9.3}$$

Here $X_{j,i,t-1}$ and $X_{j,i,t-2}$ denote the lagged values of variable $X_{j,k}$, and $e_{j,k,t}$ denotes an error term that is assumed to be iid, i.e.,

$$e \sim N(0, \sigma_{e_{j,k,t}})$$

where Σ_e is the covariance matrix of the error terms. The author points out that a better strategy might have been an $ARMA(p, q)$ or a vector autoregressive moving average model. However, the model with two independent AR(2) processes was chosen due to its simplicity.

Combining equations (9.1), (9.2), and (9.3), we have to solve a system of equations to calibrate the model using the following assumptions:

$$E_t = \begin{bmatrix} v_t \\ e_t \end{bmatrix} \sim N(0, \Sigma) \tag{9.4}$$

where

$$\Sigma = \left[\begin{array}{cc} \Sigma_v & \Sigma_{v,e} \\ \Sigma_{e,v} & \Sigma_e \end{array} \right] \tag{9.5}$$

After the estimation of equations (9.1), (9.2), and (9.3), simulations are used to calculate a macroeconomic index and, thus, conditional default probabilities. Then the unconditional or average migration matrix has to be adjusted to simulate portfolio migrations and default behavior.

We will now illustrate the adjustment procedure for the transition matrices by a simplified example using a discrete approach taken from Saunders and Allen (2002). Let us consider a transition matrix with only four rating categories A, B, C, D. Let's further assume that the unconditional or average default probability for C-rated debt is $\bar{p}_{CD} = 0.15$, while, e.g., the migration probability from state C to state B is $\bar{p}_{CB} = 0.04$ and from state C to state A is $\bar{p}_{CA} = 0.01$, as denoted in Table 9.1.

Now suppose that based on current macroeconomic conditions the estimated conditional value of the default probability for a C-rated bond given by the model equations (9.1)–(9.3) is $p_{CD,t} = 0.174$. In this case without adjusting the transition matrix we were likely to underestimate the VaR of a loan portfolio and especially the default probability of a C-rated loan. Hence, we have to adjust the transition matrix according to this estimate for $p_{CD,t}$.

With $\Delta p_{CD} = p_{CD,t} - \bar{p}_{CD} = 0.174 - 0.15 = 0.024$ a so-called diffusion term or shift parameter is determined. This parameter is then used to change the respective row in the unconditional transition matrix to obtain the conditional transition matrix. Clearly the shift in transition probabilities must be diffused throughout the row in a way ensuring that the sum of all probabilities equals one.[1] The procedure aims $\Delta p_{CC} = -0.0204$, $\Delta p_{CB} = -0.006$ and $\Delta p_{CA} = +0.0024$ and the obtained row of the conditional migration matrix as is denoted in Table 9.2.

TABLE 9.1. Unconditional or Average Transition Probabilities for Rating Category C

	A	B	C	D
A	...	...	...	...
B	...	...	...	...
C	0.01	0.04	0.80	0.15

---

[1] For a more detailed description of the procedure, we refer to Saunders and Allen (2002). Unfortunately, the described procedure contains some mistakes and does not give correct insight into how the final result is obtained.

TABLE 9.2. Conditional Transition
Matrix

	A	**B**	**C**	**D**
A	...	...	...	
B	...	...	...	...
C	0.0124	0.034	0.7796	0.174

Saunders and Allen (2002) point out that to determine the complete transition matrix, this procedure is repeated for each row of the unconditional transition matrix.

In the documentation of CreditPortfolioView, a continuous-time approach using generator matrices is applied. To describe the complete adjustment procedure, Wilson uses a so-called shift operator that redistributes the probability mass within each row of the unconditional migration matrix. The shift operator is then written in terms of a matrix $S = \{S_{ij}\}$ and the shift procedure is accomplished by

$$P^* = P_{cond} = (I + \tau S)P_{uncond}$$

Thus, the unconditional average transition matrix is multiplied by a matrix that consists of the identity matrix plus the shift matrix multiplied by a factor $\tau \geq 0$. According to Wilson the factor τ that determines the amplitude of the shift in segment j is calculated according to the following rule:

$$\tau_j = \frac{p_{jD,t}}{\bar{p}_{jD}} - 1 \quad \text{for} \quad \frac{p_{jD,t}}{\bar{p}_{jD}} \geq 1 \tag{9.6}$$

and

$$\tau_j = -\left(\frac{p_{jD,t}}{\bar{p}_{jD}} - 1\right) \quad \text{for} \quad \frac{p_{jD,t}}{\bar{p}_{jD}} < 1 \tag{9.7}$$

where p_{jD} is the unconditional default probability for the jth segment (taken from the unconditional migration matrix). Thus, the amplitude is ensured to be ≥ 1. Obviously, the shift operator (or the shift matrix) should satisfy the following conditions for the adjusted migration matrix.

- It should preserve the sum of the migration probabilities in each row to be 1; thus $\sum_{j=1}^{K} p_{ij}^* = 1$ for $i = 1, \ldots, K$.
- The shift operator should ensure that the new migration and default probabilities are all greater than or equal to zero and less than 1; thus $0 \leq p_{ij}^* \leq 1$ for $i, j = 1, \ldots, K$.

This leads, according to Wilson, to the following shift operator restrictions, given

$$P_{cond}(\tau) = (I + \tau S)P_{uncond}, \quad \tau \geq 0 \text{ and } S = \{S_{ij}\} \tag{9.8}$$

and

- $-\tau \leq s_{jj} \leq 0$ for $j = 1, \ldots, K$
- $s_{ij} \geq 0$ for all $i \neq j$
- $\sum_{i=1}^{n} s_{ij} = 0$ for $j = 1, \ldots, K$

Obviously, the conditions imposed to the shift operator matrix make it look very similar to a generator matrix. Wilson states that the conditions on S ensure that the conditional matrix P_{cond} is a valid migration matrix as long as P_{uncond} is a valid migration matrix. For the proof we refer to the technical document of CreditPortfolioView (CreditPortfolioView, 1998). The problem, however, in dealing with discrete matrices is that the boundedness condition on τ is almost impossible to guarantee for any arbitrary series of speculative default rates—especially not for historical speculative default series which have a relatively high standard deviation-to-mean ratio. Under τ violating the boundedness condition, the resulting matrix could contain negative probabilities or also probabilities greater than one. Therefore, Wilson changes from a discrete shift operator to a continuous shift operator:

$$P_{cond}(\tau + \Delta\tau) = (I + \Delta\tau S)P_{cond}(\tau) \tag{9.9}$$

Equation (9.9) leads to the differential equation

$$\frac{dP}{d\tau} = SP_{cond} \text{ with } P(0) = P_{uncond} \tag{9.10}$$

and the solution

$$P_{cond}(\tau) = exp(\tau S)P_{uncond}$$

Since we already defined how the amplitude of the shift operator is calculated, the remaining task is how to determine the shift matrix S. A right shift operator can be considered as a matrix shifting probability mass in the direction of increased downgrades and defaults. Alternatively, a left shift operator can be considered as a matrix shifting probability mass in economic expansion in the direction of higher rating grades.

Wilson defines a possible systematic right shift operator according to the following equation:

$$p_{j.}^*(\tau + \Delta\tau) = p_{j.}^*(\tau) + (s_{j-1}p_{j-1.}^*(\tau) - s_j p_{j.}^*(\tau))\Delta\tau$$

If the amplitude of the shift operator changes, the new migration probability equals the original migration probability plus a proportion from the higher class $j-1$ minus the mass that is shifted to the lower class $j+1$. Then the systematic right shift operator has the following form:

$$
S = \begin{pmatrix}
-s_1 & & \cdots & 0 \\
s_1 & -s_2 & \cdots & 0 \\
\cdots & \cdots & \cdots & \cdots \\
\cdots & s_{K-2} & -s_{K-1} & 0 \\
0 & \cdots & s_{K-1} & 0 \\
0 & \cdots & 0 & 0
\end{pmatrix}
\tag{9.11}
$$

The systematic left shift operator is defined along the lines of the right shift operator. Clearly the relation that should be expressed is that as the speculative default rate increases, credit downgrades are more likely, while upgrades have lower probabilities and vice versa. Wilson suggests defining $s_j = \alpha$ for downgrades ($j \geq r$) and $s_j = \beta$ for upgrades ($j < r$) with r being the rating class to which S relates. But in further documentation, the systematic shift operator is restricted according to $s = \alpha = \beta$ to govern the form of the left- and right-shift operators. This restriction is supposed to ensure that in the absence of macroeconomic shocks, the mean of the simulated cumulative migration matrix equals the unconditional cumulative migration matrix; see CreditPortfolioView (1998).

In addition to calibrating expected defaults by the systematic shift operator according to CreditPortfolioView, it is also important to calibrate the ratio of expected to unexpected default rates. Since investment grade segments tend to be less sensitive to cyclical movements, the amount of volatility of default rates which can be described by the systematic risk models is lower for investment grade counterparties. Thus, while one can expect defaults to vary over the cycle in a more or less predictable manner for noninvestment grade categories, default events for highly rated counterparties have to be considered as more unsystematic and surprising. Hence, in addition to the systematic shift operator, there is also added a source of uncertainty which is independent of the state of the economy. It is called the unsystematic shift operator. It affects the higher rated companies more than the lower rating categories. The probability mass is directly moved from the default entry to each entry in a row of the migration matrix or vice versa. The unsystematic right shift matrix U is of the form

$$
U = \begin{pmatrix}
-u_1 & & \cdots & 0 \\
& -u_2 & \cdots & 0 \\
\cdots & \cdots & \cdots & \cdots \\
\cdots & & -u_{K-1} & 0 \\
u_1 & u_2 & \cdots & u_{K-1} & 0
\end{pmatrix}
\tag{9.12}
$$

However, the task is not only to determine the form of S and U but also its values. Unfortunately, this part of the adjustment is not available in the published documentation of CreditPortfolioView, which has to be considered a major drawback of the model. For a simpified example of the adjustment procedure, see, e.g., Saunders and Allen (2002). In an empirical study, Wehrspohn (2004) examines the estimated long-term default probabilities by CreditPortfolioView and compares them to Standard & Poor's cumulated default probabilities. To investigate the effect of the adjustment procedure in the Wilson model, he tested model forecasts both under an average macroeconomic situation and a recession scenario. His findings are rather disenchanting. The estimated default probabilities under the average macroeconomic scenario are on average 5 times higher than the cumulative 10-year default probabilities of Standard & Poor's; for rating class A the estimated default probability is approximately 10%, and thus more than 8 times higher than the numbers provided by the rating agency. Hence, CreditPortfolioView is not able to estimate long-term default probabilities similar to the market. Further, the difference between simulated long-term default probabilities under the conditional recession and the average macroeconomic scenario are comparatively small. For the considered 10-year horizon, Wehrspohn (2004) obtained less than 10% difference, which is negligible compared to the differences in the deviations from cumulated default probabilities by the rating agencies. He concludes that the model has some deficiencies in representing market cumulative default probabilities, especially for longer time horizons, and should be refined in several ways.

9.3 Adjustment Based on Factor Model Representations

Kim (1999) developed a model for estimating conditional transition matrices. In his model he adopts a one-factor model to incorporate credit cycle dynamics into the transition matrix. Similar to CreditPortfolioView, the main idea is to improve the accuracy of credit loss simulation based on the technique of conditional transition matrices. He also points out that another goal is to yield an efficient method for stress testing according to the analyst's view of the future economic state.

To implement the technique, in a first step one builds a credit cycle index, which indicates the credit state of the financial market as a whole. The model of the credit cycle index needs to include the most relevant macroeconomic and financial series, such that the forecasted credit cycle index will represent the credit state well. Then in a next step the transition matrix is conditioned on the forecasted credit cycle index. Unlike in the one-factor default mode model, the model of conditioning the transition matrix should cover events that lead to upgrading and downgrading, as well as default. Furthermore, in the face of the animadversion on the CreditPortfolioView model, the estimated results should be stable enough to apply to forecasting or stress testing of the transition matrix.

9.3.1 Deriving an Index for the Credit Cycle

The so-called credit cycle index Z_t defines the credit state based on macroeconomic conditions shared by all obligors during period t. The index is designed to be positive in good days and to be negative in bad days. A positive index implies a lower downgrading and default probability and a higher upgrading probability and vice versa. To calibrate the index one uses the default probabilities of speculative grade bonds, since, similar to Wilson, Kim (1999) points out that highly rated bonds have very low default probabilities that are rather insensitive to the economic state.

Further, Z_t is supposed to follow a standard Gaussian distribution and is standardized according to

$$Z_t = \frac{\Phi^{-1}(SDP_t) - \mu_t}{\sigma_t} \tag{9.13}$$

where SDP_t is the speculative grade default probability of period t; μ and σ denote the historical average and the standard deviation of the inverse normal transformation of the speculative grade default probability. Since the SDP is restricted to lie between 0 and 1, a simple regression model cannot be used and a transformation is needed. Thus, the relationship between the business cycle and SDP_t is derived similarly to the CreditPortfolioView model. However, instead of the logit model suggested by Wilson (1997b), a probit model is suggested. Following CreditMetrics he assumes that the underlying, continuous credit-change indicator has a standard normal distribution:

$$SDP_t = \Phi(X_{t-1}\beta + \epsilon_t) \tag{9.14}$$

with X_{t-1} denoting a set of macroeconomic variables of the previous period and ϵ_t a random error term with $E_{t-1}(\epsilon_t) = 0$. After estimation of the coefficients $\hat{\beta}$, the forecast for the inverse normal CDF of the speculative grade default probability is

$$E(\Phi^{-1}(SDP_t)) = X_{t-1}\hat{\beta} \tag{9.15}$$

Kim points out that the probit model allows an unbiased forecast of the inverse normal CDF of SDP to be created, given recent information about the economic state and the estimated coefficient.

After testing several macroeconomic variables, the author chose the spread between Aaa and Baa bonds, the yield of 10-year treasury bonds, the quarterly CPI inflation, and the quarterly growth of GDP for X. For the estimated model all coefficients showed the signs one would expect, and in backtesting, using mean absolute error as performance criteria provided better forecasts for average SDP than simply using the average speculative grade default probabilities as a forecast.

9.3.2   Conditioning of the Migration Matrix

Similar to the CreditPortfolioView model, the second step is to adjust the transition matrix according to estimated or forecasted values of the credit cycle index. Following the one-factor model suggested by Belkin et al. (1998b) we described in the previous section, it is assumed that ratings transitions reflect an underlying, continuous credit-change indicator Y following a standard normal distribution. The credit-change indicator Y_t is assumed to have a linear relationship with the systematic credit cycle index Z_t and an idiosyncratic error term ϵ_t, so we get the one-factor model parameterization:

$$Y_t = \gamma Z_t + \sqrt{1 - \gamma^2}\epsilon_t \qquad (9.16)$$

Since both Z_t and ϵ_t are scaled to the standard normal distribution with the weights chosen to be γ and $\sqrt{1-\gamma^2}$, we get Y_t also to be standard normal. Recall that γ^2 represents the correlation between the credit change indicator Y_t and the systematic credit cycle index Z_t.

Figures 9.1 and 9.2 illustrate the effect of the shift of the credit-change indicator Y_t depending on the outcome of the credit cycle index Z_t. On average days we obtain $Z_t = 0$ for the systematic risk index and the credit-change indicator Y_t follows a standard normal distribution. If the assumed default event threshold is -2, the unconditional default probability is equal to the probability that the idiosyncratic risk factor ϵ_t is less than $\frac{-2}{\sqrt{1-0.3^2}}$. Therefore, we obtain for the unconditional PD

$$P(Y_t < -2.1945) = \Phi(\frac{-2}{\sqrt{1 - 0.3^2}}) = 0.0180 \qquad (9.17)$$

Let's now assume that the correlation γ between Y_t and Z_t is 0.3. Hence, a positive outcome of the credit cycle index $Z_t = 1.5$ shifts the credit-change indicator to the right side by $\gamma \cdot Z_t = 0.3 \cdot 1.5 = 0.5$. The conditional default probability dependent on $Z_t = 1.5$ is equal to

$$P(Y_t < -2) = P(\epsilon_t < \frac{-2.5}{\sqrt{1 - 0.3^2}}) = \Phi(\frac{-2.5}{\sqrt{1 - 0.3^2}}) = 0.0180 \qquad (9.18)$$

The lower conditional PD is illustrated by Figure 9.1.

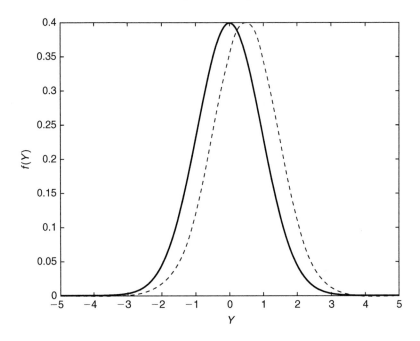

FIGURE 9.1. Average and conditional credit-change indicator for expansion scenario ($Z_t = 1.5$).

In the case of a bad outcome of the systematic credit cycle index, the distribution moves to the left side. For example, assume that $Z_t = -1.5$, so the distribution is shifted to the left by 0.5. Therefore, we get for the conditional PD

$$P(Y_t < -2) = P(\epsilon_t < \frac{-1.5}{\sqrt{1 - 0.3^2}}) = \Phi(\frac{-1.5}{\sqrt{1 - 0.3^2}}) = 0.0579 \qquad (9.19)$$

The effect on the conditional distribution for the PDs is illustrated in Figure 9.2.

To apply the above scheme to a multirating system, the author follows a procedure suggested by Belkin et al. (1998b). Following the CreditMetrics approach by Gupton et al. (1997) described in Section 4.3, it is assumed that, conditional on an initial credit rating i at the beginning of a year, one partitions values of the credit change indicator Y into a set of disjoint bins. According to Belkin et al. the bins are defined in a way that the probability that Y_t falls within a given interval equals the corresponding historical average transition rate. The mapping procedure is illustrated in Figure 9.3. The methodology can be understood as mapping a firm's future asset returns to possible ratings. The underlying assumption is that higher returns correspond to higher ratings, and vice versa. It should be noted

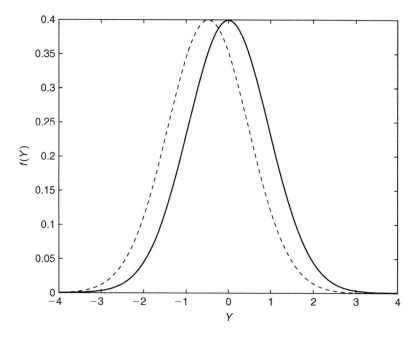

FIGURE 9.2. Average and conditional credit-change indicator for recession scenario ($Z_t = -1.5$).

that to calculate the scores, any meaningful statistical distribution could be used for the mapping. However, given the absence of preference for a particular distribution, for ease of calculation and estimation, the author chose the Gaussian distribution.

The mapping procedure is straightforward. Since the row sum in a transition matrix is always 1, one could, for each rating class in the average transition matrix, construct a sequence of joint bins covering the domain of the Gaussian variable. This can be done simply by inverting the cumulative normal distribution function starting from the default column. To illustrate the procedure, we will consider an issuer, one in the speculative grade rating class Ba. For Ba-rated issuers, we have the average transition probabilities given in Table 9.3. A default probability of 0.0141 corresponds to $x_D^{Ba} = \Phi^{-1}(0.0141) = -2.1945$. Hence, the first bin is $(-\infty, -2.1945]$. For the next entry, summing 0.0141 and 0.0111 gives us the total probability that the new rating is either C or a migration to default. The corresponding score is $x_C^{Ba} = \Phi^{-1}(0.0252) = -1.9566$, and the next bin is $(-2.1945, -1.9566]$. Repeating this procedure gives the other scores, and finally the last bin corresponding to a transition to Aaa is $(3.5402, \infty)$.

When one uses the bins calculated from the average transition matrix, it is then straightforward to calculate the conditional transition probability

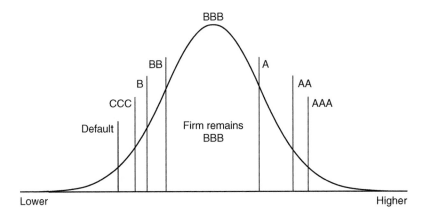

FIGURE 9.3. Corresponding credit scores to transition probabilities for a company with BBB rating [compare Belkin et al. (1998b)].

TABLE 9.3. Average One-Year Transition Probabilities (TP) and Corresponding Scores for an Issuer with Rating Baa

	Aaa	Aa	A	Baa	Ba	B	C	D
$p(Ba, i)$	0.0002	0.0011	0.0052	0.0712	0.8229	0.0742	0.0111	0.0141
$Score_{Ba}$	–	3.5402	3.0115	2.4838	1.4207	−1.2850	−1.9566	−2.1945

on the credit cycle index. In any year, the observed transition rates will deviate from the average migration matrix. It is possible to find a value of Z so that the probabilities associated with the bins defined above best approximate the given year's observed transition rates. Thus, Z_t is determined so as to minimize the weighted, mean-squared discrepancies between the model transition probabilities and the observed transition probabilities. The conditional transition probability $p_t(i, j|Z_t)$ for rating state i to another rating state j has the ordered probit model:

$$p_t(i, j|Z_t) = \Phi\left(\frac{x^i_{j+1} - \gamma Z_t}{\sqrt{1 - \gamma^2}}\right) - \Phi\left(\frac{x^i_j - \gamma Z_t}{\sqrt{1 - \gamma^2}}\right) \qquad (9.20)$$

The estimation problem then results in minimizing the following expression:

$$\min \sum_j \sum_i \frac{n_{t,j} \left[p_t(i, j) - p_t(i, j|Z_t)\right]^2}{p_t(i, j|Z_t)(1 - p_t(i, j|Z_t))} \qquad (9.21)$$

where $n_{t,j}$ denotes the number of transitions from initial grade i to j in the year t. Further observations are weighted by the inverses of the approximate sample variances $p_t(i,j|Z_t)$. For the procedure of estimating the ordered probit model, we refer to Maddala (1983). In an empirical study by Kim, estimating equation (10.5) is done by using the transition matrix and the credit cycle index of 56 quarters from 1984 to 1998. The method for estimating the ordered (multicategorical) probit model in equation (9.3) is the same except that the ordered probit model uses the bin of credit rating thresholds as intercepts of the equation. The estimated parameter γ is $\gamma_{inv} = 0.0537$ for the investment grade and $\gamma_{spec} = 0.3384$ for the speculative grade. To illustrate the adjustment procedure, we consider again the transition probabilities and related scores of a Ba-rated issuer given in Table 9.3. Suppose that the outcome of the credit cycle index for year t^* is $Z_{t^*} = 1.5$. Since the estimated correlation for speculative grade issuers is $\gamma_{spec} = 0.3384$, we get a shift of the credit-change indicator distribution by $0.3384 \cdot 1.5 = 0.5076$.

9.3.3 A Multifactor Model Extension

Wei (2003) extends the factor model representation by a multifactor, Markov chain model for rating migrations and credit spreads. The model allows transition matrices to be time varying and further driven by rating-specific latent variables. These variables can encompass a variety of economic factors including business cycles.

Similar to Wilson and Kim, Wei starts with the assumption that there exists an average transition matrix similar to $\bar{P}$, whose fixed entries represent average, per-period transition probabilities across all credit cycles. Further he assumes that the entries in a transition matrix for a particular year will deviate from the averages, and the size of the deviations is dependent on the condition of the economy. A further assumption is that the size of the deviations can be different for different rating categories.

Since in his model the author works with several variables that drive the time-variations of the transition probabilities, he defines a set of average credit scores corresponding to the average transition matrix. To reflect the period-specific transition matrices, in the following, the movement of these credit scores is modeled—not the movement of the transition probabilities. Using the same procedure as Belkin et al. (1998b) or Kim (1999), this is done by partitioning the domain of a standard normal variable by a series of z-scores. The transition matrix can then be represented as a z-score matrix. Since the upper limit of rating Aa is equivalent to the lower limit of the highest rating Aaa and it doesn't make sense to model the absorbing default state, the z-score matrix will be of dimension $(K-1) \times (K-1)$. Alternatively, given a z-score matrix, a corresponding transition matrix can also be obtained. Obviously for a given rating, a downward shift in the credit scores leads to an increase in probabilities of transitting to ratings higher than or equal to the rating in question, while an upward shift in the z-scores leads to the opposite. Table 9.4 gives the matrix of z-scores corresponding to

TABLE 9.4. Corresponding Z-Scores Matrix to Average One-Year Migration Matrix for Moody's Corporate Bond Ratings Period 1982–2001

	Aa	A	Baa	Ba	B	C	D
Aaa	-1.4583	-2.4981	-3.0327	-3.4062	$-\infty$	$-\infty$	$-\infty$
Aa	2.4890	-1.4160	-2.3931	-2.8485	-2.9926	-3.4035	-3.7643
A	3.1777	1.9987	-1.5262	-2.3688	-2.7364	-3.1758	-3.3046
Baa	3.3057	2.7128	1.5692	-1.5031	-2.1488	-2.5773	-2.7624
Ba	3.5872	3.0107	2.4813	1.4201	-1.2857	-1.9567	-2.1936
B	∞	3.0784	2.6116	2.3564	1.4908	-1.2835	-1.5448
C	3.0384	3.0384	2.6432	2.3492	1.9583	1.0928	-0.7098

the average one-year migration matrix for Moody's corporate bond ratings from 1982–2001, as reported in Table 1.1.

The next step is then to model deviations from the scores of the average transition matrix. As an extension of the model suggested by Kim, Wei assumes that the deviations are driven by K mutually independent, Gaussian distributed factors. Hence, his multifactor credit migration model is of the form

$$z_{ij} = \alpha(x + x_i) + \sqrt{1 - 2\alpha^2}\varepsilon_{ij} \qquad (9.22)$$

with rating classes $i = 1, \ldots, K - 1$ and $j = 1, \ldots, K$. The first variable x denotes the common factor for all ratings, and the x_i denote rating class specific factors, and ε_{ij} represents the idiosyncratic factor. Similar to the described one-factor model, here the factors x, x_i and ε_{ij} are also scaled to a standard normal distribution. The factors x and x_i encompass the impacts of all economic variables relevant to rating changes. Further the correlation between any two rating classes is

$$corr(z_{ij}, z_{kl}) = \alpha^2 \qquad (9.23)$$

where $i \neq k$. According to Wei, for an average year the realized deviations for all rating classes should be close to zero.

Trying to find the fitted transition matrix for each year, Wei suggests the following procedure:

In a first step the historical average transition matrix is calculated and converted into a z-score matrix. Then for each period t and for each row, the shift of the z-score matrix that minimizes the sum of deviations Δz_{it} is sought. Therefore, a key assumption of the procedure is the equal magnitude of shifts in z-scores for a particular rating class. This procedure yields a time series of z-score deviations for all rating classes and all periods Δz_{it} for all $t = 1, \ldots, T$ and $i = 1, \ldots, K - 1$. To improve the estimation results for each row, one weighs the square of deviations by the inverse of the approximate sample variance of each entry's probability estimate. Then the average of the seven shifts for each year is calculated, denoting the systematic shift for all rating classes $\bar{\Delta}z_t$ for period t. In the next step the variance $V(\bar{\Delta}z)$ of the systematic shift time series is calculated. The estimator for the α is then $\hat{\alpha} = \sqrt{V(\bar{\Delta}z)}$. Then for each period t the common shift

$$\bar{x}_t - \frac{\bar{\Delta}z_t}{\alpha} \tag{9.24}$$

is calculated. In the next step for period t and each rating class i, the rating-specific deviation is calculated. Finally, the fitted transition matrix for each period is calculated by using the average historical matrix and the z-score adjustments or deviations estimated in the previous steps.

The author points out that in the univariate model such as that of Belkin et al. (1998b), where there is no rating-specific shift, the same procedure is applied to the whole matrix for a particular year to find the common shift Δz_{it}. Then the parameter α is estimated in a similar fashion.

9.4   Other Methods

In the following we will briefly review two additional methods suggested for estimation of conditional migration matrices including ordered probit models (Nickell et al., 2000; Hu et al., 2002) and a regime-switching approach by Bangia et al. (2002). Note that both approaches will not be investigated in the empirical part.

Nickell et al. (2000) and Hu et al. (2002) propose the use of Bayesian methods in combination with an ordered probit model for conditioning credit migration matrices. The idea is to combine information from the historical average transition matrix estimate and results from other exogenous variables. The techniques are related to Bayesian methods for estimating cell probabilities in contingency tables. The transition matrix is smoothed via a function of covariates. In the first step a so-called appropriate prior is specified and then updated with a new estimator based on the observed data:

$$P_t = \lambda \cdot \bar{P} + (1 - \lambda) \cdot Q_t \tag{9.25}$$

Here $\bar{P}$ denotes some average historical transition matrix, Q_t is the estimator for the transition matrix in period t obtained by an ordered probit model, and λ a weighting coefficient. Since the matrix $\bar{P}$ is itself an estimator of the true transition matrix, updating this using other information actually corresponds to a pseudo (or empirical) Bayes approach. Clearly, the problem, next to the estimation of Q_t, is how to find an appropriate value for λ. For further explanation of the model, we refer to original articles by Nickell et al. (2000) and Hu et al. (2002). Wei (2003) points out that a large quantity of data is needed to estimate reliable parameters. Note that not only the model parameters for the probit model and λ have to be determined, but also parameters for modeling of the business cycle as a Markov chain.

A similar approach to estimate conditional migrations is suggested by Kadam and Lenk (2008). Exploring sources of heterogeneity in rating migration behavior, they adopt a Bayesian estimation procedure to estimate for each issuer profile its own continuous time Markov chain generator. While Nickell et al. (2000) employ a probit framework to compute conditional transition probabilities in a discrete-time model, Kadam and Lenk (2008) use a continuous-time model where the state durations are exponential and transition probabilities are logistic functions. Using Moody's corporate bond default database, the authors further identify significant country and industry effects with respect to rating migration volatility, default intensity, and conditional transition probabilities. They further show that other characteristics, such as how long the issuer has been in existence, may also affect the rating migration behavior.

Bangia et al. (2002) link business cycle effects and transition matrices by a regime-switching model. The authors estimate a regime-switching model for quarterly expansion and contraction classifications. Further, average expansion and contraction transition matrices are determined. For applications it is straightforward to link the regime-switching and the estimated migration matrices. Based on estimated probabilities for being either in an expansion or contraction of the economy, using the regime-switching process one-period ahead forecasts for migration matrices can be obtained. However, simulating rating distributions based on their approach, the authors find no significantly different results for short-term migration and default behavior compared to using an average migration matrix (Bangia et al., 2002).

A more advanced application of Markov mixture models can be found in Frydman and Schuermann (2008). The authors propose a parsimonious model that is a mixture of (two) Markov chains. Hereby, the mixing is on the rate of movement among credit ratings. The estimation of the model is performed using credit rating histories and an algorithm originally suggested in Frydman (2005). The authors further provide evidence that the mixture model statistically dominates the simple Markov model and that the differences between two models can be economically meaningful. Therefore, Frydman and Schuermann (2008) find further evidence for the fact that the future distribution of a firm's ratings depends not only on its current rating but also on its rating history in the past. This also confirms the results by Lando and Skødeberg (2002), Krüger et al. (2005), or in Chapter 5 of this book on the Markov property and rating drifts where migration behavior was found to exhibit higher order Markov behavior.

Of course, it is also possible to apply the adjustment methods that were reviewed in Chapter 8. Obviously, the methods were initially designed to match transition matrices with default probabilities implied in bond prices observed in the market. However, given estimates for conditional default probabilities based on the macroeconomic situation, they can also be used to adjust transition matrices subject to anticipated changes in the business cycle. Hereby, both methods implementing the adjustment based on a discrete (Jarrow et al., 1997; Kijima and Komoribayashi, 1998) or continuous-time (Lando, 2000) transition matrix can be used. Further it is also possible to carry out the adjustments using the method suggested in Lando and Mortensen (2005). In the next section an empirical analysis will be conducted that actually uses the numerical adjustment techniques originally suggested in Lando (2000) using conditional default probabilities based on a macroeconomic index.

9.5   An Empirical Study on Different Forecasting Methods

This section will provide an empirical analysis on forecasting credit migration matrices based on a business cycle credit index.[2] Hereby, we compare the in-sample and out-of-sample performance of different adjustment methods for forecasting credit migration matrices. We consider Moody's credit migration matrices for the U.S. market from 1984–1999. The in-sample period includes a history of 10 years from 1984–1993, while we use a six-year period from 1994 to 1999 to evaluate the out-of-sample forecasting ability of our models. The compared approaches include one-factor models based on the approach by Belkin et al. (1998a) and Kim (1999) as they were described in the previous section, and numerical adjustment procedures following Lando (2000). As benchmark results, we will also use the average historical migration matrices and the transition matrix of the previous period as forecasts for next year's migration matrix.

To determine one-period ahead forecasts of conditional PDs and the credit cycle index, we use a multiple regression model of the form

$$\Phi^{-1}(S_t) = c_0 + \sum_{j=1}^{d} c_j X_{j,t-1} + \varepsilon_t \quad t \in \mathbb{N} \qquad (9.26)$$

The process dynamic is influenced by the vector X_{t-1} of d exogenous macroeconomic variables of the previous period. Using equation (11.3) and (9.3), we can then calculate forecasts for the one-period ahead credit cycle index Z_t and the conditional default probabilities $\hat{p}_t(i, D|Z_t)$ for each rating class. Table 9.5 displays the included variables in the multiple regression model. Both a variety of macroeconomic variables as well as credit spreads and differences between long-term and short-term treasury bonds were

---

[2] Results of this section were originally published in Trueck (2008).

TABLE 9.5. Included Variables for the Multiple Regression Model for Credit Cycle Indices

Variable	Notation
Change in consumer price index	CPI_{t-1}
Change in GDP growth	GDP_{t-1}
Change in annual savings	SAV_{t-1}
Change in manufacturing & sales	MAN_{t-1}
Change in working output per hour	OUT_{t-1}
Change in consumption expenditures	CON_{t-1}
Change in unemployment rate	UN_{t-1}
Treasury Yields 10, 5, 3 and 1 year	$TY10_{t-1}$ etc.
Spread between 10-y and 1-y treasury	STR_{t-1}
Spreads on investment grade bonds	$SINV_{t-1}$
Spreads on speculative grade bonds	$SSPE_{t-1}$

considered. Having only 10 observations from 1984–1993 for both default probabilities and macroeconomic variables, to avoid overfitting, not more than five exogenous variables were permitted in the regression model. In the following we will now describe the procedure of model estimation and conditioning of the migration matrices.

9.5.1   Forecasts Using the Factor Model Approach

Following Kim (1999) the multiple regression model (11.3) is used for modeling and forecasting the continuous credit cycle index Z_t. It is assumed that the index follows a standardized normal distribution. Thus, a probit model will allow us to create unbiased forecasts of the inverse normal CDF of Z_t, given the recent information of the last period about the economic state and the estimated coefficients. Note that unlike Kim (1999), who uses only one credit cycle index based on speculative default probabilities, we will consider two credit cycle indices: one for speculative grade and one for investment grade issues. For the investment grade issues, we use cumulative defaults of issuers rated Aaa, Aa, A, and Baa, while for the speculative grade issues, default probabilities from Ba to C were included. Figure 9.4 exemplarily reports the observed default frequencies for the noninvestment grade rating classes Ba, B, and C that were used for estimation of the speculative grade credit cycle index.

In a second step the forecasts of the credit cycle indices are used for determining conditional migration probabilities $\hat{p}_t(i, j | Z_t)$. The adjustment is conducted following the procedure described in Section 3.1. However, for finding the optimal weights for the systematic risk indices w_{Inv} and w_{Spec}, minimizing the discrepancies between the forecasted conditional and the actually observed transition probabilities, we introduce some model

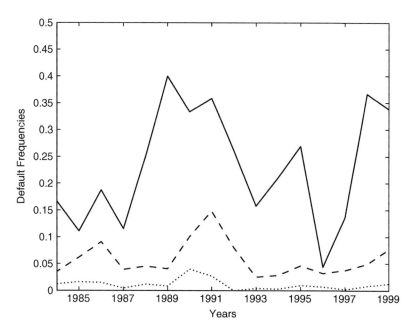

FIGURE 9.4. Moody's historical default rates for speculative rating classes Ba (*dotted*), B (*dashed*), and C (*solid*) for the period 1984–1999.

extensions. We allow for a more general weighting of the difference between forecasted and empirical observation for the transition probability in each cell. Hence, the weights for each of the cells are assigned according to some function f:

$$\min \sum_j \sum_i f(i, j, p_t(i, j), \hat{p}_t(i, j | Z_t)) \qquad (9.27)$$

where the outcome of $f(i, j, p_t(i, j), \hat{p}_t(i, j | Z_t))$ may be dependent on the row i and column j of the cell as well as on the forecasted and actually observed transition probabilities $\hat{p}_t(i, j | Z_t)$ and $p_t(i, j)$.

To achieve a better interpretation of the results, we will also use risk-sensitive difference indices suggested in Chapter 7 as optimization criteria for the distance between forecasted and actual migration matrix. Recall that based on the estimated model, the parameter w and the shifts on the migrations according to some optimization criteria are determined. In fact, this a crucial point of the model as it comes to forecasting credit migration matrices. While Belkin et al. (1998b) suggest minimizing a weighted expression of the form, Wei (2003) uses the absolute percentage deviation based on the L_1 norm or a pseudo R^2 as goodness-of-fit criteria. As it was illustrated in Chapter 7, most of the distance measures suggested in the literature so far do not quantify differences between migration matrices adequately in terms of risk. However, forecasts for transition matrices will be especially used for determining credit VaR, portfolio management, and risk management purposes. Therefore, especially risk-sensitive difference indices may be a rewarding approach for measuring the difference between forecasted and observed matrices. Following the results in Chapter 7, we suggest that the difference between a migration matrix $P = (p_{ij})$ and $Q = (q_{ij})$ can be determined in a weighted cell-by-cell calculation. Following Trueck and Rachev (2007), we will include two risk-sensitive directed difference indices in our analysis as optimization criteria:

$$D_1(P,Q) = \sum_{i=1}^{n} \sum_{j=1}^{n-1} d(i,j) + \sum_{i=1}^{n} n \cdot d(i,n) \qquad (9.28)$$

$$D_2(P,Q) = \sum_{i=1}^{n} \sum_{j=1}^{n-1} d(i,j) + \sum_{i=1}^{n} n^2 \cdot d(i,n) \qquad (9.29)$$

To compare the results with standard criteria we will consider the classic L_1 and L_2 metric

$$D_{L_1}(P,Q) = \sum_{i=1}^{n} \sum_{j=1}^{n} |p_{ij} - q_{ij}| \qquad (9.30)$$

and

$$D_{L_2}(P,Q) = \sqrt{\sum_{i=1}^{n} \sum_{j=1}^{n} (p_{ij} - q_{ij})^2} \qquad (9.31)$$

Further, the measure of so-called normalized squared differences NSD_{symm}

$$D_{NSD}(P,Q) = \sum_{i=1}^{n} \sum_{j=1}^{n} \frac{(p_{ij} - q_{ij})^2}{p_{ij}} \quad \text{for } p_{ij} \neq 0 \qquad (9.32)$$

is included in the analysis. Note that these criteria can also be used to evaluate the distance between forecasted and observed transition matrices for the numerical adjustment methods and the chosen benchmark models.

9.5.2 Forecasts Using Numerical Adjustment Methods

The second approach involves the numerical adjustment method suggested by Jarrow et al. (1997) and Lando (2000) that were reviewed in Chapter 8. Again we use a multiple regression model of the form (11.3.1). However, since the method needs estimates $\hat{p}_t(i, K)$ for the individual rating classes, for each speculative rating grade Ba, B, C as well as for the rating class Baa, a separate model is estimated. For the investment grade rating classes Aaa, Aa, A, we have to follow a different approach. Considering Moody's historical default frequencies in several years, we could observe no default for the three rating classes. To develop a regression model with only 10 observations, among them several with PD, we should avoid zero. Hence, for rating grades Aaa, Aa and A, we decided to use default probabilities from the average historical migration matrix $\bar{P}$ as estimators for the next period's PDs in these rating classes. Based on these assumptions for each year, we can estimate the vector for next year's default probabilities in the individual rating classes:

$$\hat{p} = (\hat{p}_{Aaa,D}, \hat{p}_{Aa,D}, \hat{p}_{A,D}, \hat{p}_{Baa,D}, \hat{p}_{Ba,D}, \hat{p}_{B,D}, \hat{p}_{C,D}, 1)'$$

In this section we will provide in-sample and out-of-sample results for the described models and compare them to benchmark results. Hereby, we will evaluate the performance of the chosen models against the standard approach of using historical average transitions or last year's migration matrix for the calculation of credit VaR.

9.5.3 Regression Models

In a first step, the regression models for the credit cycle index and default probability scores are estimated. Recall that in order to avoid overfitting, at the most, five explanatory variables were permitted in each regression model. The in-sample period comprised the empirical default frequencies and the suggested macroeconomic variables for the period from 1984–1993. Among the tested models, the best results for the speculative grade credit cycle index were obtained using the macroeconomic variables change in GDP growth GDP_{t-1}, change in annual savings SAV_{t-1}, the change in consumption expenditures CON_{t-1}, the change in unemployment rate UN_{t-1}, and the spread between a 10-year and 1-year treasury STR_{t-1} bond. The model gave a coefficient of determination of $R^2 = 0.98$, an F-statistic of 43.38 and a corresponding p-value of 0.001, so it was highly significant. For the investment grade credit cycle index, the best results were obtained with a model including the macroeconomic variables change in the consumer price index CPI_{t-1}, change in GDP growth GDP_{t-1}, change of consumption expenditures CON_{t-1}, and the change in unemployment rate UN_{t-1}. The model gave an R^2 statistic of 0.82, an F-statistic of 5.52, and a corresponding p-value of 0.045, so the model was still significant at the 5% level. Further, all regression coefficients were significant and showed the anticipated sign. Note that the fit for cumulated investment grade defaults was clearly worse, but it is generally accepted that investment grade defaults are less dependent on business cycle effects than

TABLE 9.6. Parameter Estimates for the Multiple Regression Model (In-Sample Period from 1984–1993)

Variable	Notation	Z_{Inv}	Z_{Spec}
Constant	β_0	−0.3973	−0.6182
Change in consumer price index	CPI_{t-1}	0.2187	−
Change in GDP growth	GDP_{t-1}	−0.9338	−0.2461
Change in annual savings	SAV_{t-1}	−	0.1838
Change in consumption expenditures	CON_{t-1}	−1.3744	−0.2509
Change in unemployment rate	UN_{t-1}	0.3616	0.2351
Spread between 10-y and 1-y treasury	STR_{t-1}	−	−0.0057

speculative grade issuers (Nickell et al., 2000; Belkin et al., 1998a). The regression coefficients for speculative and investment grade credit cycle indices Z_{Spec}, Z_{Inv} are displayed in Table 9.6. Estimation of the models for individual rating classes yield R^2 statistics between 0.79 and 0.98. Further information on parameter estimates and statistics are available on request to the author.

9.5.4   In-Sample Results

After estimation of the regression model for the credit cycle index, in the next step we will determine conditional forecasts for migration matrices based on the outcome of the credit cycle index. We first consider the results for the estimated weights of the systematic credit cycle indices Z_{Spec} and Z_{Inv}. Recall that in the chosen one-factor model approach, w is determined numerically in order to minimize the difference between the conditional forecast $\hat{p}_t(i, j|Z_t)$ and empirically observed migrations $p_t(i, j)$ for all considered transition matrices in the in-sample period. The shift in the credit change indicator and, hence, the shift in transition and default probabilities, is then an outcome of the forecasted credit cycle index of the next period and the estimated weight w for the systematic risk factor Z.

Table 9.7 provides the weights w_{Inv} and w_{Spec} for investment grade and speculative grade ratings giving the minimal distance between forecasts and observed migration matrices for the in-sample period 1984–1993. Note that depending on the chosen distance measures, we obtain different outcomes for the weights. For the speculative grade model, we find significantly higher weights of the systematic credit cycle index than for the investment grade model for all optimization criteria. We observe the lowest estimate for the weight $w_{NSD,Spec} = 0.1698$ for the NSD distance criterion, while for the other distance measures the weight for the speculative credit cycle index is estimated to be between 0.2115 and 0.2544. For investment grade issues the estimated weights range from 0.0318 to 0.1762. As mentioned previously, this is in line with previous results in the literature

TABLE 9.7. Estimated Weights w for the Credit Cycle Index Z, Representing the Influence of Z on the Change Indicators Y. Results Refer to the In-Sample Period 1984–1993 and are Estimated Based on a One-Factor Approach for Investment Grade (*Inv*) and Speculative Grade Ratings (*Spec*)

Optimization Criteria	L_1	L_2	NSD	D_1	D_2
w_{Inv}	0.0504	0.1143	0.0318	0.1089	0.1762
w_{Spec}	0.2176	0.2544	0.1698	0.2115	0.2288

(Belkin et al., 1998a; Wilson, 1997b). Especially when the shift is conducted to minimize the distance according to the L_1 and NSD distance measure, the influence of the systematic risk factor becomes very small, $w_{L_1,Inv} = 0.0318$ and $w_{NSD,Inv} = 0.0504$, respectively. This means that for these criteria the systematic risk index gives very little explanation for changes in rating behavior. The highest estimate for the weight $w_{D_2,Inv} = 0.1762$ is obtained when the distance is minimized subject to the risk-sensitive D_2 difference index criteria. It seems as if, according to D_2 changes in investment grade, migration behavior also could be explained by the systematic credit cycle index to a certain degree.

We will now investigate the in-sample one-period ahead forecast results for the different approaches. Table 9.8 provides in-sample results for mean absolute forecast errors according to the applied difference measures. As mentioned above, next to a factor-model approach (Factor) and the numerical adjustment methods (Num I, Num II), two standard benchmark methods were included in the results: using the average migration matrix of the in-sample periods (Naive I) or the transition matrix of the previous period (Naive II) as a forecast for the next period's migration matrix. Best results for each distance measure are highlighted in bold. Note that the mean error or standard deviation of the errors for different indices within the columns cannot be compared due to a different scale. However, the results in the rows can be compared and provide the forecasting performance in comparison to other approaches. For each of the considered distance criteria, the one-factor model outperforms all other approaches including the numerical adjustment procedures. In contrast to these results, the numerical adjustment methods fail to provide better results than the naive approach for the criteria L_1, L_2, and NSD. Especially Num II that was applied in the seminal work by Jarrow et al. (1997) gives rather bad one-year ahead forecasts based on the estimated default probabilities with the credit cycle index. Considering these results and the relevance of the approach in the literature, we recommend a more thorough investigation on how migration probabilities are changed by these methods in the future.

It is not surprising that the best in-sample results are obtained for the one-factor model approach. Based on the optimization procedure in (9.5)

TABLE 9.8. In-Sample Results for Mean Forecast Errors According to Applied Difference Measures and Adjustment Techniques. The Estimation Period Included 10 Years from 1984–1993. (Best results for each distance measure are highlighted in bold)

Dist.	Method	Factor	Num I	Num II	Naive I	Naive II
			Distance Statistics $D(\hat{P}, P_{obs})$			
L_1	MAE	**0.8058**	1.3461	1.7092	0.8809	1.0245
	Std	(0.2665)	(0.1415)	(0.2966)	(0.2414)	(0.3056)
L_2	MAE	**0.0580**	0.1802	0.2947	0.0725	0.1022
	Std	(0.0483)	(0.0503)	(0.0885)	(0.0510)	(0.0948)
NSD	MAE	**0.2956**	0.4773	0.8774	0.3483	0.5911
	Std	(0.1363)	(0.1356)	(0.2544)	(0.1800)	(0.4556)
D_1	MAE	**0.3218**	0.7592	1.1505	1.2417	1.4969
	Std	(0.2189)	(0.3765)	(0.9526)	(0.8903)	(0.7522)
D_2	MAE	**1.9926**	6.2919	9.4428	9.6931	10.8898
	Std	(1.3993)	(3.2154)	(4.8858)	(7.1228)	(5.5701)

that chooses the weight for the systematic risk factor in order to minimize the distance between the forecasted and empirical transition probabilities, these results could be expected. However, it is interesting to investigate how much the results improved subject to the considered optimality criteria. For the L_1, L_2 metric and the NSD difference index, we observe a reduction in the mean absolute error (MAE) by a fraction between 10% up to 50% compared to the naive approaches. The reduction for the risk-adjusted difference indices D_1 and D_2 are clearly higher. Comparing mean absolute errors between conditional and unconditional estimates for the D_1 and D_2 criteria, we find that according to the chosen criteria, the improvement is highly significant. Forecasting errors for the naive approaches are approximately 4–5 times higher; e.g., using naive approaches, the MAE for the risk-sensitive D_2 criterion are approximately $D_{2,NaiveI} = 9.6931$ and $D_{2,NaiveII} = 10.89$, while for the one-factor model, we obtain an MAE of $D_{2,Factor} = 1.99$. For these criteria also the numerical adjustment methods Num I and Num II give better results. Since more weight is allocated in the default column, the additional information of PD forecasts for the next period improves the results. Overall, in comparison to the one-factor model, for the numerical adjustment techniques, the forecast errors are still significantly higher.

We also investigated whether the improvement of the forecasting results of the one-factor model was mainly due to the speculative or investment grade rating classes of the migration matrix. Table 9.9 provides the results of the one-factor model and the naive approaches separately for initial

TABLE 9.9. In-Sample Results (Mean Absolute Errors) Separately for Speculative Grade (Ratings Ba, B, and C) and Investment Grade (Aaa, Aa, A, and Baa) Ratings

Dist.	Speculative Grade			Investment Grade		
	Factor	Naive I	Naive II	Factor	Naive I	Naive II
L_1	0.5060	0.5756	0.6558	0.2997	0.3052	0.3687
L_2	0.0423	0.0557	0.080	0.0157	0.0168	0.0222
NSD	0.1913	0.2425	0.3548	0.1043	0.1058	0.2363
D_1	0.2770	1.1620	1.3375	0.0449	0.1197	0.1628
D_2	1.6544	8.8322	8.8505	0.3382	0.8609	1.0393

speculative and investment grade ratings. We find that especially for the risk-sensitive evaluation criteria the improvement using a credit cycle index comes from better forecasts for the speculative grade default probabilities and rating changes. For the rating classes Ba–C the forecast error is reduced up to 80% when the risk-sensitive measures D_1 or D_2 are applied. Further, as it is indicated by Table 9.9, the large deviations from actual observed migration matrices take place in the speculative grade area of the matrix where more variation can be observed.

At this point we should also emphasize the advantage of the directed difference indices D_1 and D_2 as a measure for the goodness-of-fit. It concerns the question of interpretation of the results. Obviously, an MAE of 0.8058 for the L_1 norm cannot be interpreted in terms of risk. Though, using the risk-sensitive difference indices, we are able to give an interpretation of the results from a risk perspective. Trueck and Rachev (2007) show that for credit portfolios, differences between migration matrices are highly correlated with the estimated credit VaR. Using Moody's historical migration matrices, for an exemplary credit portfolio, a relationship between credit VaR and the deviation of a transition matrix from Moody's average historical migration matrix is derived. Setting the recovery rates to a constant, the relationship between VaR for the exemplary loan portfolio and D_2 is then approximately expressed by (in Mill. Euro)

$$VaR_{95\%,t} = 138.7675 + 4.7110 \cdot D_{2,t} + \varepsilon_t \qquad (9.33)$$

The estimated regression model yields an $R^2 > 0.9$ (Trueck and Rachev, 2007). Hence, due to the very high correlations between the directed difference index and credit VaR, for exemplary loan portfolios we would be able to measure our errors on migration matrix forecasts in terms of risk. This means that the mean error of 9.6931 from Table 9.8, using the average migration matrix $\bar{P}$ as an estimator, could be interpreted for the exemplary portfolio as an average misspecification of VaR of approximately $4.7110 \cdot 9.6931 \approx 45$ Mill. Euro per year. For using the migration matrix of the previous year, we obtain an approximate error of 51 Mill. Euro. When one uses the one-factor model in order to condition migration matrices to business cycle effects, the mean absolute error is reduced to 1.9926, yielding an average error on one-year VaR forecasts of 9.38 Mill. Euro for the exemplary portfolio. It is important to point out that these are just approximate numbers for an exemplary portfolio, ignoring variations in LGD figures and other components. However, as a general result, we argue that using the risk-sensitive difference indices as a goodness-of-fit measure, the forecast error may also be quantified in terms of risk. We point out that further research on this issue will be needed, especially on the sensitivity of the difference indices. Overall, the advantage of an index giving a strong interpretation in terms of risk is obvious.

9.5.5 Out-of-Sample Forecasts

Finally, we used the developed models for out-of-sample forecasting of rating migration behavior. The considered period was the subsequent years from 1994–1999. Based on a yearly re-estimation of the regression model and the weights of the systematic credit cycle index in the chosen one-factor model, and conditional PD estimates, forecasts for the migration matrix of the following year were calculated. Hereby, the in-sample estimation period was increased each year from 1984–1993 to 1984–1994, 1984–1995, ..., 1984–1998. Results for the yearly re-estimated weights w_{Inv} and w_{Spec} of the systematic credit cycle index using D_2 are described in Table 9.10. Results for the other distance measures are available on request from the author. As it could be expected, the weights change through time and vary between 0.234 and 0.191 for the speculative grade issuers and between 0.168 and 0.149 for the investment grade credit cycle index. Generally, the weight of the systematic credit cycle index decreases for both investment categories through time.

Table 9.11 finally investigates the out-of sample performance of the considered models. We find that especially for the conditional approaches

TABLE 9.10. Re-Estimated Weights of the Credit Cycle Index for Investment and Speculative Grade Ratings in the One-Factor Model Approach Using the Distance Index D_2

Year	1994	1995	1996	1997	1998	1999
			Speculative Grade			
D_2	0.2340	0.2058	0.2005	0.1914	0.1961	0.1964
			Investment Grade			
D_2	0.1663	0.1681	0.1579	0.1493	0.1529	0.1489

TABLE 9.11. Out-of-Sample Results for Mean Absolute Forecast Errors According to Applied Difference Measures D_2 and Adjustment Techniques. The Out-of-Sample Period Included Six Years from 1994–1999. (Best results for each year are highlighted in bold)

Method	Factor	Num I	Num II	Naive I	Naive II
Year	Distance Statistics $D_2(\hat{P}, P_{obs})$				
1994	**3.2563**	6.9856	9.2745	8.7058	4.4462
1995	1.9834	3.5110	4.2809	**1.0289**	7.6769
1996	**8.8284**	14.3459	21.7397	18.9697	17.9408
1997	**5.2049**	10.8375	14.5619	12.4049	6.5649
1998	**2.5774**	8.9729	8.0307	5.5436	17.9484
1999	3.1936	7.2204	9.7712	8.5408	**2.9973**
Average	**4.1740**	8.6456	11.2765	9.1989	9.5958

(Factor, Num I, and Num II) that use the credit cycle index, the results are not as good as for the in-sample period. This can be explained by the decreasing influence of the systematic credit cycle index, for the out-of-sample period that was reported in Table 9.11. Still the factor model significantly outperforms the numerical adjustment methods Num I and Num II and the benchmark models Naive I and Naive II. Except for the years 1996 and 1999, it gives the best forecasts of next year's migration matrix in each year. Further, clearly the lowest average forecast error is obtained using the factor model approach. However, compared to the in-sample estimation, the average forecasting error is higher, and we obtain a mean absolute error of 4.1740. For the naive models the results for in-sample and out-of-sample periods are similar, while for the numerical adjustment methods, the error increased as well. Note that Num II provides the worst results of all models and is outperformed even by the naive approaches.

We point out that the results could have been improved by changing the variables of the macroeconomic forecasting model for the credit cycle index. However, in order to guarantee a genuine out-of-sample test of the model, we choose the macroeconomic variables to be the same for in-sample and out-of-sample model evaluation. Still we conclude that a regular re-estimation of the model for the credit cycle indices may be recommendable.

10

Dependence Modeling and Credit Migrations

10.1 Introduction

The traditional and often discussed starting point in approaching credit risk issues is a single loan or bond. This special case makes it fairly easy to derive meaningful statistics like the expected loss, the likelihood of default in a given period of time or the expected loss, VaR, etc., that allow us to quantify inherent credit risk.

But when it comes to the question of how to proceed in the case of a portfolio of such instruments where diversification or concentration effects play an important role, methodology starts to differ considerably. All approaches, though, have one thing in common: in order to capture portfolio effects, they all consider implicitly or explicitly some interdependence between different items in the portfolio. When dealing with more than one random variable at a time, one immediately faces the problem of understanding and modeling the dependence between them. The first, and maybe decisive, step to tackle this problem is the understanding of the statistical concept of dependence, and a precise definition of terms.

This chapter focuses on dependence as an issue of special interest in credit risk. First a simple example is used to illustrate the importance and the impact of dependence when it comes to assessing a portfolio. Then we compare the notions of correlation and dependence and capturing the dependence structure. Then we provide a brief review on the definition and structure of copulas. In subsequent sections we investigate the use of copulas in modeling rating transitions and examine how correlated and dependent migrations can be modeled in a Markov chain framework. Assessing credit risk on a portfolio level requires the combination of two components: information on the risk of all portfolio items, and information on the level and structure of interaction between them. Conversely, the final goal of portfolio risk considerations—the distribution function of the portfolio value for the risk horizon—will be substantially determined and influenced by these components.

In order to illustrate the impact of the degree of dependence between the portfolio items, consider the following example:

We assume a portfolio of 50 different items that are all subject to default risk. Let every individual item have a default probability of $p = 0.2$—this corresponds roughly to the one that has a CCC-rated bond or loan—and a survivorship probability of $(1 - p)$ over some given time period T. In the case of independence of the individual defaults, we can calculate the distribution of the defaults by using a binomial distribution with $n = 50$ and $p = 0.2$.

We now focus on the probability distribution of the sum of surviving firms, X, and observe changes in the shape of this distribution when changing the degree of dependence between the portfolio items. Note that it is straightforward to extend this example and consider the probability distribution of portfolio value by assuming some value V for every surviving firm.

10.1.1 Independence

As the sum of independent Bernoulli distributed random variables is binomially distributed, we obtain a $Bin(50, 0.8)$ distribution here. The expected value for the number of survivors is $E = n(1 - p) = 40$ and the variance is $Var = n(1 - p)p = 8$. See Figure 10.1 for the corresponding histogram for this case.

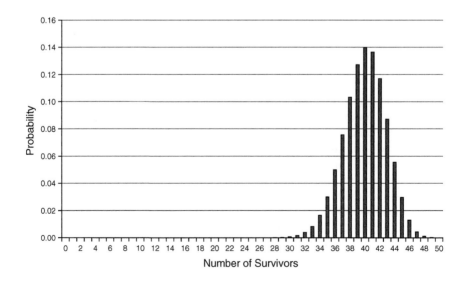

FIGURE 10.1. Histogram for the case of independence.

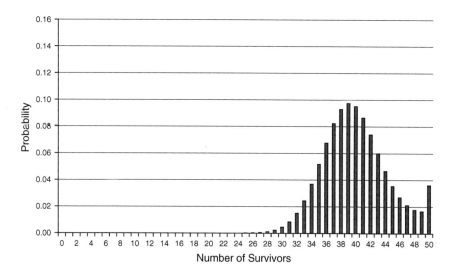

FIGURE 10.2. Histogram for $\beta = 0.95$.

10.1.2 Dependence

Now we include some dependence to the marginals. In our example the dependence is modeled by applying a Gumbel copula with parameter $\beta \in (0, 1]$.[1] For a choice of $\beta = 1$, the defaults are independent and the results correspond to the case discussed above. As β approaches zero, the dependence between the items increases. Note that irrespective of β, all sum-of-survivor distributions have a mean of 40.

Figure 10.2 plots the histogram for $\beta = 0.95$. In comparison to the $\beta = 1$ case, we obtain a flatter distribution with more probability mass to the right. Note the substantial increase for the probability of all firms surviving from 0.00143 to 0.036.

This effect can be explained by decomposing the sum into successive Bernoulli draws. Now consider the conditional probability for the remaining firms if the outcome of the Bernoulli game is already known for some firms. In the case of independence, the conditional probability remains the same, irrespective of the number of defaults that have already occurred. Whereas in the case of dependence, the fact that all firms have survived so far influences the next Bernoulli draw and increases the probability of survival for the next firm.

The distribution obtained when decreasing β to 0.8 can be seen in Figure 10.3. Here, one can observe that the mass of the distribution also

---

[1] See Section 10.3 for further discussion on copulas and the definition of the Gumbel copula.

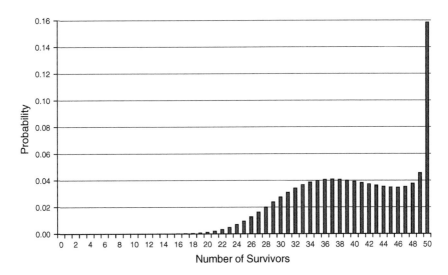

FIGURE 10.3. Histogram for $\beta = 0.8$.

TABLE 10.1. Statistical Parameters for Different Values of β

β	1	0.95	0.8	0.4	0.2	0.05	$\to 0^+$
μ	40	40	40	40	40	40	40
σ^2	8	19.4	58.7	203.0	295.7	373.0	400

moves partially to the left when increasing β, which translates into a pronounced left tail. Comparing, for example, $P(X \leq 30)$ for both distributions yields $P(X_{\beta=1} \leq 30) = 0.00093$ and $P(X_{\beta=0.8} \leq 30) = 0.128$.

Driven by the distribution's tendency to broaden and spread to the extremes, the variance increases. Table 10.1 gives an overview over the mean and variance for different values of β.

As β approaches zero, the distribution converges towards a two-point distribution with

$$P(X = 0) = 0.2 \quad \text{and} \quad P(X = 50) = 0.8$$

where the probabilities for *no default* and *total default* correspond to the default and nondefault probabilities of the individual items in the portfolio, respectively. The case $\beta = 0.05$ comes close to this extreme (see Figure 10.4).

This example has shown that the distribution of the number of defaults in the portfolio—and at the same time the distribution of overall portfolio default loss—is substantially influenced by the degree of dependence between the items in the portfolio.

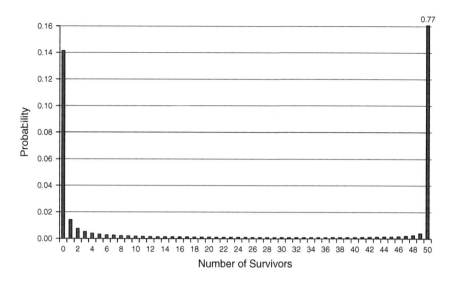

FIGURE 10.4. Histogram for $\beta = 0.05$.

10.2   Capturing the Structure of Dependence

Intuitively, two events A and B are independent, if the fact that B has occurred alters nothing about the chance of A occurring. In formula notation

$$P(A \,|\, B) = P(A)$$

However, this definition of independence requires $P(B) > 0$ and therefore we use the more general definition on the basis of the probability of the joint occurrence of A and B here:

Definition 10.1 *Two events A and B are said to be independent if*

$$P(A \cap B) = P(A) \cdot P(B)$$

Often, more than two events will be of interest and definition 10.1 is generalized to

Definition 10.2 *Let $B = \{B_\lambda : \lambda \in \Lambda\}$ be a set of events. These events are said to be independent if for every positive integer n and each n distinct elements $\lambda_1, \ldots, \lambda_n$ in the indexing set Λ we have*

$$P(B_{\lambda_1} \cap \cdots \cap B_{\lambda_n}) = \prod_{j=1}^{n} P(B_{\lambda_j})$$

Transferring the concept of independence from events to random variables (rv's), one defines

Definition 10.3 *Let $\{X_\lambda : \lambda \in \Lambda\}$ be a family of rv's. They are said to be independent if for every integer $n \geq 1$ and every n distinct $\lambda_1, \ldots, \lambda_n \in \Lambda$,*

$$F_{X_{\lambda_1}, \ldots, X_{\lambda_n}}(x_1, \ldots, x_n) = \prod_{j=1}^{n} F_{X_{\lambda_j}}(x_j) \qquad \forall x_j \in \mathbb{R}, \ j = 1, \ldots, n$$

This definition can be transformed into a well-known lemma stating that for independent rv's, their joint (multivariate) distribution function (df) is just the product over their individual (univariate) df's:

Lemma 10.4 *The rv's $X_1, \ldots, X_n$ are independent if*

$$F_{X_1, \ldots, X_n}(x_1, \ldots, x_n) = \prod_{j=1}^{n} F_{X_j}(x_j) \qquad \forall x_j \in \mathbb{R}, \ j = 1, \ldots, n$$

When one is dealing with real-world cases, independence is often assumed in order to obtain models that are mathematically and statistically easy to handle. However, this assumption is a very strong one and has to be tested for. Especially in the area of risk, where effects of diversification and concentration exist and have to be considered with care, the assumption of independence is often untenable. For this reason, concepts of how to incorporate the structure of dependence into statistical modeling are needed. In the next section, we take a closer look at the measurement and modeling of dependence.

Although commonly used as a synonym for *dependence*, the term *correlation* in the original meaning of the word stands for a measure of dependence between two rv's. Here, we consider *linear correlation* and *rank correlation*.

Linear correlation is a measure of *linear* dependence between rv's. It is important to bear in mind that nonlinear dependence structures are not captured by this statistical parameter. Its definition is

Definition 10.5 *The linear correlation coefficient between the real-valued, nondegenerate rv's X and Y with finite variances is*

$$\rho(X, Y) = \frac{cov(X, Y)}{\sqrt{VAR(X)VAR(Y)}} \tag{10.1}$$

Some properties of linear correlation are used in the following:

- If the rv's X and Y are independent, then $\rho(X, Y) = 0$; whereas the reverse is not necessarily true.

- In the case of perfect linear dependence, i.e.,

$$Y = aX + b \quad \text{a.s.} \quad a \in \mathbb{R}\setminus\{0\}, b \in \mathbb{R}$$

  we have $\rho(X, Y) = \pm 1$.

- Finally, linear correlation fulfills the linearity property

$$\rho(aX + b, cY + d) = \text{sgn}(a \cdot c)\rho(X, Y) \quad a, c \in \mathbb{R}\setminus\{0\}; b, d \in \mathbb{R} \quad (10.2)$$

For a generalization of more than two rv's, pairwise correlations between two rv's are considered and combined to a correlation matrix. Let $\mathbf{X} = (X_1, \ldots, X_n)^t$ be a vector of rv's with finite variances. Then

$$\rho_{n \times n} := \begin{pmatrix} \rho(X_1, X_1) & \cdots & \rho(X_1, X_n) \\ \vdots & \ddots & \vdots \\ \rho(X_n, X_1) & \cdots & \rho(X_n, X_n) \end{pmatrix}$$

Correlation matrices have the property of being symmetric and positive semi-definite.

Although rank correlation is somewhat more difficult to handle in certain contexts than linear correlation, and for this reason is not as popular as the latter, it has some substantial advantages. It does not require finite variances, is invariant under nonlinear transformations of the rv's, and indicates co(counter)monotonicity by taking values of ± 1. The concept of comonotonicity indicates that each random variable within a vector of random variables is a strictly increasing function of any of the others; see, e.g., McNeil et al. (2005).

The definition of Spearman's rank correlation coefficient is

$$\rho_S(X_i, X_j) = \rho(F_i(X_i), F_j(X_j))$$

where $\rho(X, Y)$ is the linear correlation coefficient as defined in equation (10.1).

However, rank correlation is just another scalar measure of dependence and therefore not able to fully describe a dependence structure. Furthermore, there remain some profound deficiencies, like the fact that a correlation of zero does not generally imply independence.

For this reason, and for the fact that linear correlation is much more frequently used in credit risk modeling issues, rank correlation will not be treated with more detail in this paper. Thus, henceforth, whenever talking about correlation, we refer to it as *linear correlation*.

Linear correlation is one particular measure of (linear) stochastic dependence amongst many. Under certain circumstances, however, the linear correlation coefficient gains additional meaning.

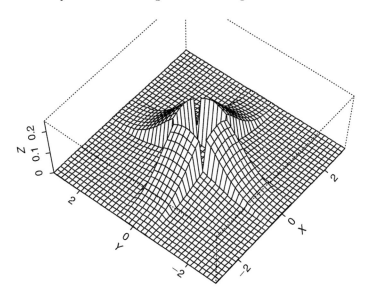

FIGURE 10.5. Density of a nonbivariate normal distribution with standard normal marginals.

If the joint distribution function of two rv's X and Y is bivariate normal, the linear correlation coefficient $\rho_{X,Y}$ contains all information about the dependence structure between them.

- $\rho_{X,Y} = 0 \quad \Longleftrightarrow \quad X$ and Y are independent

- The parameters of the marginal distributions (these are univariate normal) μ_X, σ_X and μ_Y, σ_Y together with $\rho_{X,Y}$ fully and uniquely determine the joint bivariate distribution.

At this point it is important to note the fact that two rv's X and Y are both (univariate) normally distributed and that $\rho_{X,Y}$ exists does **not** imply that the joint (bivariate) distribution function is bivariate normal.

Consider Figure 10.5 for a graphical illustration of this point.[2] The figure illustrates the two-dimensional plot of the density of a bivariate distribution that is clearly not bivariate normal. Nevertheless, the marginal distributions for X and Y are univariate standard normal and a finite $\rho_{X,Y}$ exists. This distribution has been constructed by using a copula for modeling dependence structure between the two marginals. We will further investigate copulas in Section 10.3.

The class of spherical distributions is a family of symmetric distributions for uncorrelated random vectors with mean zero whose density is constant

---

[2] The example and the graph were taken from Embrechts et al. (1999).

on spheres. This class extends and comprises the standard multivariate normal distribution. A further generalization leads to the class of elliptical distributions whose density is constant on ellipsoids. In this environment, the matrix of linear correlation coefficients fully captures the dependence structure amongst rv's. Note however, that the property of the multivariate normal case where zero correlation implies independence is not valid for the generalized case.

However, in the elliptical world the variance-covariance approach to optimizing portfolios makes sense, and VAR is a coherent measure of risk here. For this reason, the class of elliptical distributions represents an ideal environment for standard (market) risk managing approaches. When it comes to credit risk issues, however, the elliptical distribution assumption often underestimates the joint occurrence of extreme events.

10.2.1   Under General Multivariate Distributions

Unfortunately, for various multivariate distributions, correlation generally gives no indication about the degree or structure of dependence. A list of deficiencies and problems in the general case shall illustrate this point; see, e.g., McNeil et al. (2005); Rachev et al. (2005):

1. Correlation is simply a scalar measure of dependency; it cannot tell us everything we would like to know about the dependence structure of risks.

2. Possible values of correlation depend on the marginal distribution of the risks. All values between -1 and 1 are not necessarily attainable.

3. Perfectly positively dependent risks do not necessarily have a correlation of 1; perfectly negatively dependent risks do not necessarily have a correlation of -1.

4. A correlation of zero does not indicate independence of risks.

5. Correlation is not invariant under transformations of the risks. For example, $\log(X)$ and $\log(Y)$ generally do not have the same correlation as X and Y.

6. Correlation is defined only when the variances of the risks are finite. It is not an appropriate dependence measure for very heavy-tailed risks where variances appear infinite.

An illustration of point 2 and 4 is, for example, provided in Embrechts et al. (1999), where two rv's X and Y following a lognormal distribution with $\mu_X = \mu_Y = 0$, $\sigma_X = 1$, and $\sigma_Y = 2$ are considered. The authors show that by an arbitrary specification of the joint distribution with the given marginals, it is not possible to attain any correlation in $[-1, 1]$. In fact, there exist boundaries for a maximal and a minimal attainable correlation $[\rho_{min}, \rho_{max}]$ which in the given case is $[-0.090, 0.666]$. Allowing

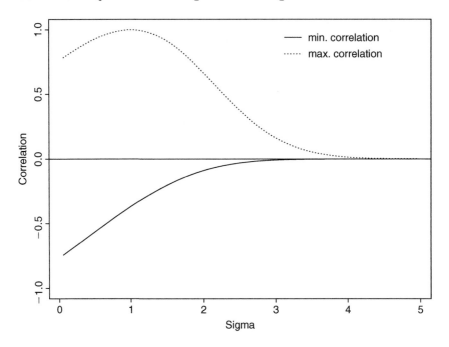

FIGURE 10.6. Maximum and minimum attainable correlation for $X \sim$ Lognormal$(0, 1)$ and $Y \sim$ Lognormal$(0, \text{sigma})$.

σ_Y to increase, this interval becomes arbitrarily small, as one can see in Figure 10.6. Hereby, it is interesting to note that the two boundaries represent the case where the two rv's are perfectly positive dependent (the max. correlation line) or perfectly negative dependent (the min. correlation line), respectively. Thus, although the attainable interval for ρ as $\sigma_Y > 1$ converges to zero from both sides, the dependence between X and Y is by no means weak. This indicates that for general multivariate distributions, it might be wrong to interpret low values of the correlation also as weak dependence.

In the following section we will therefore provide a brief overview on a more general specification of dependence between random variables by using copulas.

10.3 Copulas

As we saw in the previous section, in general, linear correlation will not be able to capture entirely the dependence structure between two random variables. At this point a general concept of describing the dependence structure within multivariate distributions is needed. Since marginal distributions are very illustrative, easy to handle, and often used as basic building blocks for the design of a multivariate distribution, the idea of separating the description of the joint multivariate distribution into the marginal behavior and the dependence structure is very attractive. One representation of the dependence structure that satisfies this concept is a copula. A copula is a function that combines the marginal distributions to form the joint multivariate distribution that was initially introduced by Sklar (1959); Schweizer and Sklar (1983). For an introduction to copulas, see Nelsen (1999); for applications to various issues in financial econometrics and risk management, see Cherubini et al. (2004); McNeil et al. (2005); Frey and McNeil (2003); Hull and White (2004); Mashal et al. (2003), and Schönbucher and Schubert (2001), to name a few.

Definition 10.6 *A copula is the distribution function of a random vector in $\mathbb{R}^n$ with standard uniform marginals.*

One can alternatively define a copula as a function and impose certain restrictions.

Definition 10.7 *A copula is any real valued function $C : [0,1]^n \to [0,1]$, i.e., a mapping of the unit hypercube into the unit interval, which has the following three properties:*

1. *$C(u_1, \ldots, u_n)$ is increasing in each component of u_i.*

2. *$C(1, \ldots, 1, u_i, 1, \ldots, 1) = u_i$ for all $i \in \{1, \ldots, n\}$, $u_i \in [0,1]$.*

3. *For all $(a_1, \ldots, a_n), (b_1, \ldots, b_n) \in [0,1]^n$ with $a_i \leq b_i$:*

$$\sum_{i_1=1}^{2} \cdots \sum_{i_n=1}^{2} (-1)^{i_1 + \cdots + i_n} C(u_{1i_1}, \ldots, u_{ni_n}) \geq 0$$

where $u_{j1} = a_j$ and $u_{j2} = b_j$ for all $j \in \{1, \ldots, n\}$.

Let $X = (X_1, \ldots, X_n)'$ be a random vector of real-valued rv's whose dependence structure is completely described by the joint distribution function

$$F(x_1, \ldots, x_n) = P(X_1 < x_1, \ldots, X_n < x_n) \tag{10.3}$$

Each rv X_i has a marginal distribution of F_i that is assumed to be continuous for simplicity. Recall that the transformation of a continuous rv X with its own distribution function F results in an rv $F(X)$, which is standardly uniformly distributed. Thus, transforming equation (10.3) component-wise yields

$$
\begin{aligned}
F(x_1, \ldots, x_n) &= P(X_1 < x_1, \ldots, X_n < x_n) \\
&= P[F_1(X_1) < F_1(x_1), \ldots, F_n(X_n) < F_n(x_n)] \\
&= C(F_1(x_1), \ldots, F_n(x_n)) \quad\quad\quad (10.4)
\end{aligned}
$$

where the function C can be identified as a joint distribution function with standard uniform marginals—the copula of the random vector X. In equation (10.4), one can clearly see how the copula combines the marginals to the joint distribution.

Sklar's theorem provides a theoretic foundation for the copula concept (Schweizer and Sklar, 1983).

Theorem 10.8 (Sklar's theorem) *Let F be a joint distribution function with continuous margins $F_1, \ldots, F_n$. Then there exists a unique copula $C :$ $[0,1]^n \rightarrow [0,1]$ such that for all $x_1, \ldots, x_n$ in $\mathbb{R} = [-\infty, \infty]$ (10.4) holds. Conversely, if C is a copula and $F_1, \ldots, F_n$ are distribution functions, then the function F given by (10.4) is a joint distribution function with margins $F_1, \ldots, F_n$.*

For the case that the marginals F_i are not all continuous, it can be shown (Schweizer and Sklar, 1983) that the joint distribution function can also be expressed as in equation (10.4), although C is no longer unique in this case.

10.3.1 Examples of Copulas

1. If the rv's X_i are independent, then the copula is just the product over the F_i

$$
C^{ind}(x_1, \ldots, x_n) = x_1, \ldots, x_n
$$

2. The *Gaussian* copula is

$$
C_\rho^{Ga}(x, y) = \int_{-\infty}^{\Phi^{-1}(x)} \int_{-\infty}^{\Phi^{-1}(y)} \frac{1}{2\pi\sqrt{(1-\rho^2)}} \exp \frac{-(s^2 - 2\rho st + t^2)}{2(1-\rho^2)} \, ds dt,
$$

where $\rho \in (-1, 1)$ and $\Phi^{-1}(\alpha) = \inf\{x \mid \Phi(x) \geq \alpha\}$ is the univariate inverse standard normal distribution function. Applying C_ρ^{Ga} to two univariate standard normally distributed rv's results in a standard bivariate normal distribution with correlation coefficient ρ.

Note that, since the copula and the marginals can be arbitrarily combined, this (and any other) copula can be applied to *any* set of univariate rv's. The outcome will then surely not be multivariate normal, but the resulting multivariate distribution has inherited the dependence structure from the multivariate normal distribution.

3. Similar to the Gaussian copula, we can also define the multivariate Student t copula:

$$T_{\Sigma,v}(u_1, u_2, \ldots, u_n) = t_{\Sigma,v}(t_v^{-1}(u_1), t_v^{-1}(u_1), \ldots, t_v^{-1}(u_n))$$

where $t_{\sigma,v}$ is the multivariate Student t distribution with correlation matrix Σ.

4. As a last example, the *Gumbel* or *logistic* copula

$$C_\beta^{Gu}(x, y) = \exp\left[-\left\{(-\log x)^{\frac{1}{\beta}} + (-\log y)^{\frac{1}{\beta}}\right\}^\beta\right],$$

where $\beta \in (0, 1]$ indicates the dependence between X and Y. $\beta = 1$ gives independence and $\beta \to 0^+$ leads to perfect dependence.

10.3.2   *Properties of Copulas*

According to theorem 10.8, a multivariate distribution is fully determined by its marginal distributions and a copula. Therefore, the copula contains all information about the dependence structure between the associated random variables. In the case where all marginal distributions are continuous, the copula is unique and therefore often referred to as the dependence structure for the given combination of multivariate and marginal distribution. If the copula is not unique because at least one of the marginal distributions is not continuous, it can still be called a possible representation of the dependence structure.

A very useful feature of a copula is the fact that it is invariant under increasing and continuous transformation of the marginals.

Lemma   10.9 *If* $(X_1, \ldots, X_n)^t$ *has copula* C *and* $T_1, \ldots, T_n$ *are increasing continuous functions, then* $(T_1(X_1), \ldots, T_n(X_n))^t$ *also has copula* C.

For the proof we refer to Embrechts et al. (1999). One application of lemma 10.9 would be that the transition from the representation of a random variable to its logarithmic representation does not change the copula. Note that the linear correlation coefficient does not have this property. It is only invariant under linear transformations as stated in equation (10.2).

10.3.3   Constructing Multivariate Distributions with Copulas

From the concept of a copula, it is immediately clear that the easiest way to construct a multivariate distribution using a copula is to assume some marginal distributions and apply the copula. A practical problem, however, will be set up the other way round: The multivariate distribution has to be estimated by fitting the copula to data. A discussion of this topic is beyond the scope of this chapter; we refer to McNeil et al. (2005) for further discussion. In the following, we provide some examples for different copulas for illustration purposes.

Example 10.10 [3] *Let X and Y be two rv's that are both identical gamma (3,1) distributed. Now we apply two different copulas and compare the characteristics by simulating 1000 bivariate draws from both models. First, we use a Gaussian copula with parameter $\rho_{Ga} = 0.7$. The second distribution is then derived by applying a Gumbel copula whose parameter β is adjusted in a way that the linear correlation coefficient for the resulting bivariate distribution is also $\rho_{Gu} = 0.7$.*

Figure 10.7 shows the scatter plot of the 1000 draws for both distributions. The 99% quantile $q_{0.99}$ for the marginal Gamma distribution has been added as an indicator line for extreme values.

Note that despite the fact that both distributions have the same linear correlation coefficient, the dependence between X and Y is obviously quite different in both models. Using the Gumbel copula, extreme events have a tendency to occur together, as one can observe by comparing the number of draws where x and y exceed $q_{0.99}$ simultaneously. Those are 12 for the Gumbel and 3 for the Gaussian case.

Additionally, the probability of Y exceeding $q_{0.99}$ given that X has exceeded $q_{0.99}$ can be roughly estimated from the figure:

$$\hat{P}_{Ga}(X > q_{0.99}|Y > q_{0.99}) = \frac{3}{9} = 0.\bar{3}$$

$$\hat{P}_{Gu}(X > q_{0.99}|Y > q_{0.99}) = \frac{12}{16} = 0.75$$

This is another indicator of the increased probability for the joint occurrence of extreme events.

In the previous section we considered a bivariate distribution to show that marginal distributions and correlation are insufficient information to fully specify the joint distribution. This example was constructed in the following way, using a copula.

---

[3] The example and the graph were taken from Embrechts et al. (1999), pages 2 and 22f.

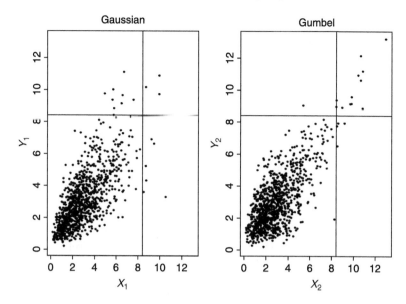

FIGURE 10.7. In this example, 1000 draws from two distributions that were constructed using Gamma(3,1) marginals and two different copulas, both having a linear correlation of $\rho = 0.7$.

Let X and Y be two rv's with standard normal distributions. Obviously the outcome for the bivariate distribution when applying an arbitrary copula is not bivariate normal in general. This is only the case when choosing the Gaussian copula $C = C_\rho^{Ga}$.

Thus, the following copula has been constructed:

$$f(x) = \mathbf{1}_{\{(\gamma, 1-\gamma)\}}(x) + \frac{2\gamma - 1}{2\gamma} \mathbf{1}_{\{(\gamma, 1-\gamma)^c\}}(x)$$

$$g(y) = -\mathbf{1}_{\{(\gamma, 1-\gamma)\}}(y) - \frac{2\gamma - 1}{2\gamma} \mathbf{1}_{\{(\gamma, 1-\gamma)^c\}}(y)$$

with $\gamma \in [\frac{1}{4}, \frac{1}{2}]$. For $\gamma < \frac{1}{2}$, the joint density disappears on the square $[\gamma, 1 - \gamma]^2$ which can be seen in Figure 10.5. This shows that the joint distribution is surely not bivariate normal. However, the linear correlation coefficient between X and Y exists. From symmetry considerations $(C(u, v) = c(1 - u, v), 0 \le u, v \le 1)$ it can be deduced that $\rho_{X,Y} = 0$, irrespective of γ. Therefore, uncountably many bivariate distributions with standard normal marginals and zero correlation exist that are not bivariate normal.

10.4   Modeling Dependent Defaults

While in this book we will concentrate on how dependent credit migrations can be modeled in a Markov chain framework; we will at least briefly discuss the use of copulas in modeling dependent defaults. There has been a large number of publications on the issue with a variety of different techniques. An excellent overview on different methods for modeling dependent defaults can be found, e.g., in Lando (2004); McNeil et al. (2005); or Bluhm and Overbeck (2007). The latter concentrate on the application of the techniques to structured credit portfolio analysis and CDOs.

A common approach to model dependent defaults are mixed binomial models. As illustrated in the introductory section of this chapter, the binomial distribution is a straightforward approach to study the number of defaults in a portfolio over a given period of time. A mixture distribution is then used to add a dependence structure randomizing the default probabilities of the binomial distribution. This can be interpreted as having a background variable conditioning the probability of default and affecting a number of companies in the portfolio. The higher the variablility in the mixture distribution, the higher will be the possible correlation of defaults and the more weight will be given to the tails of the loss distribution. It is further possible to set up the model in a way that the losses in case of default are a function of the background variable.

An approach based on the binomial distribution that was initially suggested by the industry is so-called diversity scores (Moody's Investment Service, 1997; Cifuentes et al., 1998). Moody's diversity scores go back to a so-called binominal expansion technique, first introduced by Moody's Investment Service (1997). The idea behind this technique is to approximate the number of losses of a large portfolio of N correlated loans with the losses on a smaller number D of independent loans with larger face value. This number equals the diversity score D which translates the portfolio into an equivalent number of uncorrelated defaults. The approximation portfolio is determined by assuming that each of the D firms in the portfolio with independent defaults has the same face value and same default probability. Then by matching the total promised principal, the mean, and variance of the loss of the principal of the model portfolio with the original portfolio, one can determine D and F. Usually, for calculation of the diversity scores, it is assumed that issuers in the same industry sector are related, while issuers in different industry sectors are treated as independent. For further details on diversity scores dependent on the number of firms in each industry, we refer to Moody's Investment Service (1997). However, it should be noted that diversity scores will give the same approximating portfolio with D independent firms and F to portfolios that might actually exhibit large variations in their tail probabilities. Therefore, the accuracy of the approximation of the original portfolio might be of significantly different quality depending on the nature of dependence. Especially when the underlying portfolio is very heterogenous in terms of credit quality, diversity scores may not provide an accurate approximation.

An alternative popular approach is the binomial contagion or infectious default model that is suggested in Davis and Lo (2001). Hereby, it is distinguished between direct defaults and defaults triggered through a so-called contagion event. A contagion event can be interpreted as the default of a firm also bringing down other companies and making them default. Given the basic infection model within a group of n bonds, the authors also extend the model to a more complex setup with several different subsets. Here, default infection is allowed within any subset but not across different subsets. This represents the notion that bonds in different industry sectors default independently, whereas infection patterns exist within each industry. For further reading on how the binomial model can be extended to a continuous-time dynamic version using a pure-death process, we refer to Lando (2004). More on binomial, Bernoulli, and factor mixture models can also be found in McNeil et al. (2005).

An intensity based model of dependent defaults is suggested in Duffie and Garleanu (2001). Default intensity models generally assume that an obligor defaults with a certain intensity during a given period of time and go back to Duffie and Singleton, 1999; Jarrow and Turnbull, 1995; Madan and Ünal, 1998. In the model of Duffie and Garleanu (2001), the intensity is governed by basic affine processes. The basic notion is that at each time t before the default time of the individual obligor, the default arrives at some intensity. The intensity is modeled as a mean reverting process with jumps. Immediately after default, the intensity drops to zero and the default probability becomes zero. As opposed to the infectious default models, this model is dynamic as the intensity also allows for stochastic variations over time. Correlations across obligors are modeled through correlation in the stochastic processes for the default intensities. One of the key results used in the model is that the sums of basic affine processes are also basic affine; i.e., the class of basic affine function is closed against summation. Therefore, when applying the basic model for one obligor to a multi-obligor model, one exploits the fact that a basic affine model can be written as the sum of independent basic affine models, having the same intensity process in common; see Duffie and Garleanu (2001) for further details.

Finally, copulas have become a very popular tool to model dependent defaults. Initially suggested by Vasicek (1987); Li (2000), a substantial number of publications has been dedicated to the topic in recent years. References include Frey and McNeil (2003); Giesecke (2004); Laurent and Gregory (2005); Hull and White (2004); Mashal and Naldi (2002); Schönbucher and Schubert (2001); Schönbucher (2003), just to name a few. An excellent treatment on the issue can also be found in McNeil et al. (2005). While Li (2000) suggests the use of of the Gaussian copula, a variety of copulas has been applied to model the dependence structure of defaults by other authors. Frey and McNeil (2003) and Mashal and Naldi (2002) suggest the use of the Student t-copula, while Schönbucher and Schubert (2001) propose the Clayton copula for dependent defaults. Applications of factor copulas can be found in Laurent and Gregory (2005), while Giesecke (2004) suggests an approach linking the marginal survival function with a joint survival function, the so-called survival copula. Hull and White (2004) show how many different copula models can be generated by assuming different distributional assumptions within a factor model approach and find that a model using Student t-copulas fits CDO market prices reasonably well.

Overall, a large number of publications has been dedicated to modeling dependent defaults. Unfortunately, the same interest seems to be lacking in modeling joint or dependent migrations in a Markov chain framework. In the following section we will provide some techniques that focus on modeling dependencies in rating transitions within a factor model approach.

10.5   Modeling Dependent Migrations

To model dependent migrations in a credit portfolio, one has to have some approach for including the dependence structure in migrations. As mentioned above, there is only a limited number of publications focusing on dependencies in credit migrations. While there are several applications of copulas in credit risk for modeling joint defaults, they lack the same interest towards modeling dependence in rating migrations. Exceptions include Hamilton et al. (2002) who apply a framework using copulas for credit migrations in an intensity based framework and use them to price credit derivatives. Further investigating the issue, Gagliardini and Gourieroux (2005a,b) present a general framework for rating dynamics, based on stochastic migration matrices. In an empirical study using French corporate data, they focus on serial correlation between migration matrices. McNeil and Wendin (2006) provide a standard statistical framework for ordered categorical variables and induce dependence between migrations by means of latent risk factors. The dynamics of the risk factors are assumed to follow a Markov process; therefore, the model can be interpreted as a state space model. The authors argue that latent risk factors with serial dependence should be able to also capture the effects of cross-sectional dependence. Then an ordered logit model with serially correlated latent factors is fitted using computational Bayesian techniques for model inference by Gibbs sampling (McNeil and Wendin, 2006).

In the following we will suggest a simpler approach to integrate the dependence structure either by using correlations or a copula framework. We will start with an approach using correlations initially suggested by Belkin et al. (1998b) and Kim (1999) and illustrated in the previous chapter for forecasting conditional transition matrices. Hereby, credit migrations are modeled as being dependent on a systematic risk factor and an idiosyncratic, firm-specific factor. The dependence in credit migrations can then be triggered by the degree of correlation with the systematic risk factor. We also suggest the use of copulas for modeling the joint dynamics of credit rating changes. Hereby, the Gaussian and Student t-copula will be used to show the effects of different assumptions about the degree of dependence and the choice of the copula.

10.5.1 Dependence Based on a Credit Cycle Index

Let us first consider an approach based on a factor model including a systematic and idiosyncratic risk component as it suggested in Belkin et al. (1998b), Finger (2001), and Kim (1999). As illustrated in the previous chapter, the model was initially designed to adjust migration matrices for business cycle effects and derive conditional transition matrices instead of using average historical ones. Recall that in the first step the so-called credit cycle index Z_t is determined, which defines the credit state based on macroeconomic conditions shared by all obligors during period t. The index is designed to be positive in good days and to be negative in bad days. A positive index implies a lower PD and downgrading probability but a higher upgrading probability and vice versa. A forecast of the index Z_t is then calculated based on the outcome of some macroeconomic variables.

Different degrees of dependence in migration behavior can then be added by adjusting the transition matrix according to an estimated or forecasted value of the credit cycle index. Hereby, it is assumed that rating transitions reflect an underlying continuous credit-change indicator Y_t following a standard normal distribution. Further, the credit-change indicator is assumed to be influenced by both a systematic and unsystematic risk component. Therefore, Y_t has a linear relationship with the systematic credit cycle index Z_t and an idiosyncratic error term u_t. Recall from previous Chapters 3 and 9 that the typical one-factor model parameterization (Belkin et al., 1998a; Finger, 2001) can then be denoted by

$$Y_t = wZ_t + \sqrt{1 - w^2}u_t \tag{10.5}$$

Since both Z_t and u_t are scaled to the standard normal distribution, with the weights chosen to be w and $\sqrt{1 - w^2}$, Y_t is also standard normally distributed. Hereby, w^2 provides a straightforward interpretation as the correlation between the the systematic credit cycle index Z_t and the credit change indicator Y_t. The probability distribution for the rating change of a company then takes place according to the outcome of the systematic risk index. In particular, default happens when the value of Y_t drops below a defined threshold T:

$$P(Y_t < T) = P(wZ_t + \sqrt{1 - w^2}u_t < T) \tag{10.6}$$

$$= P\left(u_t < \frac{T - wZ_t}{\sqrt{1 - w^2}}\right) = \Phi\left(\frac{T - wZ_t}{\sqrt{1 - w^2}}\right)$$

In the previous chapter it was illustrated how the shift of the credit-change indicator Y_t depended on the outcome of the credit cycle index

Z_t. To extend this scheme to a multirating system, it is assumed that conditional on an initial credit rating i at the beginning of a year, one partitions values of the credit change indicator Y_t into a set of disjoint bins. The bins are defined in a way that the probability of Y_t falling in a given interval equals the corresponding historical average transition rate. This can be done by simply inverting the cumulative normal distribution function starting from the default column, which is illustrated in Figure 9.4. The bins for the credit migrations can then be calculated by partitioning $(-\infty, \infty)$ into K subintervals for each rating class i:

$$
\begin{aligned}
t_1 &= \Phi^{-1}(1 - p_{i,1}) \\
t_2 &= \Phi^{-1}(1 - (p_{i,1} + p_{i,2})) \\
&\cdots \\
t_j &= \Phi^{-1}(1 - \textstyle\sum_{k=1}^{j} p_{i,k}) \\
&\cdots \\
t_{K-1} &= \Phi^{-1}(1 - \textstyle\sum_{k=1}^{K-1} p_{i,k})
\end{aligned}
\tag{10.7}
$$

The migrations can then be described by the following function $f : [0,1] \to S$:

$$
f_s =
\begin{cases}
S_1, & \text{for } u_t \in (t_1, -\infty) \\
S_2 & \text{for } u_t \in (t_2, t_1] \\
\cdots & \cdots \\
S_j & \text{for } u_t \in (t_j, t_{j-1}] \\
\cdots & \cdots \\
S_K & \text{for } u_t \in (t_{K-1}, \infty]
\end{cases}
\tag{10.8}
$$

Using the bins calculated from the average historical transition matrix, one can calculate the conditional transition probabilities based on the outcome of the credit cycle index Z_t. On average days, one obtains $Z_t = 0$ for the systematic risk index. A positive outcome of the credit cycle index Z_t shifts the credit-change indicator to the right side, while in the case of a bad outcome of the systematic risk index, the distribution moves to the left side. Thus, for each year with a positive or negative outcome of the systematic credit cycle index, the conditional transition rates will deviate from the average historical migration matrix.

10.5.2 Dependence Based on Individual Transitions

Alternatively to the changes in migration behavior due to a credit cycle index, one can also add dependence between migration by using correlated random numbers u_t for the simulation. Assume that a conditional or unconditional migration matrix has been calculated according to the predicted outcome of the credit cycle index Z_t. Then, when we use the thresholds (10.7) and the function (10.8), it is straightforward to simulate individual migrations for a loan or bond portfolio. In the case of the u_i being uncorrelated, we can generate them by drawing iid. random numbers $(u_1, u_2, \ldots, u_n)$ from a standard normal distribution function Φ. However, when we use the Cholesky decomposition, it is straightforward to also include a dependence structure to the migrations. Let us, therefore, denote the correlation matrix for the u_i by C. Then C is a positive definite matrix, and we can use the Cholesky decomposition to obtain matrices A and A^T such that

$$C = A^T A \qquad (10.9)$$

The matrix A can then be used to transform a vector of uncorrelated random variates $(u_1, u_2, \ldots, u_n)$ into correlated random numbers $(u_1^c, u_2^c, \ldots, u_n^c)$ by

$$(u_1^c, u_2^c, \ldots, u_n^c) = (u_1, u_2, \ldots, u_n) \cdot A \qquad (10.10)$$

To simulate correlated credit migrations, then one simply applies function (10.8) to determine the outcome of the next rating state.

10.5.3 Approaches Using Copulas

As illustrated in previous sections, often a single statistical parameter like the linear correlation coefficient will not be able to capture the entire dependence structure between two random variables in the general case. In this case a general concept of describing the dependence structure within multivariate distributions is needed. Since marginal distributions are very illustrative, easy to handle, and often used as basic building blocks for the design of a multivariate distribution, the idea of separating the description of the joint multivariate distribution into the marginal behavior and the dependence structure is very attractive also for dependent migrations. Then the dependence between the individual marginal distributions is modeled by a copula. As mentioned above, the literature provides many suggestions of copulae for credit risk (Frey and McNeil, 2003; Giesecke, 2004; Laurent and Gregory, 2005; Hull and White, 2004; Li, 2000; Mashal and Naldi, 2002; Schönbucher and Schubert, 2001; Schönbucher, 2003) that will permit various dependence structures among the rating migrations. In the following we will restrict ourselves to the use of the Gaussian copula and the Student t-copula to simulate dependent credit migrations. However, the extension of the approach to using various other copulas is straightforward.

Recall the multivariate Gaussian copula as probably the simplest example:

$$C^{Normal}(u_1, \ldots, u_n) = \Phi_{\Sigma}^n(\Phi^{-1}(u_1), \ldots, \Phi^{-1}(u_n)) \qquad (10.11)$$

Hereby, Φ denotes the standard normal cumulative distribution function, Φ^{-1} the inverse of the standard normal cumulative distribution function, and Φ^n_Σ the standard multivariate normal distribution with correlation matrix Σ. As it was mentioned above, the multivariate normal copula correlates the random variables rather near the mean and not in the tails and, therefore, fails to incorporate tail dependence. To add more dependence in the tails, alternatively, we also provide the framework using the Student t-copula. To generate correlated uniform numbers $(u_1, \ldots, u_n)$, we can use the Cholesky decomposition; see, e.g., Cherubini et al. (2004). Let therefore R denote the correlation matrix for the u_i. Then R is a positive definite matrix, and we can use the Cholesky decomposition to obtain matrices A and A^T such that

$$R = A^T A \tag{10.12}$$

The matrix A^T can then be used to generate random variates from the Gaussian or Student t-copula. An algorithm for generating random numbers from the Gaussian copula is provided, e.g., in Cherubini et al. (2004):

1. Find the Cholesky decomposition of $R = A^T A$.

2. Simulate n independent random numbers $(z_1, z_2, \ldots, z_n)$ from $N(0, 1)$.

3. Set

$$(x_1, x_2, \ldots, x_n) = A^T \cdot (z_1, z_2, \ldots, z_n)'$$

4. Set $(u_1^R, u_2^R, \ldots, u_n^R) = (\Phi(x_1), \Phi(x_2), \ldots, \Phi(x_n))$ where Φ denotes distribution function of univariate standard normal distribution.

On the other hand, to generate random numbers from the Student t-copula with v degrees of freedom, we can use the following algorithm:

1. Find the Cholesky decomposition of $R = A^T A$.

2. Simulate n independent random numbers $(z_1, z_2, \ldots, z_n)$ from $N(0, 1)$.

3. Simulate a random number s from χ^2_v independent of z.

4. Set $(y_1, y_2, \ldots, y_n) = A^T \cdot (z_1, z_2, \ldots, z_n)'$.

5. Set $(x_1, x_2, \ldots, x_n) = \sqrt{(v/s)} \cdot (y_1, y_2, \ldots, y_n)$.

6. Set $u_i = T_v(x_i)$ for $i = 1, \ldots, n$ where T_v denotes the univariate Student t distribution function.

Similar algorithms are available to simulate random numbers from other copulas like the Gumbel, Clayton, or Frank copula. While the Gaussian

TABLE 10.2. Ratings and Exposures for the Considered Credit Portfolio

Rating	AAA	AA	A	BBB	BB	B	CCC
No.	11	106	260	299	241	95	148
Average Exposure (Mio. Euro)	20	15	15	10	10	5	5

and Student t-copula are symmetric, alternative copulas will also allow for more complex dependence structures for rating migrations. As the results in the next section indicate, not only the estimated degree of dependence, but also the choice of the copula significantly affects the results on credit migrations.

10.6 An Empirical Study on Dependent Migrations

This section presents empirical results on simulating dependent migrations using the Gaussian and Student t-copula.[4] We compare the different simulation methods in the following way: using an exemplary portfolio and the average historical migration matrix introduced in Section 6.4, we apply the Gaussian and Student t-copula to simulate dependent credit migrations for a one-year time horizon and compare these results to independently simulated transitions. Recall that the exemplary loan portfolio consists of 1120 companies with rating distribution and exposures according to Table 10.2. After a copula correlation parameter ρ is chosen for the Gaussian and Student t-copula, for each scenario $n = 1000$ simulations for the portfolio were run.

10.6.1   Distribution of Defaults

In the first step we investigate the distribution of the number of defaults in the portfolio dependent on the chosen copula correlation parameter. Hereby, we illustrate the case of independent migrations as well as dependent migrations from the Gaussian and t-copula model for different choices of the copula correlation parameter ρ. For our study we decided to compare three different cases for the correlation parameter: $\rho = 0.1$, $\rho = 0.2$, and finally $\rho = 0.5$. Note that the latter will be rather unrealistic in empirical applications; however, to illustrate the significant effect, dependencies

---

[4]The structure of this section will follow the results initially provided in Trueck (2007). In the original publication results for alternative time horizons and copulas are also provided.

in migration behavior may have, we decided to also allow for such a comparably high value of the copula correlation parameter.

Figure 10.8 provides the number of defaults in the portfolio after one year for independent migrations, dependent migrations from the Gaussian and Student t-copula for the different copula correlation parameters $\rho = 0.1$, $\rho = 0.2$, and $\rho = 0.5$. The corresponding descriptive statistics are given

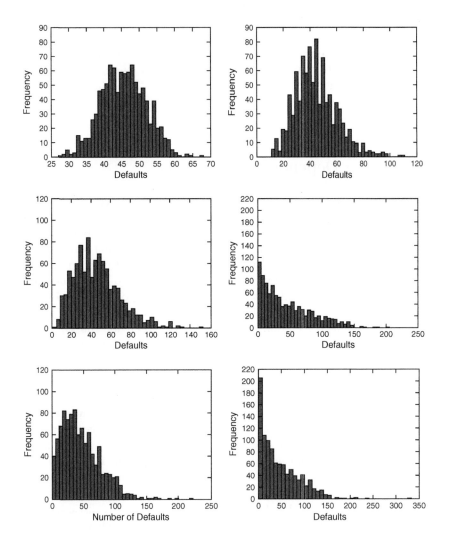

FIGURE 10.8. Number of defaults in the portfolio after one year for independent migrations (*upper left panel*), for dependent migrations from Gaussian copula $\rho = 0.1$ (*upper right panel*), $\rho = 0.2$ (*mid left panel*), and $\rho = 0.5$ (*mid right panel*) and for dependent migrations using the Student t-copula with $\rho = 0.2$ (*lower left panel*) and $\rho = 0.5$ (*lower right panel*).

TABLE 10.3. Descriptive Statistics for the Simulated Distribution of the Number of Defaults in the Portfolio After One Year for Independent Migrations and Dependent Migrations from Gaussian and Student t-copula

Dependence	Number of Defaults					
	$q_{0.01}$	$q_{0.05}$	Mean	$q_{0.95}$	$q_{0.99}$	Std
$\rho = 0$	31	35	45.6100	56	59	6.2436
Gaussian $\rho = 0.1$	15	22	45.1000	74	90	16.0518
Gaussian $\rho = 0.2$	9	14	46.0860	90	118	23.3681
Gaussian $\rho = 0.5$	0	3	45.4780	121	143	38.2871
Student t $\rho = 0.1$	6	11	45.9920	92	127	25.2758
Student t $\rho = 0.2$	1	7	46.9270	104	139	31.5953
Student t $\rho = 0.5$	0	1	46.0300	125	157	42.0739

in Table 10.3. Obviously we find that the simulated distribution for the number of defaults is almost symmetric in the case of independence. We observe a mean of approximately 46 defaults and a 90% confidence interval for the number of defaults would be [35, 56]. What we observe from Figure 10.8 is that the higher the copula correlation parameter, the more right-skewed becomes the distribution of defaults and the higher becomes the standard deviation of the distribution. While for the case of independent migration the simulated distribution has a standard deviation of $\sigma = 6.24$, for an increase in the copula correlation parameter the corresponding numbers are 16.05 (for $\rho = 0.1$), 23.37 (for $\rho = 0.2$), and 38.29 (for $\rho = 0.5$). This also has a dramatic effect on the confidence intervals for the number of defaults: for $\rho = 0.5$ the 90% confidence interval for the number of defaults is [3, 121].

The effects are even more pronounced when the Student t-copula is used adding more dependence in the tails. Choosing $\rho = 0.5$ for a small number of simulations, one could observe even more than 200 defaults for the portfolio. In general, the distribution of defaults is even more skewed and exhibits higher variance than for the Gaussian copula with the same coefficient of correlation. Note, however, that despite the substantial changes in the shape and variance of the distribution, the average number of defaults for all simulation experiments is around 46. So the mean number of defaults is not affected by the copula or correlation parameter. On the other hand, for the distribution and calculated default quantiles, both the choice of the copula and the correlation parameter yield significantly different results. Still, these results are not surprising and could also be obtained by using copulas just to model dependent defaults only. Therefore, we will now also have a look at the distribution of ratings for the exemplary portfolio, which usually can not be investigated by modeling dependent defaults.

10.6.2 The Distribution of Rating Changes

Let us first have a look at the distribution of ratings for noninvestment grade rating class C that is displayed in Table 10.4. Recall that for the usual portfolio there were approximately 150 companies in this rating state. Figure 10.9 displays the number of companies in the rating state after one

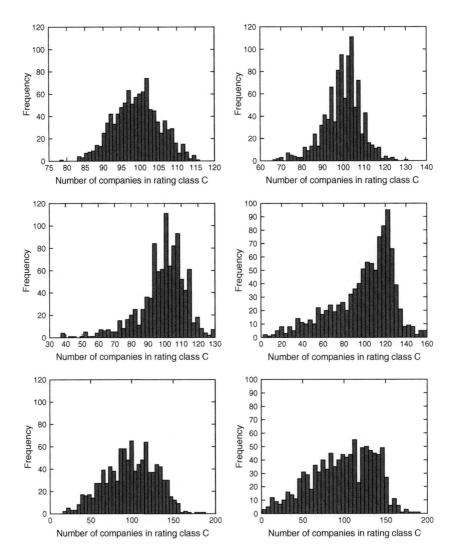

FIGURE 10.9. Number of companies in rating state C after one year for independent migrations (*upper left panel*), for dependent migrations from Gaussian copula $\rho = 0.1$ (*upper right panel*), $\rho = 0.2$ (*mid left panel*), and $\rho = 0.5$ (*mid right panel*) and for dependent migrations using the Student t-copula with $\rho = 0.2$ (*lower left panel*) and $\rho = 0.5$ (*lower right panel*).

year. Again the simulation results are provided for independent migrations and for dependent migrations from the Gaussian copula and Student t-copula with different correlation parameters. In the case of independence, the simulated distribution for the number of companies in rating state C is quiet symmetric. Again we find for the Gaussian copula that the higher the choice of the correlation parameter, the more skewed and volatile becomes the distribution. Note, however, that in this case the distribution is skewed to the left and not to the right. Again, for the Student t-distribution the effects on the volatility of the rating distribution are more pronounced. The standard deviation of the number of companies in rating class C ranges from approximately 29.75 to 37.54 depending on the choice of the copula correlation parameter. In comparison, the standard deviation for independently simulated transitions is 6.40. Despite the higher volatility for the Student t-copula, the simulated distributions of companies in rating class C are less skewed than for the Gaussian copula. Overall, we find that when applying a model with independent individual migrations, the number of companies in rating state C would be expected to be reduced from 148 to somewhere between 89 and 110 with 90% confidence. Assuming that credit migrations show a dependence structure that could be modeled by a Gaussian or Student t-copula, this interval becomes substantially wider. The simulated 90% confidence interval, for example, is $[72, 117]$ for a Gaussian copula with correlation parameter $\rho = 0.2$, while it increases to $[45, 144]$ when a Student t-copula with the same copula correlation parameter is used. This means that while the expected value of companies in a rating state stays approximately the same, confidence intervals significantly become wider when the dependence for credit migrations is increased or when a copula with more dependence in the tails is used.

We finally investigate the results for companies in the investment grade rating state A that are provided in Table 10.5. Initially, there

TABLE 10.4. Descriptive Statistics for the Simulated Distribution of the Number of Companies in Rating State C After One Year for Independent Migrations and Dependent Migrations from Gaussian and Student t-copula

| Dependence | Companies in C | | | | | |
	$q_{0.01}$	$q_{0.05}$	Mean	$q_{0.95}$	$q_{0.99}$	Std
$\rho = 0$	85	89	99.2760	110	113	6.4041
Gaussian $\rho = 0.1$	73	84	99.8740	114	120	8.9141
Gaussian $\rho = 0.2$	52	72	98.8960	117	125	14.0366
Gaussian $\rho = 0.5$	17	38	98.8940	134	152	29.5456
Student t $\rho = 0.1$	28	47	99.3500	144	156	29.7486
Student t $\rho = 0.2$	29	45	98.3220	144	157	30.2874
Student t $\rho = 0.5$	12	30	97.9860	150	165	37.5379

were 260 companies in this rating state. Figure 10.10 displays the number of companies in rating state A after one year. Also here the simulation results are provided for independent migrations, for dependent migrations from Gaussian copula and Student t-copula with the

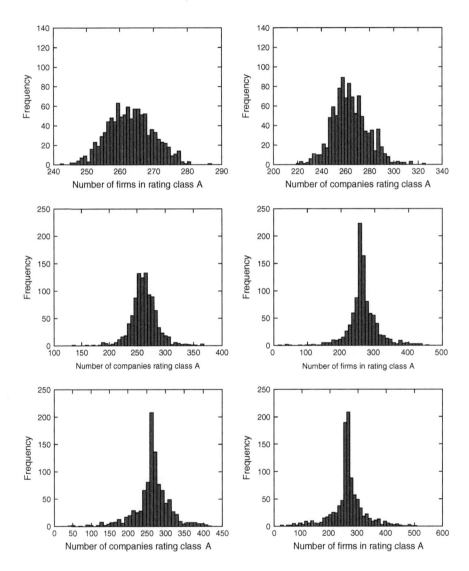

FIGURE 10.10. Number of companies in rating state A after one year for independent migrations (*upper left panel*), for dependent migrations from Gaussian copula $\rho = 0.1$ (*upper right panel*), $\rho = 0.2$ (*mid left panel*), and $\rho = 0.5$ (*mid right panel*) and for dependent migrations using the Student t-copula with $\rho = 0.2$ (*lower left panel*) and $\rho = 0.5$ (*lower right panel*).

same correlation parameters $\rho = 0.1$, $\rho = 0.2$ and $\rho = 0.5$. For all simulation experiments the expected value of companies in the rating state after one year is slightly increased to a number between 262 and 265. However, while the mean of the distribution remains approximately the same, the shape of the distribution is substantially affected by the chosen copula and the correlation parameter. For the Gaussian copula, we find that the higher the choice of ρ, the more leptokurtic the distribution becomes. Further the standard deviation of the distribution increases substantially from $\sigma = 6.78$ in case of independent migrations to $\sigma = 45.35$ when the Gaussian copula with $\rho = 0.5$ is applied (see Table 10.5). However, unlike for the number of defaults or companies in rating state C, we find that the distribution remains rather symmetric in this case. As expected, for the Student t-copula the distribution is more leptokurtic and exhibits even higher standard deviation. Simulated 90% confidence intervals now range from $[253, 275]$ for independence to $[146, 370]$ when a Student t-copula with copula correlation parameter $\rho = 0.5$ is used. Note that this interval is approximately 10 times wider than in the case of independence.

Overall, the results point out the substantial effects of dependent credit migrations. Hereby, unlike for models that concentrate on dependent defaults only, a simulation model for dependent credit migrations is able to provide results on the number of companies that are expected to be in a certain rating class after an arbitrary number of periods. In our analysis, only results for $t = 1$ year were provided; however, it is straightforward to extend the time horizon. We find that, while both for the number of defaults and number of companies in a rating state, the expected value stays approximately the same, simulated confidence intervals are significantly wider when the copula correlation parameter is increased or a copula with more tail dependence is used. Further the shape of the distribution changes

TABLE 10.5. Descriptive Statistics for the Simulated Distribution of the Number of Companies in Rating State A After One Year for Independent Migrations and Dependent Migrations from Gaussian and Student t-copula

	Companies in A					
Dependence	$q_{0.01}$	$q_{0.05}$	Mean	$q_{0.95}$	$q_{0.99}$	Std
$\rho = 0$	249	253	263.5820	275	278	6.7798
Gaussian $\rho = 0.1$	231	241	263.7470	289	303	14.6565
Gaussian $\rho = 0.2$	191	227	262.5520	300	331	23.4282
Gaussian $\rho = 0.5$	131	197	265.0690	339	411	45.3503
Student t $\rho = 0.1$	101	178	263.2730	330	364	44.5682
Student t $\rho = 0.2$	116	180	265.0640	333	390	46.8939
Student t $\rho = 0.5$	73	146	263.4040	370	443	60.9158

significantly and becomes either more skewed or leptokurtic, dependent on the rating state. This will have substantial effects not only for the VaR of a credit portfolio, but also when rating changes are considered for a mark-to-market evaluation of the portfolio. We conclude that it might be beneficial to investigate the use of different copulas for modeling dependent credit migrations; see, e.g., Trueck (2007).

11

Credit Derivatives

11.1 Introduction

Credit derivatives may be defined as a specific class of financial instruments whose value is derived from an underlying asset bearing a credit risk of private or sovereign debt issuers. The rationales behind credit derivatives are various, depending on the types of players on the market. The banks, which are the largest group of users of credit derivatives, intend to free up capital, optimize their balance sheet, manage loan exposure without the consent of the debtor, and compile to the regulatory offsets as well as for risk reduction and diversification. Institutional investors like insurance companies and fund managers, on the other hand, have the opportunity to access new classes of credit assets, such as bank loans, which have not been directly available to nonbank investors as a result of the absence of necessary origination and infrastructure. In addition to that, these investor groups also aim to hedge and diversify their portfolios and to reduce the risk by buying credit derivative instruments.

Although the market for credit derivatives has a well diversified group of participants with differing needs, it has been a very young market. The market appears to have arisen out of the market for secondary loan trading in the early 1990s. The earliest transactions appear to have been completed around 1991/1992. The first transactions were settled with the intention to isolate and transfer credit risk, access new classes of assets such as bank loans, and increase returns by investing in credit risk through credit derivatives. As the market has evolved, other types of transactions have emerged with the goals to increase the credit risk spectrum (types of risk, recovery rates, and combinations of different debt characteristics) and to manage a credit portfolio actively. The key factors for the development can be summarized as the following:

- concern about concentration of credit risk in bank asset portfolios;

- developments in the management of credit risk;

- focus on overcoming the inefficiency and illiquidity of available structures for transferring and trading credit risk;

- incompleteness of the credit risk spectrum; and

- recognition of the need to develop structures which would facilitate attracting new investment risk capital into assumption of credit risk.

Despite the substantial growth of credit derivative products and the industry, appropriate models for pricing or hedging these products might still have to be developed. The recent subprime mortgage crisis has explicitly illustrated how dangerous it can be to underestimate the risk arising from credit derivative transactions and how difficult it is to price this risk. This section aims to provide a brief overview on participants and a variety of products in the credit derivatives market.

Market Participants: There are several key players on the market for credit derivatives. By far, large commercial banks and investment banks/securities houses followed by insurance companies are the biggest participants. While commercial banks and investment banks/securities houses act both as sellers and buyers of protection, insurance companies sell more protection than purchase it, using their knowledge of risk assessment. Other key players include hedge funds, pension and investment funds, and corporates.

Commercial Banks: Banks use credit derivatives to transfer credit risk without selling the underlying asset, mostly a loan to a client. Thus, the relationship with the client is preserved and the client does not even have to be informed about the transaction. In addition to that, the risk of the bank's credit portfolio can be easily hedged by purchasing default protection such as portfolio default swap or basket swap. The portfolio is managed actively with low transaction costs, as credit derivatives may be purchased or sold to achieve the desired risk level without buying new assets and selling the existing ones. An important motivation for commercial banks is regulatory capital requirements. Under the current Basel Accord, the bank is generally required to hold 8% of its exposure to a corporate borrower as capital reserve. If the bank is involved in a credit derivatives transaction to reduce the risk of its credit exposure and the bank's counterparty is again a bank in an OECD country, providing the evidence that the risk has effectively been transferred to the counterparty, the bank has to hold regulatory capital of only 1.6% instead of 8%.

Investment Banks/Securities Houses: These intermediaries sell and buy default protection in order to provide liquidity to clients and to trade for their own account. While trading for their own account, they buy protection against counterparty risk arising from their credit exposure to clients or other OTC derivatives such as interest rate swaps. One key role played by the investment banks and securities houses is bridging the needs of protection buyers and sellers. Legal and regulatory requirements in some countries may restrict or even prohibit the exposure of insurance companies to credit derivatives. However, the insurance companies may sell protection to other insurance companies that sell default protection such as credit default swaps. Investment banks and securities houses enter the game here, founding insurance companies in financial centers like Bermuda that allow insurers to enter the derivatives market. Thus, they just pass the credit insurance to the protection buyer and the insurance premium to the insurance company that is prevented from being involved in derivatives contracts.

Insurance Companies: Insurance companies are net sellers of protection and their share in the market has been increasing. By selling protection, they intend to participate in the bank's loan market where they have been nonexistent. They focus on creating synthetic exposure to credit markets, especially to high yield bonds and emerging market debt, and by assuming credit risk, the insurance companies aim for yield enhancement. Credit derivatives also reduce the transaction costs of constructing a well-diversified credit book.

Pension/Investment Funds and Hedge Funds: The motivation of this group is somewhat similar to insurance companies. Like them, the pension/investment funds and hedge funds are also net protection sellers, although hedge funds have been increasingly buying protection in recent years, especially on lower rated bonds of U.S. companies. Hedge funds also try to use the arbitrage opportunities between the money and derivatives markets.

Corporates: The participation of this group has been limited to a few large multinationals with excellent credit ratings. These companies usually buy credit default swaps against credit risk associated with their customers or suppliers.

Overall, the credit derivatives market brings together different investor and industry groups who have varying expectations of entering a derivatives transaction.

11.1.1 Types of Credit Derivatives

Credit derivatives can be roughly classified into two main groups: *Single-name instruments* provide protection against default by a single reference entity, i.e., underlying credit asset such as a bank loan or bond. *Multiname instruments* contracts contingent on default result in a pool of reference units, thus allowing the investors to transfer the risk of a credit portfolio instead of dealing with every security separately. Single-name products make up the majority of the market; however, multiname products have been substantially increasing their share in recent years. In the following two subsections, we will introduce some of the most common products in the credit derivatives market.

Single-Name Credit Derivatives

Credit Default Swaps (CDS): CDS are the most common products in the credit derivatives market. In a vanilla CDS, the protection buyer agrees to make periodic payments (swap spread or premium), generally quarterly, to the protection seller over the lifetime of the CDS (three-, five-, and ten-year maturities are the most common ones). In exchange for this protection, the seller is obliged to make a payment in case the reference entity defaults. If no default occurs during the maturity of the CDS, the protection seller just receives the premium.

In case of default, CDS are settled either physically or in cash depending on the contract specifications. In a physically settled CDS, the protection seller must buy the defaulted asset for the face value. In a cash settled swap, the protection seller pays the difference between the face value of the defaulted asset and the recovery value determined by a poll among the market participants. In the United States, for example, the majority of CDS are physically settled.

One major factor for the development and the size of CDS is the standardization of the CDS transactions using the master agreements of the International Swaps and Derivatives Association (ISDA). This has increased the liquidity and transparency in this segment, thus reducing the transaction costs and the insurance premium paid. However, there are still disputes concerning the legal definition of default and the treatment of debt restructuring.

Asset Swaps: In an asset swap the investor purchases a fixed-rate liability issued by a reference entity; i.e., the investor receives periodic payments at a fixed rate. She simultaneously enters an interest rate (fixed-for-floating) swap with another counterparty such as a bank, where the investor is obliged to make fixed payments at predetermined dates while receiving payments at a floating rate (usually spread over a short-term LIBOR, called asset swap spread). The important point here is that the fixed payments of the asset swap exactly match those of the reference asset. Thus, the investor is protected against the interest rate risk of the fixed-rate liability, which is transferred to the asset swap counterparty. The investor merely holds the credit risk component of the reference asset.

Credit Spread Options: Credit spread options are "derivative contracts where the payoff is dependent on the credit spread of the reference entity to some strike level." The credit spread is defined either as the spread relative to the risk-free benchmark (the absolute spread) or to another credit-sensitive asset (the relative spread).

A credit spread put option gives the holder the right to sell the reference asset to the writer of the option if the spread increases above the strike level. As an example, think of a bond of a corporate and a bond investor. If the credit quality of the corporate declines, the bond price will go down, resulting in a higher yield and thus a higher spread over, let's say, the risk-free U.S. Treasury bonds. If the spread is over the strike level, the holder of the credit spread put will exercise the option at the prespecified strike level, selling the bond to the writer at a higher price than its market value. Generally, it has to be distinguished between the physical and the cash settlement. While the physical settlement is similar as described above, in a cash settlement, the difference between the current spread and the strike spread is weighted with the remaining time-to-maturity of the underlying and multiplied with its face value.

Credit spread put options are popular among insurance companies that are restricted to invest in speculative grade bonds. Thus, if the reference credit is downgraded from an initial investment grade to speculative grade, the holder of such a put option can get rid of the junk bond for a higher price than it can sell at the market. A credit spread call option, in contrast, gives the holder the right to buy a credit asset if the spread decreases below a strike level, enabling the holder to purchase the asset cheaper than its market value.

Total Return Swaps: In a total return swap contract, the investor receives all the cash flows associated with a credit asset without actually owning it. The counterparty of the contract, e.g., a bank, passes through the cash flows of the credit asset to the investor. In exchange for these cash flows, the investor pays a spread over short-term LIBOR.

In a total return swap, the investor takes over the entire credit risk. Should the issuer of the credit asset default, the investor bears the loss. Held until the maturity of the swap contract (usually three to five years), the investor receives a payment from the counterparty if the market value of the underlying credit asset has appreciated since the inception date of the swap. If not, the investor is required to pay the difference resulting from the depreciation.

Total return swaps facilitate the purchase or sale of a credit asset in a synthetic format. A good example is the bank loan market. Total return swaps make it possible for nonbanks such as insurance companies to participate in the bank loan market and assume the full credit risk and the cash flows. A bank, on the other hand, has the chance to reduce its exposure to a client or a specific industry, free some capital, and manage its credit lines better.

Multiname Credit Derivatives

In the following we will describe a number of multiname credit derivatives. For a more detailed description of such products and various pricing techniques, see, e.g., Bluhm and Overbeck (2007b).

Basket Swaps: A basket swap is a derivative written on a portfolio or basket of credit assets. A common example is the "first-to-default" basket. In this case, the protection seller has to make a payment when an asset from the basket defaults. The payment is either the face value of the asset in exchange for the asset or the difference between the face value and the estimated recovery value by market participants. In exchange for this insurance, the protection seller receives periodic premiums. A first-to-default basket is terminated after the first default. More risk-averse investors may purchase second-to-default, third-to-default, or nth to default basket contracts where they also are protected against the second, third, or nth default in the basket.

An investor purchasing a basket swap transfers some of the credit risk to the protection seller, which is especially useful when the investor's portfolio is not well diversified due to high transaction costs.

Portfolio Default Swaps: Portfolio default swaps differ from basket swaps in the sense that the protection payment is not triggered by the number of defaults in the underlying portfolio but the size of the default-related loss in the portfolio. For instance, a first-loss tranche of 10% protects the investors against defaults leading to a cumulated 10% loss in the portfolio. After that, the contract is terminated.

11.1.2   Collateralized Debt Obligations (CDO)

A CDO is a debt security issued by a special-purpose vehicle (SPV) and backed by a diversified loan or bond portfolio. CDOs can roughly be classified by the following criteria:

- Underlying assets: Most CDOs are based on corporate bonds *(CBOs)* and commercial loans *(CLOs)*. Further underlying assets are structured products, such as asset-backed securities and other CDOs (called *CDO squared*), and emerging market debt.

- Purpose: *Arbitrage CDOs* aim to profit from price differences between the components included in the CDO and the sale price of the CDO tranches. They securitize traded assets like bonds and credit default swaps. *Balance sheet CDOs* aim to shrink the balance sheet and reduce required economic or regulatory capital.

- Credit structure: While the portfolio of a *cash flow CDO* is not actively traded, *market value CDOs* include actively traded assets where the portfolio manager has to meet fixed requirements concerning, for example, credit quality of the assets or diversification.

- In opposition to cash CDOs, *synthetic CDOs (CSOs)* are constructed using credit default swaps. There is no true sale of an underlying portfolio, but the issuer sells credit default swaps on a synthetic portfolio.

Traditionally, SPV either purchases the portfolio of bond and loan securities in the secondary market or from the balance sheet of a bank. Then,

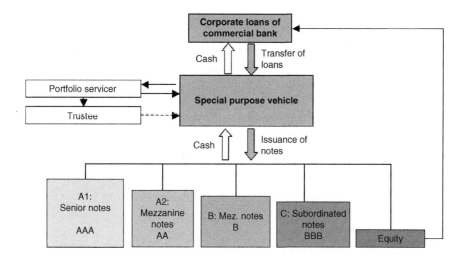

FIGURE 11.1. The structure of an exemplary CDO.

SPV issues CDOs divided into various tranches to satisfy the risk preferences of different investors backed by the cash flows of this reference portfolio. Typically, the risk is tranched in a senior position rated AAA, one or several mezzanine positions, and a first-loss position, usually rated below BBB. Figure 11.1 depicts the transactions settled in an exemplary CDO.

Note that very often the SPV also enters into a portfolio default swap contract with a protection buyer such as a bank to assume the credit risk of the underlying portfolio. This setup is called "synthetic CDO." At the same time, it issues CDOs to investors (who are the end-sellers of protection) and invests the proceeds in highly rated collateral securities like G7 government bonds. The investors then receive the returns on these securities with portfolio default swap premium. In case of default on the reference portfolio, these payments are reduced and the protection buyer has a claim on SPV backed by the collateral.

Credit-Linked Notes (CLN): CLNs allow investors, who are prohibited to enter directly into derivatives contracts, to benefit from the advantages of credit derivatives. CLNs are debt obligations with an embedded credit derivative. The idea behind CLNs may be best understood by the following example:

Assume an insurance company A, two banks B1 and B2, and a risky company C. Assume that the insurance company wants to take some credit risk associated with the debt of company C. However, assume further, there is no publicly traded bond of C available and its entire liabilities consist of bank loans given by bank B1. In addition to that, A's investment policy prevents it from entering into the derivatives market by selling CDS. A can then purchase CLNs worth 100 million Euros, referenced to company C and issued by bank B2. Bank B2 invests this amount into highly rated collateral securities and at the same time enters into a CDS contract with bank B1, selling protection against a default by company C. From now on, B2 will simply pass the CDS premiums received from bank B1 to insurance company A. If company C defaults, B2 will pay the face value of A's debt to B1. Insurance company A, however, will receive only the recovery value of C's debt, meaning if the recovery rate is 40%, C will get only 40 million Euros back instead of the initial investment of 100 million Euros. The CLN is then terminated. If no default occurs, insurance company C will continue to receive the CDS premiums until the maturity date of CLN.

11.2   Pricing Single-Named Credit Derivatives

In the following we will provide an overview on how credit migration matrices can be used to price single-named credit derivatives. Generally for this purpose, the main task is the derivation of a well-calibrated PD term structure or credit curve, since this can be used to determine the probability distribution of default times for an obligor. In this section we will describe how this can be done using credit migration matrices. For a more general introduction to PD term structures, we refer to Bluhm et al. (2003), for their application to structured credit products, e.g., to Bluhm and Overbeck (2007b). In general, every bank has its way to calibrate credit curves to their internal and external data.

The PD term structure for some obligor with rating class i can be defined the following way; see, e.g., Bluhm and Overbeck (2007b):

$$p_i(t) = P(D_i \leq t) \text{ for } t \geq 0 \tag{11.1}$$

where D_i simply denotes the probability that obligor i defaults. Thus, $p_i(t)$ is the probability that obligor i defaults within the time interval $[0, t]$. Then the curve of these cumulative default probabilities provides the PD term structure of the considered obligor. Note that the credit curve is naturally increasing with increasing time. Further,

$$s_i(t) = 1 - p_i(t) = P(D_i > t) \text{ for } t \geq 0 \tag{11.2}$$

denotes the survival probability of an obligor up to time t. Obviously, it can be expected that for different rating classes these curves will look quite different. To illustrate the derivation of credit curves for different rating states based on a transition matrix, let us consider a numerical example. Note that in this example the derivation of the credit curves is based on using a historical transition matrix, while in real-world applications credit curves may be calibrated based on risk-neutral and time-inhomogeneous migration matrices; see, e.g., Bluhm and Overbeck (2007a); Jarrow et al. (1997). We will return to this issue later on. For the moment to illustrate the calculation of the PD term structure, we stick to the most simple case of assuming a given one-year transition matrix P for the eight rating states $AAA, AA, A, BBB, BB, BB, CCC, D$ and the assumption of a homogeneous model. The assumed exemplary transition matrix is provided in Table 11.1.

Since the PD term structure is denoted in continuous time, the corresponding generator matrix Λ has to be used to derive the corresponding cumulative PDs. Note that for the transition matrix, the series (5.4) converges to a generator matrix with negative off-diagonal elements that is presented in Table 11.2. Since this matrix would provide negative transition matrices for short term periods, it is not economically meaningful. Therefore, we use one of the methods suggested by Israel et al. (2000) illustrated in Section 5.3 to find an adequate approximation of the generator matrix. We decided to use the second method that replaces the negative

TABLE 11.1. Assumed Average One Year Transition Matrix P for Calculation of PD Term Structure

	AAA	AA	A	BBB	BB	B	CCC	D
AAA	0.9276	0.0661	0.0050	0.0009	0.0003	0.0000	0.0000	0.0000
AA	0.0064	0.9152	0.0700	0.0062	0.0008	0.0011	0.0002	0.0001
A	0.0007	0.0221	0.9137	0.0546	0.0058	0.0024	0.0003	0.0005
BBB	0.0005	0.0029	0.0550	0.8753	0.0506	0.0108	0.0021	0.0029
BB	0.0002	0.0011	0.0052	0.0712	0.8229	0.0741	0.0111	0.0141
B	0.0000	0.0010	0.0035	0.0047	0.0588	0.8323	0.0385	0.0612
CCC	0.0012	0.0000	0.0029	0.0053	0.0157	0.1121	0.6238	0.2389
D	0.0000	0.0000	0.0000	0.0000	0.0000	0.0000	0.0000	1.0000

TABLE 11.2. Corresponding Generator Matrix Λ to P with Negative Off-Diagonal Elements

	AAA	AA	A	BBB	BB	B	CCC	D
AAA	−0.0754	0.0718	0.0027	0.0007	0.0003	−0.0001	0.0000	0.0000
AA	0.0069	−0.0898	0.0765	0.0045	0.0005	0.0010	0.0003	0.0000
A	0.0007	0.0241	−0.0930	0.0609	0.0048	0.0021	0.0002	0.0003
BBB	0.0005	0.0024	0.0614	−0.1376	0.0592	0.0099	0.0021	0.0021
BB	0.0002	0.0011	0.0032	0.0839	−0.2007	0.0885	0.0129	0.0110
B	0.0000	0.0011	0.0036	0.0023	0.0708	−0.1904	0.0529	0.0598
CCC	0.0016	−0.0002	0.0033	0.0060	0.0159	0.1548	−0.4765	0.2951
D	0.0000	0.0000	0.0000	0.0000	0.0000	0.0000	0.0000	0.0000

entries by zero and adds the appropriate value back into all entries of the row proportional to their absolute values. The result for the approximate generator $\tilde{\Lambda}$ is given in Table 11.3 and the corresponding approximation $\tilde{P}$ for P is provided in Table 11.4. Obviously, $\tilde{P}$ is very close to the original transition matrix P.

The approximate generator matrix can then be used to calculate the PD term structures for the individual rating classes. Figure 11.2 provides the credit curves derived from the approximate continuous-time generator matrix $\tilde{\Lambda}$ for investment grade rating states AAA, AA, A, and BBB. Figure 11.3 provides the same curves for speculative grade rating states BB, C, and CCC. The corresponding curves for the survival probabilities are displayed in Figures 11.4 and 11.5. The PD term structures for the speculative grade ratings show the typical shape of a decreasing growth rate. This is due to the fact that, conditional on having survived for some time, the chances for further survival actually improve. Remember that this behavior is also often reflected in the term structure of credit spreads; see, e.g., Chapter 4 and the empricial results provided by Fons (1994). For investment grade rating states, we observe the opposite effect. Since companies with a very high rating have no further upside potential but are

TABLE 11.3. The Approximated Generator Matrix $\tilde{\Lambda}$

	AAA	AA	A	BBB	BB	B	CCC	D
AAA	−0.0754	0.0717	0.0027	0.0007	0.0003	0.0000	0.0000	0.0000
AA	0.0069	−0.0898	0.0765	0.0045	0.0005	0.0010	0.0003	0.0000
A	0.0007	0.0241	−0.0930	0.0609	0.0048	0.0021	0.0002	0.0003
BBB	0.0005	0.0024	0.0614	−0.1376	0.0592	0.0099	0.0021	0.0021
BB	0.0002	0.0011	0.0032	0.0839	−0.2007	0.0885	0.0129	0.0110
B	0.0000	0.0011	0.0036	0.0023	0.0708	−0.1904	0.0529	0.0597
CCC	0.0016	0.0000	0.0033	0.0060	0.0159	0.1548	−0.4766	0.2951
D	0.0000	0.0000	0.0000	0.0000	0.0000	0.0000	0.0000	0.0000

TABLE 11.4. Approximation $\tilde{P}$ for Discrete-Time Average One Year Transition Matrix P

	AAA	AA	A	BBB	BB	B	CCC	D
AAA	0.9276	0.0661	0.0050	0.0009	0.0003	0.0001	0.0000	0.0000
AA	0.0064	0.9152	0.0700	0.0062	0.0008	0.0011	0.0002	0.0001
A	0.0007	0.0221	0.9137	0.0546	0.0058	0.0024	0.0003	0.0005
BBB	0.0005	0.0029	0.0550	0.8753	0.0506	0.0108	0.0021	0.0029
BB	0.0002	0.0011	0.0052	0.0712	0.8229	0.0741	0.0111	0.0141
B	0.0000	0.0010	0.0035	0.0047	0.0588	0.8323	0.0385	0.0612
CCC	0.0012	0.0002	0.0029	0.0053	0.0157	0.1121	0.6238	0.2388
D	0.0000	0.0000	0.0000	0.0000	0.0000	0.0000	0.0000	1.0000

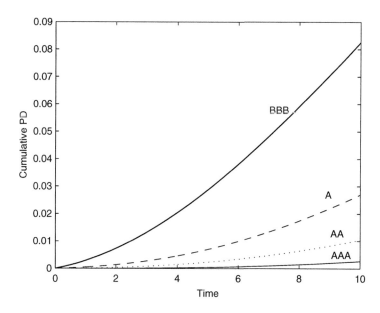

FIGURE 11.2. Cumulative default probabilities derived from the considered continuous-time generator matrix for investment grade rating states AAA (*solid line*), AA (*dotted line*), A (*dashed line*), and BBB (*bold line*).

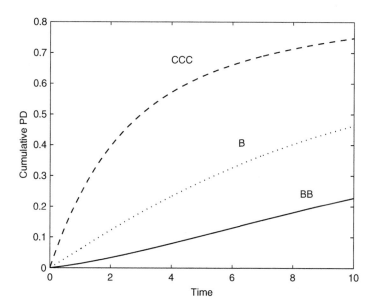

FIGURE 11.3. Cumulative default probabilities derived from the considered continuous-time generator matrix for speculative grade rating states BB (*solid line*), B (*dotted line*), and CCC (*dashed line*).

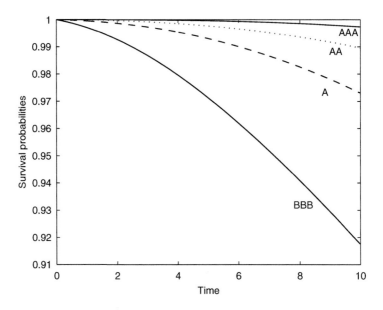

FIGURE 11.4. Corresponding survival probabilities derived from the considered continuous-time generator matrix for investment grade rating states AAA (*solid line*), AA (*dotted line*), A (*dashed line*), and BBB (*bold line*).

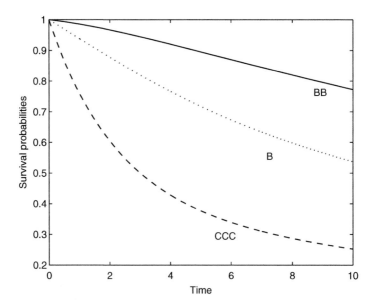

FIGURE 11.5. Corresponding survival probabilities derived from the considered continuous-time generator matrix for speculative grade rating states BB (*solid line*), B (*dotted line*), and CCC (*dashed line*).

more likely to be downgraded with the passage of time, conditional on their survival for some time, the probability of surviving further decreases due to a potential deterioration of their rating over time. Further investigating the issue and calculating quarterly forward PDs, Bluhm and Overbeck (2007b) find a mean reversion effect in PD term structures that is also in line with findings of the rating agency Moody's KMV.

The derived PD term structure can then be used to derive the density of the default time distribution by simply calculating the derivative of the credit curve:

$$f_i(t) = \frac{d}{dt} p_i(t) \tag{11.3}$$

Having a density of the default time distribution, it is then straightforward to calculate prices for single-name credit derivatives such as CDS for different maturities. It may also be interesting to use the density function of the default times to determine descriptive statistics like the mean or the variance of the default times for a rating class i:

$$E(D_i) = \int_0^\infty t \cdot f_i(t) dt \tag{11.4}$$

$$\sigma_{D_i}^2 = \int_0^\infty (t - E(D_i)) \cdot f_i(t) dt \tag{11.5}$$

Overall, the continuous-time homogeneous Markov chain framework provides a simple method to construct the PD term structure, survival curves, and the density of default time distributions for individual rating classes i. However, comparing the derived PD term structure from the homogeneous continuous-time Markov chain model with empirically observed credit curves, the curves do not match that well; see, e.g., Bluhm and Overbeck (2007a). The authors therefore suggest using a non-homogeneous continuous-time Markov chain approach of the following form:

Starting with a time-homogeneous generator $\Lambda = (\lambda_{ij})$ with $1 \leq i, j \leq K$, they relax the assumption of constant transition rates λ_{ij}. Instead they suggest a time-dependent generator matrix Λ_t of the following form:

$$\Lambda_t = \Phi_t \times \Lambda \tag{11.6}$$

where $\times$ denotes matrix multiplication. Further $\Phi_t = (\varphi_{ij}(t))$ for $1 \leq i, j \leq K$ denotes a diagonal matrix of the following form:

$$\varphi_{ij}(t) = \begin{cases} 0 & for \ i \neq j \\ \varphi_{\alpha_i, \beta_i}(t) & for \ i = j \end{cases} \tag{11.7}$$

Since Φ_t is a diagonal matrix, multiplying Λ with Φ_t is basically a scaling of the row i of Λ with $\varphi_{\alpha_i,\beta_i}(t)$. Bluhm and Overbeck (2007a) further define $\varphi_{\alpha,\beta}(t)$ as normalized and increasing functions according to

$$\varphi_{\alpha,\beta}(t) = \frac{(1 - e^{-\alpha t})t^{\beta - 1}}{1 - e^{-\alpha}} \qquad \text{for } t \geq 0 \qquad (11.8)$$

The term "normalized" refers to the fact that $\varphi_{\alpha,\beta}(t) = 1$, so for $t = 1$ we obtain the same one-year migration matrix that was initially used for calculating the generator matrix Λ. Note that the term $(1 - e^{-\alpha t})$ of the function corresponds to the distribution function of an exponential distribution with parameter α, while the second term $t^{\beta - 1}$ is an adjustment term. For $\beta > 1$, it can be considered as time-accelerating, while for $\beta < 1$ as a time-slowing-down term. Finally, the term $1 - e^{-\alpha}$ in the denominator is simply a normalizing term to guarantee $\varphi_{\alpha,\beta}(t) = 1$. The authors point out that $\varphi_{\alpha,\beta}(t)$ has some resemblance with the Gamma distribution (Bluhm and Overbeck, 2007b). The function can then be used to define time-dependent generator matrices according to expression (11.2) that can be used to derive PD term structures. It can also be used to calculate migration matrices for any given time period $[0, t]$ according to

$$P_t = exp(t\Lambda_t) \qquad \text{for } t \geq 0. \qquad (11.9)$$

Based on expression (11.2), the time-dependent generator matrix Λ_t can be determined by the two vectors $(\alpha_1, \ldots, \alpha_K)$ and $(\beta_1, \ldots, \beta_K)$. As it was said before, PD term structures derived using a time-homogeneous Markov chain approach did not show the same shape as empirically observed cumulative PDs as they are provided, e.g., by the major rating agencies. However, using the time-dependent approach suggested above, the authors use empirically observed cumulative PDs for the different rating classes (Standard & Poor's, 2005) to calibrate the two vectors $(\alpha_1, \ldots, \alpha_K)$ and $(\beta_1, \ldots, \beta_K)$. This is done by minimizing the mean-squared distance between empirically observed cumulative PDs and the model PDs based on the time-dependent generator. Obviously, the parameters for the default state α_8 and β_8 are meaningless for the approach so they are set to $\alpha_8 = \beta_8 = 1$. For the other rating states, they report the optimized α- and β-vectors provided in Table 11.5.

The authors show that by using Standard & Poor's adjusted one-year migration matrix (Standard & Poor's, 2005), the corresponding approximated generator matrix Λ and the optimized α- and β-vectors for time-bending functions $\varphi_{\alpha,\beta}(t)$ given in Table 11.5, credit curves matching empirically observed multiple-year default frequencies can be matched. However, the authors point out that the approach may be quite sensitive

TABLE 11.5. Optimized α- and β-Vectors for Time-Bending Functions $\varphi_{\alpha,\beta}(t)$ According to Bluhm and Overbeck (2007a)

Rating State	α	β
AAA	0.34	0.89
AA	0.11	0.26
A	0.81	0.65
BBB	0.23	0.30
BB	0.32	0.56
B	0.23	0.40
CCC	2.15	0.46

to the model inputs and do not recommend it for extrapolation beyond the observed time horizon of cumulative default probabilities (Bluhm and Overbeck, 2007b).

Overall, the PD term structure obtained by a continuous-time homogeneous or nonhomogeneous Markov chain approach can be used in a straightforward manner to price single-named credit derivatives like credit default swaps or credit-linked notes. For the pricing of more complex credit derivatives like CDOs, portfolio or basket default swaps in addition to the PD term structure for individual obligors, a dependence structure needs to be introduced. We will further investigate the issue in the following section.

11.3   Modeling and Pricing of Collateralized Debt Obligations and Basket Credit Derivatives

In the previous section we were mainly concentrating on the use of credit migrations for deriving PD term structures that can be used for the pricing of single-named credit derivatives. Generally, for the extension of the approach to basket derivatives and CDOs, the nature of the introduced dependence structure is decisive. Hereby, various dependence structures can be assumed using copula models. In the following we will examine the use of transition matrices for the pricing of such complex instruments like CDOs and portfolio or basket default swaps. While the term structure of cumulative PDs might still be an essential tool for pricing these instruments, major focus also has to be put on the issue of dependence between the obligors, in particular dependent defaults.

Figure 11.6 illustrates the loss distribution for an exemplary loan portfolio dependent on the assumed degree of dependence. Herby, the Gaussian copula approach for dependent migrations discussed in Chapter 10 was assumed for modeling the dependent migrations with a copula correlation

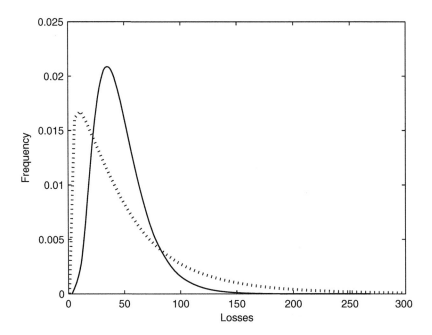

FIGURE 11.6. Loss distribution for different degrees of correlation $\rho = 0.1$ (*solid line*) and $\rho = 0.4$ (*dotted line*) for an exemplary loan portfolio. The loss distribution was simulated using the dependent migration approach suggested in Chapter 10.

parameter of $\rho = 0.1$ and $\rho = 0.4$. Obviously, the distribution with the higher copula correlation parameter yields a significantly higher probability for extreme losses in the portfolio.

In this section we will mainly focus on the use of credit migration matrices and derived PD term structures for determining the loss distribution and the effects on tranche losses in a CDO. Note that this approach somehow deviates from the very popular concept of implied correlations for CDOs. Before we illustrate the approach based on credit migrations, let us first briefly review the idea of implied correlations.

Implied correlations are a consequence of the the availability of market quotes of standard tranches like the iTraxx and the CDX. Quotes of standardized tranches also provide a market view of default correlation between the individual credits in the portfolio at different points in the capital structure. Often market participants are quoting rather the so-called implied correlation instead of the spread or the price of a CDO tranche. The implied correlation of a tranche is the uniform asset correlation number such that the fair or theoretical value of a tranche equals its market quote. Quoted correlations are always based on an underlying model assumption. The most common models used to price synthetic CDOs are currently variants of the one-factor Gaussian copula model (Li, 2000) which is often also referred to as the large pool model. Until recently, the concept could be considered as the industry standard approach for the pricing of basket credit derivatives.

The homogeneous large pool Gaussian copula model, or simply the large pool model, is a model very similar to the risk factor model applied in the new Basel Capital Accord that was described in Chapter 3. It generally employs the following assumptions:

- The default of an obligor is triggered when its asset value falls below a certain threshold.
- The asset value is driven by one standard normally distributed factor, which can be viewed to represent the market or the general state of economy, and its idiosyncratic risk.
- The portfolio consists of a large number of credits of uniform size, uniform recovery rate, and uniform probability of default.

Thus, we can describe the normalized asset value of the ith obligor x_i by a one-factor model:

$$x_i = \sqrt{\rho}m + \sqrt{1 - \rho}z_i \tag{11.10}$$

where m denotes the normalized return of the single factor and z_i is the idiosyncratic risk with $m, z_i \sim \Phi(0,1)$, and thus also $x_i \sim \Phi(0,1)$. $\sqrt{\rho}$ is the correlation of each obligor with the market factor and ρ the uniform pairwise correlation between the obligors. Let p denote the probability of default; thus, the threshold of default equals $\Phi^{-1}(p)$. Then we can denote the expected percentage portfolio loss given m according to the following formula (Li, 2000; Bluhm, 2003):

$$p(m) = \phi\left(\frac{\phi^{-1}(p) - \sqrt{\rho}m}{\sqrt{1 - \rho}}\right) \tag{11.11}$$

From this, an analytic expression for the portfolio loss distribution can be derived. In the most simple case of a recovery rate of 0%, the function of portfolio losses can be calculated using the following expression (Bluhm et al., 2003):

$$f_{p,\rho}(x) = \sqrt{\frac{1-\rho}{\rho}}exp[\frac{1}{2}(\phi^{-1}(x))^2 - \frac{1}{2\rho}(\phi^{-1}(p) - \sqrt{1 - \rho}\phi^{-1}(x))^2] \tag{11.12}$$

Based on the determined loss distribution of the portfolio, the expected losses for the individual tranches can also be determined. To illustrate the concept of implied correlations, let us consider the iTraxx Europe. It consists of the 125 most liquidly traded European CDS which are assigned to six different industry groups. The market agreed to quoted standard tranches which are responsible for 0% to 3%, 3% to 6%, 6% to 9%, 9% to 12%, and 12% to 22% of the losses. As these tranche quotes are a function of supply and demand, they reflect a market view of the correlation of the underlying portfolio. From this, the concept of implied correlation, or "the market view of correlation," emerged.

Mashal et al. (2004) define the implied correlation of a tranche as the uniform asset correlation number that makes the fair or theoretical value of a tranche equal to its market quote. In other words, Hull and White (2004), for example, define the implied correlation for a tranche as the correlation that causes the value of the tranche to be zero. Due to its analytical tractability and small number of parameters, the large pool model initially constituted the market standard for calculating implied correlation; see, for example, McGinty and Ahluwalia (2004a). The concept enables market participants to calculate and quote implied default correlation, to trade correlation, and to use implied default correlation for relative value considerations when comparing alternative investments in synthetic CDO tranches or to make use of implied correlation for arbitrage opportunities. For further reading on implied correlations, the distinction between compound and base correlations, the limitations of the approach, etc., we refer to Bluhm and Overbeck (2007b), Bluhm et al. (2003), Lehnert et al. (2006), McGinty and Ahluwalia (2004a,b), Willemann (2004), and the literature mentioned there. We should also point out that various extensions of the approach with different copulas have been suggested in the literature. References include Frey and McNeil (2003), Giesecke (2004), Laurent and Gregory (2005), Hull and White (2004), Mashal and Naldi (2002), Schönbucher and Schubert (2001), and Schönbucher (2003), just to mention some of them. Some of the approaches also focus on the consequences of the chosen copula on the pricing of CDOs. For example, Hull and White (2004) illustrate how various copula models can be generated by assuming different distributional assumptions within a factor model approach and find that a model using Student t-copulas fitting CDO provides a reasonable fit to market prices.

In several recent publications, the effect of credit migrations on credit derivative pricing has been examined by several authors, among others by Bielecki et al. (2003), Hrvatin et al. (2006), Hurd and Kuznetsov (2005), and Picone (2005). Hereby, Hrvatin et al. (2006) investigated CDO near-term rating stability of different CDO tranches depending on different factors. Next to the granularity of the portfolio, in particular, credit migrations in the underlying reference portfolio are considered to have an impact on the stability of CDO tranche ratings. Pointing out the influence of changes in credit migrations, Picone (2005) developed a time-inhomogeneous intensity model for valuing cash-flow CDOs. His approach explicitly incorporates the credit rating of the firms in the collateral portfolio by applying a set of transition matrices, calibrated to historical default probabilities. Finally, Hurd and Kuznetsov (2005) show that credit basket derivatives can be

modeled in a parsimonious and computationally efficient manner within
the affine Markov chain framework for multifirm credit migration, while
Bielecki et al. (2003) concentrate on dependent migrations and defaults in
a Markovian market model and the effects on the valuation of basket credit
derivatives.

In this section we will suggest an alternative approach using a conditional continuous-time rating migration model with stable risk factors that
can be used for CDO evaluation purposes. The approach is quite similar to
the continuous time-inhomogeneous Markov chain approach suggested in
Bluhm and Overbeck (2007b) or Picone (2005). The model is based on the
adjustment methods suggested in Chapter 9 and a continuous time simulation approach as it was introduced in Chapter 5 for modeling the transitions
within a period. We point out that the model is typically designed for the
evaluation of CDOs consisting of SME loans or companies that are not
traded on the stock market. Usually for such companies only quarterly or
even yearly *data* on asset returns or changes in creditworthiness are available. Therefore, it is difficult to model asset correlations of such companies
based on a systematic risk factor like, e.g., returns of a stock market index.
So in this section we rather rely on the use of macroeconomic variables to
improve the estimates on forecasted default probabilities for SMEs.

11.3.1 Estimation of Macroeconomic Risk Factors

This section briefly describes a new model with conditional rating migrations in a continuous-time framework for determining the loss distribution
of a CDO. Since usually CDOs issued by banks consist of loans having a
maturity of several years, the model will make use of a multiperiod rating
migration model and not consider only a one-year time horizon. Therefore,
multiperiod simulations of the considered risk factors will be needed. In
comparison to the approach suggested in Chapter 9, we will consider an
extension of the model allowing for skewness and heavy tails in the risk
factors. As the natural extension of the Gaussian distribution, the class of
α-stable is used to describe the return distribution of the considered risk
factors. Fur further reading on α-stable distributions and their applications
in financial models and credit risk, we refer to Rachev and Mittnik (1999)
and Rachev et al. (2001). Thus, we suggest the macroeconomic variables
available on a quarterly or yearly basis to follow a stable ARMA(p, q)
process:

$$X_{i,t} = c_0 + \sum_{j=1}^{p} a_j X_{i,t-j} + \sum_{j=1}^{q} b_j \varepsilon_{t-j} + \varepsilon_t, \quad t \in \mathbb{N}.$$

The residuals of the process follow an α-stable distribution with $\varepsilon_t \sim$
$S_\alpha(\beta, \sigma, 0)$. For variables available on a daily basis, we propose an ARMAX-
process with α-stable GARCH-residuals (see Menn and Rachev, 2004), as

TABLE 11.6. Parameters of Fit of the Stable
Distribution to VIX Returns

VIX	1.5833	0.0777	0.6555	−0.0032

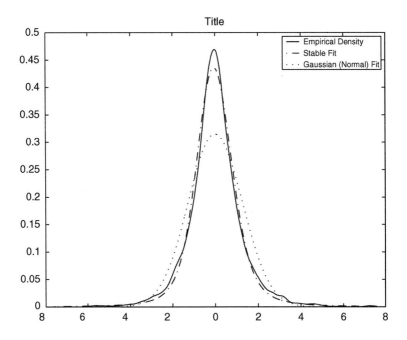

FIGURE 11.7. Fit of stable distribution to returns of VIX.

an adequate discrete-time stochastic process for modeling the evolution of
future outcomes of the variable $Y = (Y_t)_{t \in \mathbb{N}}$.

$$Y_t = c_0 + \sum_{j=1}^{d} c_j X_t^{(j)} + \sum_{j=1}^{n} a_j Y_{t-j} + \sum_{j=1}^{m} b_j \varepsilon_{t-j} + \varepsilon_t \quad t \in \mathbb{N} \qquad (11.13)$$

Consider, for example, the CBOE volatility index providing extraordinarily
good forecasts for recovery rates and default probabilities of PDs for speculative grade loans. Investigating the assumption of normally distributed
returns for the variables, we observe phenomena like heavy tails and excess
kurtosis for this variable. Figure 11.7 illustrates stable and Gaussian fit to
the volatility index for the period from 01.01.1990 to 31.12.2003. We find
that returns of the variable VIX exhibit heavy tails, and using maximum
likelihood estimation, we obtain the following parameters:

With $\alpha = 1.5833$ we observe an index of stability $\alpha << 2$. This indicates the necessity of a stochastic process that can also capture heavy tails in the return distribution. As a consequence, the proposed ARMAX model with GARCH-residuals can be considered as an adequate model for this risk factor.

In Chapter 9 we described the use of a continuous credit change indicator in each rating class $Y_{i,t}$, or in speculative grade and investment grade rating classes, respectively, to be dependent on macroeconomic variables X_{t-1} of the previous periods, see Trueck (2008). Thus, based on the estimated model and simulated macroeconomic risk factors, we propose a model

$$Y_{i,t} = c_0 + \sum_{j=1}^{d} c_j X_{t-1} + \varepsilon_t \quad t \in \mathbb{N}$$

for the credit change indicator for rating class i. The conditioning of the migration matrix is conducted using the procedure described in Chapter 9. As optimality criteria for the numerical adjustment procedure, we suggest the use of the risk-sensitive difference indices suggested in Chapter 6.

11.3.2 Modeling of Conditional Migrations and Recovery Rates

For simulation of the loss distribution, we use a so-called *conditional continuous-time rating migration model*, similar to the model suggested in Bluhm and Overbeck (2007b). Note, however, that in our approach the adjustment is made according to the credit change indicator that is based on observed macroeconomic conditions. Further, note that the dependence enters via the shift in credit migration and an additionally introduced dependence based on dependent migrations according to a Gaussian or Student t copula model. Based on an average transition matrix P_{avg} and estimated credit change indicators $Y_{i,t}$ for time t, we adjust the transition matrix using one of the risk-sensitive optimality criteria suggested in Chapter 6. As a result conditional migration matrices $\hat{P}_t$ are obtained. The next step is to calculate the corresponding conditional generator matrix for period t $\hat{\Lambda}_t$:

$$\hat{\Lambda}_t = \begin{pmatrix} \hat{\lambda}_{11} & \hat{\lambda}_{12} & \cdots & \hat{\lambda}_{1K} \\ \hat{\lambda}_{21} & \hat{\lambda}_{22} & \cdots & \hat{\lambda}_{2K} \\ \cdots & \cdots & \cdots & \cdots \\ \hat{\lambda}_{K-1,1} & \hat{\lambda}_{K-1,2} & \cdots & \hat{\lambda}_{K-1,K} \\ 0 & 0 & \cdots & 0 \end{pmatrix} \tag{11.14}$$

where $\hat{\lambda}_{ij} \geq 0$, for all i, j and $\hat{\lambda}_{ii} = -\sum_{\substack{j=1 \\ j \neq i}}^{K} \hat{\lambda}_{ij}$, for $i = 1, \ldots, K$ and the off-diagonal elements representing the intensities for a jump to rating j from rating i. Based on the forecasts of the conditional migration matrix, we obtain different generators for each time period. Therefore, simulations of credit migrations will also be based on the forecasts for the macroeconomic situation.

For modeling the recovery rates we will use an ex-ante regression model that can also be used for forecasting recovery rates of future periods. The main input variables for the model were the volatility index (VIX) and some macroeconomic variables like, for example, the weekly spreads on investment grade AA bonds. It should be pointed out that the recovery rates obtained by this method are estimates for average recovery rates in a market.

11.3.3   Some Empirical Results

In the following we will apply the suggested macroeconomic continuous-time rating migration model. We will illustrate preliminary results for the suggested models for evaluation of an exemplary CDO consisting of loans of SMEs. We point out that further research on real CDO markets will be necessary.

The portfolio consists of loans of mainly small and medium-sized enterprises. Further, due to political reasons the portfolio is divided into two subportfolios of different structure. In the following we will apply the developed model to determine the CDO loss distribution under different market scenarios. The total volume of the considered CDO is assumed to be 300 million Euros. The portfolio actually consists of two subportfolios. The first one includes greater exposures for 30 loans, with an exposure of approximately 9 − 11 million Euros each. The first subportfolio consists of investment grade companies only. Let the target distribution of ratings for the considered subportfolio be as displayed in Table 11.7.

The second subportfolio consists of 30 small firms of speculative grade rating class BB. For simplicity, we assume that the average exposure for the second subportfolio is approximately 1 million Euros for each loan. The portfolio is refinanced in the so-called build-up phase through an equity tranche of 45 million Euros (15% of the target volume) and a credit line divided into a mezzanine and senior line. The equity tranche itself is divided into a so-called first loss piece of 15 million Euros and a second loss piece of 30 million Euros taken by the second loss investors. For the sake of completeness we point out that one third of the equity tranche as well as

TABLE 11.7. Target Distribution of Ratings for the First Subportfolio of the SME CDO

Rating	AAA	AA	A	BBB
No. of firms	0	5	10	15
Average Exposure (Million Euros)	0	11	10	9

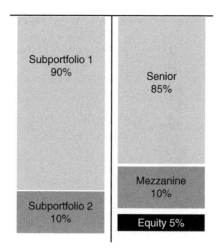

FIGURE 11.8. Structure of the considered CDO.

5% of the total volume is taken by the bank. The structure of the portfolio is displayed in Figure 11.8.

After the build-up phase of the portfolio, a maturity horizon of eight years is assumed before the debt will be paid back by the obligors. Making allowance for the high numbers of obligors in subinvestment grade rating classes, we should expect several defaults to happen. Also the loss distribution of the CDO will be very much dependent on the macroeconomic situation at the issuance time. In the following we provide some simulation results for the loss distribution based on the introduced multiperiod continuous-time migration model. Let us first illustrate the effect of the initial situation for the business cycle when the CDO is issued.

Figure 11.9 illustrates a typical loss distribution for the portfolio under an average macroeconomic scenario. We also provided the quantiles of the loss distribution in order to illustrate the probability for the equity tranche to be completely eaten away as well as the probabilities that the mezzanine or even the senior tranche will be affected. The mean loss of the considered CDO is 9.93 million Euros, while the 0.5-quantile is 9.1 million Euros. The difference is due to the fact that the loss distribution is skewed to the right. We obtain a skewness parameter of $\beta = 0.81$ and a kurtosis of $k = 3.61$. We find that under the considered macroeconomic scenario the probability for the equity tranche to be eaten completely and thus the probability for a mezzanine investor to be hit is approximately 20%. The observed maximum of the loss distribution running 10,000 simulations with our multiperiod continuous-time migration model gives a value of 38.2 million Euros. We conclude that under the average market scenario the senior tranche of the CDO was never hit.

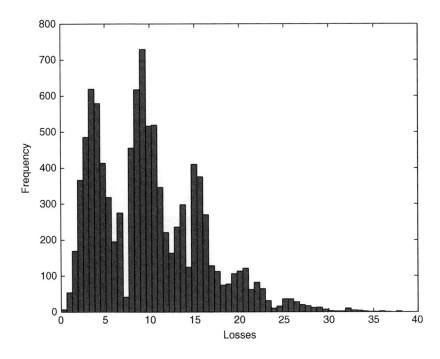

FIGURE 11.9. Sample loss distribution for the portfolio based on an average economic scenario situation.

Figure 11.10 illustrates how based on the obtained loss distribution the effect and finally credit spreads for the tranches can be obtained. The loss in a tranche is a piecewise linear function that can be determined in a straight-forward manner. We illustrate the procedure for the mezzanine tranche of the portfolio. For losses below 15 million Euros investors in the mezza-nine tranche will not be affected at all. Beginning from 15 million the loss in the tranche increases linearly until the portfolio loss reaches 45 million Euros. In this case the complete tranche is eaten and the senior tranche will be affected. Thus, dependent on the loss distribution, we will be able to determine expected and unexpected losses in each tranche.

For a scenario where the CDO was initially issued in an expansion of the economy, we obtain other results; see Figure 11.11 and Table 11.8. Now the mean loss of the distribution is 4.15 million Euros while the 0.5-quantile under an initial economic expansion scenario is 2.8 million Euros. This is due to the extremely right-skewed and leptokurtic distribution with $\beta = 1.38$ and $k = 5.05$. To exceed a loss of 15 million Euros affecting the mezzanine tranche has a probability of only 1.1%. We obtain a maximum of the loss distribution of 26.3 million Euros. Effects on tranche spreads will be substantial comparing the average macroeconomic scenario and the expansion scenario.

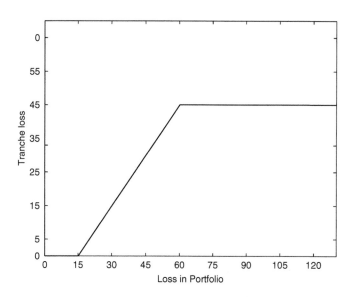

FIGURE 11.10. Relationship between portfolio loss and mezzanine tranche loss.

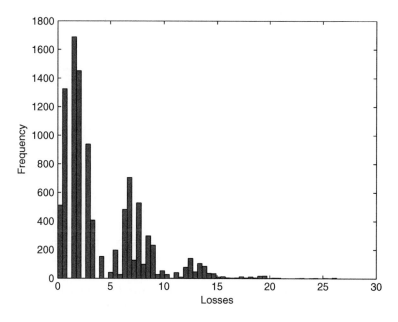

FIGURE 11.11. Sample loss distribution for the CDO under an expansion scenario of the macroeconomic situation.

TABLE 11.8. Selected Quantiles of the CDO Loss Distribution According to the Tranche Specification Under Average Macroeconomic Scenario

Quantile	0.5	0.802	0.95	0.99	Max
Loss	9.1 million	15 million	21 million	27 million	38.2 million

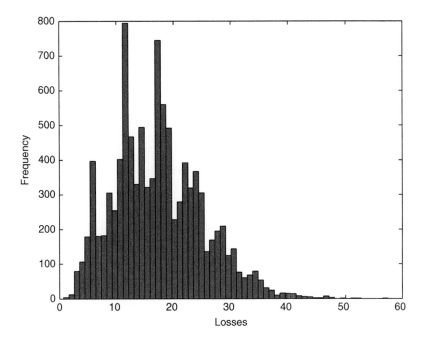

FIGURE 11.12. Sample loss distribution for the CDO under an expansion scenario of the macroeconomic situation.

Finally, Figure 11.12 displays a sample loss distribution for the CDO when it is issued under a recession scenario of the macroeconomic situation. We find the distribution to be less skewed $\beta = 0.5382$ and with a kurtosis of $k = 3.16$ close to that of the normal. However, the probability for the mezzanine tranche to be hit is approximately 52%, while for the first time there is also a probability of 15 basis points to hit the senior tranche. The maximum loss occurred was 57.5 million Euros denoting a loss in the senior tranche of more than 12.5 million Euros. Even the investors in the most secure tranche could be affected by the losses.

We conclude that the suggested multiperiod continuous-time migration model based on adjustments of the transition matrix according to business cycle effects is a model that can also be used for calculating CDO

TABLE 11.9. Selected Quantiles of the CDO Loss Distribution According to the Tranche Specification Under Initial Economic Expansion and Recession Scenario

Quantile	0.418	0.5	0.95	0.99	0.9985	Max
Loss (rec)	15 million	16.8 million	30.8 million	37.1 million	45 million	57.5 million
Loss (exp)	2.1 million	2.8 million	12.6 million	15.4 million	20.7 million	26.3 million

TABLE 11.10. Descriptive Statistics for CDO Loss Distribution Dependent on Initial Macroeconomic Scenario

	Mean	σ	Skewness	Kurtosis
Average Scenario	9.9345	5.8811	0.8115	3.6117
Expansion Scenario	4.1512	3.8536	1.3824	5.0523
Recession	17.2916	7.7167	0.5382	3.1646

tranche loss distributions. Due to correlation with a systematic risk factor, the model has the crucial advantage over a one-factor model that rating migrations to nondefault states can be included. The model further explicitly showed the effect of the initial stage of the economy when the CDO was issued. A next step would be to use the model for CDO pricing to examine its performance on real market data.

11.4 Pricing Step-Up Bonds

Another credit derivative where the use of historical or risk-neutral transition matrices is of particular help is so-called step-up bonds. For these instruments, the coupon depends on the issuer's rating or possibly also on the rating of its long-term debt. To compensate investors for a possible decline in the credit quality, the bonds offer the following feature if the rating of the issuer deteriorates and hits a predefined level, the coupon rises with a predefined number of basis points. In the following we will illustrate how transition matrices might be used to price step-up bonds, i.e., corporate bonds with a step-up provision. In our analysis we will follow the methods and techniques outlined in Lando and Mortensen (2005) and Houweling et al. (2004). Both studies concentrate on telecom bonds in the Euro zone. While Houweling et al. (2004) focus on a comparison of different valuation models, Lando and Mortensen (2005) investigate to what extent step-up bonds are priced at a discount relative to fixed-coupon bonds. In the following, we will briefly illustrate how historical and derived risk-neutral transition matrices can be used to price bonds with such step-up provisions.

11.4.1 Step-Up Bonds

Step-up bonds offer a way of linking credit quality of the issuer of a bond to cash flows. They can be considered as a special case of credit-sensitive notes, which were first issued in the late 1980s. Recently, they have been popular in particular in the telecom sector with quite a large volume of issuance. An advantage of this high volume is that the secondary market for these bonds is quite liquid. As mentioned above, the coupon of a step-up bond is dependent on the issuer's rating or the rating of its long-term debt and rises when the rating deteriorates and hits a predefined level. Depending on the type of step-up coupon, the coupon can rise even a consecutive number of times if the rating further deteriorates. On the other hand, for many step-up bonds, the coupon is also reduced if the issuer's rating improves again. This is then the so-called step-down feature. Note, however, that for all types of step-up bonds in the market so far, the coupon can never go below the original level at issuance.

The different step-up conditions can be used for a classification of the bonds. Hereby, a possible discriminating condition of the step-up bonds is the definition of a rating change: whether both Moody's and S&P have to downgrade the issuer or only one of them before the step-up trigger is hit. Another discriminating condition can be based on whether the coupon can step up and down or only step up. Further criteria could be the rating-trigger level and the number of basis points of the step-up. For more on the classification and definition of step-up bonds, see, e.g., McAdie et al. (2000) or Marchakitus et al. (2001). In the following we will describe the basic framework that can be used to price step-up bonds based on a historical migration matrix and observed market credit spreads (Houweling et al., 2004; Lando and Mortensen, 2005).

11.4.2 Pricing of Step-Up Bonds

In this section we will briefly describe the approach of Houweling et al. (2004) that can be used to price step-up bonds. Generally for pricing of a bond, it is assumed that the value of the bond equals the sum of the discounted, expected cash flows. The difference between a plain vanilla bond and a step-up bond's coupons is that in the latter case the coupons are a function of the issuer's rating. Therefore, it is necessary to model the issuer's rating transition process. Hereby, the company's credit rating R_t is initially modeled as a Markov chain on a finite state space $S = 1, \ldots, K$ under the historical probability measure. Since we are interested in pricing the bond, the migration process should be modeled under the equivalent martingale measure such that the Jarrow et al. (1997) model can be used as an appropriate framework. Following the described model in Section 8.1, it is therefore assumed the existence of a unique equivalent martingale measure makes all default-free and defaultable bond prices martingales. Further, the rating process is assumed to be independent of default-free interest rates. As pointed out in Chapter 8, various techniques have been suggested to calculate risk-neutral transition matrices from actually observed real-world ones. Houweling et al. (2004) follow an approach similar to the one suggested by Kijima and Komoribayashi (1998); however, they model "cumulative" probabilities $\tilde{q}_{ij}(t,T)$ instead of the usually suggested "forward" probabilities $\tilde{q}_{ij}(t,t+1)$; see, e.g., Jarrow et al. (1997), Kijima and Komoribayashi (1998), and Lando and Mortensen (2005).

Therefore, the entries of the risk-neutral transition matrix $\tilde{Q}(t,T)$ are derived by

$$\tilde{q}_{ij}(t,T) = \begin{cases} \pi(t,T)q_{ij}(t,T) & \text{for } j \neq K \\ 1 - \pi(t,T)(1 - q_{iK}(t,T)) & \text{for } j = K \end{cases} \tag{11.15}$$

for some risk premium $\pi(t,T)$ that can be calculated by

$$\pi(t,T) = \frac{1 - \tilde{q}_{R_t,K}(t,T)}{1 - q_{R_t,K}(t,T)} \tag{11.16}$$

Note that hereby the authors use only one risk premium for all rating categories because each Euro-denominated telecom issuer does not cover the full rating spectrum. Therefore, only the risk premium derived from the issuer's current rating can be calculated and is applied to all rating states. The determined risk-neutral transition matrices are then used for the valuation of the step-up bonds.

Let us therefore consider a step-up and step-down bond with n remaining coupon payments at times $t_j (j = 2, \ldots, n)$ and a face value of 1. Of course, the coupon payment j is made only if the bond has not defaulted before t_j. Dependent on the rating r at time t_j, the coupon payment is equal to c_r for $r = 1, \ldots, K$. Further, the step-up bond's principal amount is paid at maturity t_n, again only if the issuer has not defaulted beforehand. In case the issuer does default before maturity, a constant recovery rate δ is paid at the default time. Note that this assumption implies that the recovery rate δ applies to the principal only and not to the coupons.

Then the risk-neutral valuation principle is applied to the cash flows from coupons, principal, and recovery rate, yielding the price of the step-up bond at time t. Assuming that default can happen only at the coupon payment dates, the value of a rating-triggered step-up and step-down bond can be determined according to the following expression [see Houweling et al. (2004) for the derivation of the expression]:

$$B(t, \mathbf{t}, \mathbf{c}) = p(t, t_1)(1 - \tilde{q}_{R_t, K}(t, t_1))c_{R_{t_0}}$$

$$+ \sum_{j=2}^{n} \left[p(t, t_j) \sum_{k=1}^{K} \tilde{q}_{R_t, k}(t, t_{j-1})(1 - \tilde{q}_{k, K}(t_j - 1, t_j))c_k \right]$$

$$+ p(t, t_n)(1 - \tilde{q}_{R_t, K}(t, t_n))$$

$$+ \sum_{j=1}^{n} p(t, t_j)(\tilde{q}_{R_t, K}(t, t_j) - \tilde{q}_{R_t, K}(t, t_{j-1}))\delta \qquad (11.17)$$

In comparison the pricing equation for a similar plain vanilla bond without a step-up or step-down provision would be

$$B^{PV}(t, \mathbf{t}, \mathbf{c}) = \sum_{j=1}^{n} p(t, t_j)(1 - \tilde{q}_{R_t, K}(t, t_j))c$$

$$+ p(t, t_n)(1 - \tilde{q}_{R_t, K}(t, t_n))$$

$$+ \sum_{j=1}^{n} p(t, t_j)(\tilde{q}_{R_t, K}(t, t_j) - \tilde{q}_{R_t, K}(t, t_{j-1}))\delta \quad (11.18)$$

An alternative method is suggested by McAdie et al. (2000) or Fumagalli and Tauren (2001). The authors suggest using the zero-coupon curve of the telecom company to discount expected coupons. In their application, however, the expectation is calculated with historical transition probabilities instead of using risk-neutral ones. Using the issuers time-t discount factor $v(t, T)$ for time T and assuming that the first coupon payment is known, the pricing equation becomes

$$B^H(t, \mathbf{t}, \mathbf{c}) = v(t, t_1)c_{R_{t_0}} + \sum_{j=2}^{n} [v(t, t_j) \sum_{k=1}^{K} \tilde{q}_{R_t, k}(t, t_{j-1})c_k] + v(t, t_n)$$

For empirical results of the approach, we refer to the original paper by Houweling et al. (2004) and also to Lando and Mortensen (2005). Overall, the step-up bonds are one of the credit derivatives where rating changes and credit migrations to another state are of particular interest. As mentioned before, one should keep in mind that important information related to a single company might be ignored when transition matrices are used to price credit derivatives. By using the rating of the company and the corresponding migration probabilities as input variables, one measures the dynamics of the rating class but not those of the individual firm. Unfortunately, many characteristics of a company affecting the default process or rating changes may not be captured by the rating class. To overcome this problem, one might decide to consider only the bond of the particular issuer and conduct the adjustment based on the observed spread and implied default probability.

Bibliography

Albanese, C., Chen, O., 2006. Implied migrations rates from credit barrier models. *Journal of Banking and Finance* 30, 607–626.

Alessandrini, F., 1999. Credit risk, interest rate risk, and the business cycle. *Journal of Fixed Income* 9(2), 42–53.

Allen, L., Saunders, A., 2003. A survey of cyclical effects in credit risk measurement model. BIS Working Paper 126.

Altman, E., 1968. Financial ratios, discriminant analysis, and the prediction of corporate bankruptcy. *Journal of Finance* 23(4), 589–609.

Altman, E., 1983. *Corporate Financial Distress. A Complete Guide to Predicting, Avoiding, and Dealing with Bankruptcy*. John Wiley & Sons Inc., New York.

Altman, E., Brady, B., Resti, A., Sironi, A., 2005. The link between default and recovery rates: Theory, empirical evidence and implications. *Journal of Business* 78(6), 2203–2227.

Altman, E., Kao, D., 1992a. The implications of corporate bond rating drift. *Financial Analysts Journal* 48(3), 64–75.

Altman, E., Kao, D., 1992b. Rating drift in high yield bonds. *Journal of Fixed Income* 1(4), 15–20.

Altman, E., Kishore, V., 1996. Almost everything you wanted to know about recoveries on defaulted bonds. *Financial Analysts Journal* 52(6), 57–64.

Altman, E., Narayanan, P., 1997. An international survey of business failure classification models. *Financial Markets, Instruments and Institutions* 6(2), 1–57.

Altman, E., Rijken, H., 2006. A point-in-time perspective on through-the-cycle ratings. *Financial Analysts Journal* 62(1), 54–70.

Altman, E., Saunders, A., 1998. Credit risk measurement: Developments over the last 20 years. *Journal of Banking and Finance* 21, 1721–1742.

Amato, J., Furfine, C., 2004. Are credit ratings procyclical? *Journal of Banking and Finance* 28(11), 2641–2677.

Ammann, E., 2002. *Credit risk valuation: Methods, Models and Applications*. Springer.

Anderson, T., Goodman, L., 1957. Statistical inference about Markov chains. *Annals of Mathematical Statistics* 28(1).

Araten, M., Angbazo, L., 1997. *Roots of Transition Matrices: Application to Settlement Risk*. Chase Manhattan Bank, Practical Paper.

Araten, M., Jacobs Jr., M., Varshney, P., Pellegrino, C., 2004. An internal ratings migration study. *RMA Journal* (April), 92–97.

Arvanitis, A., Gregory, J., 2001. *Credit—The Complete Guide to Pricing, Hedging and Risk Management*. Risk Books, London.

Arvanitis, A., Gregory, J., Laurent, J. -P., 1999. Building models for credit spreads. *Journal of Derivatives* 6(3), 27–43.

Atiya, A., 1997. Bankruptcy prediction for credit risk using neural networks: A survey and new results. *IEEE Transactions on Neural Networks* 12(4), 929–935.

Balcaena, S., Oogh, H., 2006. 35 years of studies on business failure: An overview of the classic statistical methodologies and their related problems. *The British Accounting Review* 38(1), 63–93.

Bangia, A., Diebold, F., Kronimus, A., Schagen, C., Schuermann, T., 2002. Ratings migration and the business cycle, with application to credit portfolio stress testing. *Journal of Banking and Finance* 26, 445–474.

Bank of Japan, 2005. *Advancing Credit Risk Management through Internal Rating Systems*. Report.

Basel Committee on Banking Supervision, 2001. *The New Basel Capital Accord*, Second Consultative Document.

Basel Committee on Banking Supervision, 2004. *The New Basel Capital Accord, International Convergence of Capital Measurement and Capital Standards: A Revised Framework*. BIS Working paper.

Basel Committee on Banking Supervision, 2005. *Studies on Validation of Internal Rating Systems*. BIS Working paper 14.

Beaver, W., 1966. Financial ratios as predictors of failure. *Journal of Accounting Research, Supplement on Empirical Research in Accounting* 4, 77–111.

Belkin, B., Forest, L., Suchower, S., 1998a. The effect of systematic credit risk on loan portfolio value-at-risk and loan pricing. CreditMetrics Monitor (1st Quarter).

Belkin, B., Forest, L., Suchower, S., 1998b. A one-parameter representation of credit risk and transition matrices. CreditMetrics Monitor (3rd Quarter), 46–56.

Bielecki, T., Crepey, S., Jeanblanc, M., Rutkowski, M., 2003. *Valuation of Basket Credit Derivatives in the Credit Migrations Framework*. Working paper, Universite D'Evry.

Bielecki, T., Rutkowski, M., 2002. *Credit risk: Modeling, valuation and hedging*. Springer Finance, Berlin.

Billingsley, P., 1961. Statistical methods in Markov chains. *Annals of Mathematical Statistics* 32(1), 12–40.

Billingsley, R., Lamy, R., Marr, M., Thompson, G., 1985. Split ratings and bond reoffering yields. *Financial Management* 14(2), 59–65.

Bluhm, C., 2003. *CDO Modeling: Techniques, Examples and Applications*. Working paper, Hypovereinsbank.

Bluhm, C., Overbeck, L., 2007a. Calibration of pd term structures: To be Markov or not to be. *Risk* (November).

Bluhm, C., Overbeck, L., 2007b. *Structured Credit Portfolio Analysis, Baskets and CDOs*. Chapman & Hall/CRC Financial Mathematics Series.

Bluhm, C., Overbeck, L., Wagner, C., 2003. *An Introduction to Credit Risk Modeling.* Chapman & Hall/CRC Financial Mathematics Series.

Cantor, R., Packer, F., Cole, K., 2005. Split ratings and the pricing of credit risk. *Journal of Fixed Income* 7(3), 72–82.

Cherubini, U., Luciano, E., Vecchiato, W., 2004. *Copula Methods in Finance.* Wiley Finance Series, New York.

Christensen, J., Hansen, E., Lando, D., 2004. Confidence sets for continuous time rating transition probabilities. *Journal of Banking and Finance* 28, 2575–2602.

Cifuentes, A., Efrat, I., Gluck, J., Murphy, E., 1998. Buying and selling credit risk. Credit derivatives. Applications for risk management, investment and portfolio optimization, *Risk Magazine.*

Cossin, D., Pirotte, H., 2001. *Advanced Credit Risk Analysis—Financial Approaches and Mathematical Models to Assess, Price and Manage Credit Risk.* Wiley, New York.

Cowell, F., Racheva, B., Trueck, S., 2007. *Recent Advances in Credit Risk Management.* Physica, Heidelberg.

Credit Suisse Financial Products, 1997. *Credit Risk$^+$: A Credit Risk Management Framework.*

Credit Suisse Financial Products, 1998. *Credit Risk$^+$: A Credit Risk Management Framework.* Credit Suisse, technical report.

CreditPortfolioView, 1998. CreditPortfolioView—Approach Document and Users Manual. McKinsey, technical report.

Crosbie, P., Bohn, J., 2002. *Modeling Default Risk.* Working paper, KMV Corporation.

Crouhy, M., Jarrow, R., Turnbull, S., 2008. The subprime credit crisis of 07, Working paper.

Dartsch, A., Weinrich, G., 2002. Das gesamtprojekt internes rating. In: Hofmann, G. (Ed.), *Basel II und MaK—Vorgaben, bankinterne Verfahren, Bewertungen.* Bankakademie-Verlag, pp. 131–145.

Davis, M., Lo, V., 2001. Infectious defaults. *Quantitative Finance* 1, 382–387.

Dhar, V., Stein, R., 1997. *Seven Methods of Transforming Corporate Data into Business Intelligence.* Prentice-Hall, Inc., Upper Saddle River, NJ, USA.

Dietsch, M., Petey, J., 2004. Should SME exposures be treated as retail or corporate exposures? A comparative analysis of default probabilities and asset correlations in French and German SMEs. *Journal of Banking and Finance* 28, 773–788.

Duffie, D., Garleanu, N., 2001. Risk and valuation of collateralized debt obligations. *Financial Analysts Journal* 57(1), 41–59.

Duffie, D., Singleton, K., 1999. Modeling term structures of defaultable bonds. *Review of Financial Studies* (12), 687–720.

Duffie, D., Singleton, K., 2003. *Credit Risk: Pricing Measurement and Management.* Princeton University Press, Princeton, NJ.

Düllmann, K., Scheule, H., 2003. *Determinants of the Asset Correlations of German Corporations and Implications for Regulatory Capital.* Working paper, University of Regensburg.

Efron, B., Tibshirani, R., 1993. *An Introduction to the Bootstrap.* Chapman & Hall, New York.

Elizalde, A., 2006. *Credit Risk Models II: Structural Models.* CEMFI Working paper No. 0606.

Embrechts, P., McNeil, A., Straumann, D., 1999. Correlation and dependence in risk management: Properties and pitfalls. In: *Risk Management: Value at Risk and Beyond*, ed. Dempster, M. Kluwer Academic Publishers, Norwell, MA, USA.

Engelmann, B., Hayden, E., Tasche, D., January 2003. Testing rating accuracy. *Risk* (16)1, 82–86.

European Central Bank, 2004. Market dynamics associated with credit ratings: A literature review. *Occasional Paper Series* (16), 1–37.

Fabozzi, F., 2006a. *Bond Markets, Analysis and Strategies*, 6th edition. Prentice-Hall.

Fabozzi, F., 2006b. *Fixed Income Mathematics*, 4th edition. McGraw-Hill.

Finger, C., 2001. The one-factor CreditMetrics model in the New Basel Capital Accord. *RiskMetrics Journal* 2(1), 9–18.

Fitzpatrick, 1932. Comparison of ratios of successful industrial enterprises with those of failed firms. *Certified Public Accountant* (October), 598–605.

Fons, J. S., 1994. Using default rates to model the term structure of credit risk. *Financial Analysts Journal* (Sept-Oct), 25–33.

Frey, R., McNeil, A., 2003. Dependent defaults in models of portfolio credit risk. *Journal of Risk* 6(1), 59–92.

Frydman, H., 2005. Estimation in the mixture of Markov chains moving with different speeds. *Journal of the American Statistical Association* 100 (Sept), 1046–1053.

Frydman, H., Schuermann, T., 2008. Credit rating dynamics and Markov mixture models. *Journal of Banking and Finance* (Forthcoming).

Fumagalli, R., Tauren, M., 2001. *Valuing bonds with step-up coupons.* European credit research, credit strategy, Schroder Salomon Smith Barney.

Gagliardini, P., Gourieroux, C., 2005a. Migration correlation: Definition and efficient estimation. *Journal of Banking and Finance* 29, 865–894.

Gagliardini, P., Gourieroux, C., 2005b. Stochastic migration models with application to corporate risk. *Journal of Financial Econometrics* 3(2), 188–226.

Geweke, J., Marshall, R. G. Z., 1986. Mobility indices in continuous time Markov chains. *Econometrica* 54(6), 1407–1423.

Giesecke, K., 2004. Correlated default with incomplete information. *Journal of Banking and Finance* 28, 1521–1545.

Glasserman, P., 1992. Derivative estimates from simulation of continuous-time Markov chains. *Operations Research*, 40(2), 292–308.

Goodman, L., 1958. Simplified runs tests and likelihood ratio tests for Markov chains. *Biometrica* 45, 181–197.

Gordy, M., 2002. *A Risk-Factor Model Foundation for Ratings Based Capital Rules.* Working paper, Board of Governors of the Federal Reserve System.

Greene, H., 1993. *Econometric Analysis.* Prentice-Hall, New York.

Gupton, G., Finger, C., Bhatia, M., 1997. *A Jump-Diffusion Approach to Modeling Credit Risk and Valuing Defautable Securities.* Credit Metrics—technical document, JP Morgan & Co. Incorporated.

Hamerle, A., Liebig, T., Scheule, H., 2004. Forecasting credit portfolio risk. *Deutsche Bundesbank Discussion Paper Series: Banking and Financial Studies* 1.

Hamilton, D., James, J., Webber, N., 2002. *Copula Methods and the Analysis of Credit Risk.* Working paper.

Helwege, J., Kleiman, P., 1997. Understanding aggregate default rates of high-yield bonds. *Journal of Fixed Income* 7(1), 55–61.

Henneke, J., Trueck, S., 2006. Asset correlations and capital requirements for SMEs under the revised Basel II framework. *Banks and Bank Systems* 1(1).

Hosmer, D., Lemeshow, S., 1989. *Applied Logistic Regression.* Wiley, New York.

Houweling, P., Mentink, A., Vorst, T., 2004. Valuing Euro rating-triggered step-up telecom bonds. *Journal of Derivatives* 11 (3), 63–80.

Hrvatin, R., Neugebauer, M., Stoyle, G., 2006. The analysis of short-term rating migration in synthetic CDOs. *The Journal of Structured Finance* (Fall).

Hu, Y., Kiesel, R., Perraudin, J., 2002. The estimation of transition matrices for sovereign credit ratings. *Journal of Banking and Finance* 26, 1383–1406.

Hull, J., White, A., 2004. Valuation of a CDO and an nth to default CDS without Monte Carlo simulation. *Journal of Derivatives* 12(2), 8–23.

Hurd, T., Kuznetsov, A., 2005. *Fast CDO Computations in the Affine Markov Chain Model.* Working Paper, McMaster University, Canada.

Israel, R., Rosenthal, J., Wei, J., 2000. Finding generators for Markov chains via empirical transition matrices, with application to credit ratings. *Mathematical Finance* 11, 245–265.

Jackson, R., Murray, A., 2004. Alternative input-output matrix updating formulations. *Economic Systems Research* 16, 135–148.

Jacobson, T., Lind, J., Roszbach, K., 2006. Internal ratings systems, implied credit risk and the consistency of banks' risk classification policies. *Journal of Banking and Finance* 30, 1899–1926.

Jafry, Y., Schuermann, T., 2004. Measurement, estimation and comparison of credit migration matrices. *Journal of Banking and Finance* 28, 2603–2639.

Jarrow, R., Lando, D., Turnbull, S., 1997. A Markov model for the term structure of credit risk spreads. *Review of Financial Studies* 10, 481–523.

Jarrow, R., Turnbull, S., 1995. Pricing derivatives on financial securities subject to credit risk. *Journal of Finance* 50, 53–85.

Jones, F., 1987. Current techniques in bankruptcy prediction. *Journal of Accounting Literature* 6, 131–164.

Kadam, A., Lenk, P., 2008. Bayesian inference for heterogeneity in credit rating migrations. *Journal of Banking and Finance* (Forthcoming).

Kijima, M., Komoribayashi, K., 1998. A Markov chain model for valuing credit risk derivatives. *Journal of Derivatives* 6, 97–108.

Kim, J., 1999. Conditioning the transition matrix. *Risk Credit Risk Special Report*, 37–40.

Kreinin, A., Sidelnikova, M., 2001. Regularization algorithms for transition matrices. *Algo Research Quarterly* 4, 23–40.

Krüger, U., Stötzel, M., Trueck, S., 2005. Time series properties of a rating system based on financial ratios. *Deutsche Bundesbank Discussion Paper Series: Banking and Financial Studies* 14, 1–60.

Küchler, U., Sorensen, M., 1997. *Exponential Families of Stochastic Processes*. Springer, New York.

Lahr, M., 2001. A strategy for producing hybrid regional input-output tables. In: Lahr, M., Dietzenbacher, E. (Eds.), *Input-Output Analysis: Frontiers and Extensions*. Palgrave, pp. 182–191.

Lando, D., 1998. On cox processes and credit risky securities. *Derivatives Research* 2(2–3), 99–120.

Lando, D., 2000. *Some Elements of Rating Based Credit Risk Modeling*. Wiley, New York, pp. 193–215.

Lando, D., 2004. *Credit Risk Modeling: Theory and Applications*. Princeton University Press, New Jersey.

Lando, D., Mortensen, A., 2005. On the pricing of step-up bonds in the European telecom sector. *Journal of Credit Risk* 1(1), 71–110.

Lando, D., Skødeberg, T., 2002. Analyzing rating transitions and rating drift with continuous observations. *Journal of Banking and Finance* 26(2), 423–444.

Laurent, J., Gregory, J., 2005. Basket default swaps, CDO's and factor copulas. *Journal of Risk* 7(4), 103–122.

Lehnert, N., Altrock, F., Rachev, S., Trueck, S., Wilch, A., 2006. *Implied Correlations in CDO Tranches*. Working paper.

Li, D., 2000. On default correlation: A copula function approach. *Journal of Fixed Income* 9, 43–54.

Löffler, G., 2004. An anatomy of rating through the cycle. *Journal of Banking and Finance* 28(3), 695–720.

Löffler, G., 2005. Avoiding the rating bounce: Why rating agencies are slow to react to new information. *Journal of Economic Behavior and Organisation* 56(3), 365–381.

Longstaff, F., Schwartz, E., 1995. A simple approach to valuing risky fixed and floating rate debt. *Journal of Finance* 50, 789–819.

Lopez, J., 2004. The empirical relationship between average asset correlation, firm probability of default and asset size. *Journal of Financial Intermediation* 13(2), 265–283.

Madan, D., Unal, H., 1998. Pricing the risks of default. *Review of Derivatives Research* 2, 121–160.

Maddala, G. S., 1983. *Limited-Dependent and Qualitative Variables in Econometrics*. Cambridge University Press, Cambridge, UK.

Marchakitus, S., Soderberg, M., Bramley, A., 2001. *European Telecoms Update, Watch Your Step*. Credit Research Sector Report, JP Morgan Securities Ltd.

Mashal, R., Naldi, M., 2002. Extreme events and default baskets. *Risk* June, 119–122.

Mashal, R., Naldi, M., Tejwani, G., 2004. *The Implications of Implied Correlation*. Lehman brothers, quantitative credit research, Working paper.

Mashal, R., Naldi, M., Zeevi, A., 2003. Extreme events and multiname credit derivatives. In: *Credit Derivatives the Definitive Guide*, Risk Waters Group, Great Britain, 313–338.

Matuszewski, T. P. P., Sawyer, J. A., 1964. Linear programming estimates of changes in input-output coefficients. *Canadian Journal of Economics and Political Science* 30, 203–210.

McAdie, R., Martin, S., O'Kane, D., 2000. *Credit-sensitive Telecom Bonds: A Framework for Valuation*. European Credit Strategy & Research Market Analysis, Lehman Brothers.

McCullagh, P., Nelder, J., 1989. *Generalized Linear Models*. Chapman and Hall, London.

McGinty, L., Ahluwalia, R., 2004a. *Credit Correlation: A Guide*. Credit Derivatives Strategy, JP Morgan.

McGinty, L., Ahluwalia, R., 2004b. *A Relative Value Framework for Credit Correlation*. Credit Derivatives Strategy, JP Morgan.

McNeil, A., Frey, R., Embrechts, P., 2005. *Quantitative Risk Management: Concepts, Techniques and Tools*. Princeton University Press, New Jersey.

McNeil, A., Wendin, J., 2006. Dependent credit migrations. *Journal of Credit Risk* 2(3), 87–114.

Menn, C., Rachev, S., 2004. *A New Class of Probability Distributions and Its Application to Finance*. Working paper.

Merton, R., 1974. On the pricing of corporate debt: The risk structure of interest rates. *Journal of Finance* 29, 449–470.

Moody's Investment Service, 1997. The binominal expansion technique. *Moody's Special Report* July.

Moody's KMV, 2004. Moody's RiskCalcTM v3.1 Model. *Moody's KMV* April.

Nagpal, K., Bahar, R., 2000. Modeling the dynamics of rating transition. *Credit* March, 57–63.

Nelsen, R., 1999. *An Introduction to Copulas*. Springer, New York.

Nickell, P., Varotto, S., 2000. Stability of rating transitions. *Journal of Banking and Finance* 1–2, 203–227.

Noris, J., 1998. *Markov Chains*. Cambridge University Press, Cambridge, UK.

Ohlson, J., 1980. Financial ratios and the probabilistic prediction of bankruptcy. *Journal of Accounting Research* 18(1), 109–131.

Perry, L., Liu, P., Evans, D., 1988. Rev. ed. 2008. Modified bond ratings: Further evidence on the effect of split ratings on corporate bond yields. *Journal of Business Finance and Accounting* 15(2), 231–241.

Picone, D., 2005. *Structuring and Rating Cash-Flow CDOs with Rating Transition Matrices*. Working paper, Cass Business School.

Platt, H., Platt, M., 1991. A note on the use of industry-relative ratios in bankruptcy prediction. *Journal of Banking and Finance* 15(6), 1183–1194.

Press, J., Wilson, S., 1978. Choosing between logistic regression and discriminant analysis. *Journal of the American Statistical Association* 73.

Prokopczuk, M., Trueck, S., 2008. *Risk Neutral Migration Matrices*. Working paper.

Rachev, S., 1991. *Probability Metrics and the Stability of Stochastic Models*. Wiley, Chichester, New York.

Rachev, S., Menn, C., Fabozzi, F., 2005. *Fat-Tailed and Skewed Asset Return Distributions—Implications for Risk Management, Portfolio Selection and Option Pricing*. John Wiley and Sons, New York.

Rachev, S., Mittnik, S., 1999. *Stable Paretian Models in Finance*. John Wiley and Sons, Chichester, West Sussex, UK.

Rachev, S., Schwartz, E., Khindanova, I., 2001. Stable modeling of credit risk. *Proceedings of the American Statistical Association Conference*.

Rösch, D., 2002. *Correlations and Business Cycles of Credit Risk: Evidence from Bankruptcies in Germany*. Working paper, University of Regensburg.

Saunders, A., Allen, L., 2002. *Credit Risk Measurement*. John Wiley, New York.

Schönbucher, P., 2003. *Credit Derivatives Pricing Models: Models, Pricing and Implementation*. Wiley, Chichester, UK.

Schönbucher, P., Schubert, D., 2001. *Copula Dependent Default Risk in Intensity Models*. Technical report, University of Bonn.

Schuermann, T., 2004. What do we know about loss given default? In Shimko, D. (ed.), *Credit Risk Models and Management*, 2nd ed., Risk Books, London.

Schuermann, T., Hanson, T., 2004. *Estimating Probabilities of Default*. Federal Reserve Bank of New York Staff Reports.

Schweizer, B., Sklar, A., 1983. *Probabilistic Metric Spaces*. North Holland Elsevier, New York.

Servigny, A., Renault, O., 2004. *Measuring and Managing Credit Risk*. McGraw Hill, New York.

Singer, B., Spilerman, S., 1976. The representation of social processes by Markov models. Fonctions de réparation à n dimensions et leurs marges. *American Journal of Sociology* 82, 1–54.

Sklar, A., 1959. Fonctions de répartition à n dimensions et leurs marges. *Publications de l'Institut de Statistique de L'Université de Paris* 8, 229–231.

Sobehart, J., Keenan, S., Stein, R., 2000. Benchmarking quantitative default risk models: A validation methodology. *Risk Management Services Rating Methodology* March 2000.

Somers, R., Kendall, M., 1938. A new measure of rank correlation. *Biometrika* 30, 81–93.

Somers, R., 1962a. A new asymmetric measure of association for ordinal variables. *American Sociological Review* 27(6), 799–811.

Somers, R., 1962b. A similarity between Goodman and Kruskal's tau and Kendall's tau. *Journal of the American Statistical Association* 57(300), 804–812.

Standard & Poor's, 2000. Corporate Rating Criteria.

Standard & Poor's, 2005. *Annual global corporate default study: Corporate defaults poised to rise in 2005.* Standard & Poor's Global Fixed Income Research.

Strang, G., 1988. *Linear Algebra and Its Applications.* Thomson Learning, Inc.

Trueck, S., 2005. *Measures for Comparing Transition Matrices from a Value-at-Risk Perspective.* Working paper, Institute of Statistics and Mathematical Economics, University of Karlsruhe.

Trueck, S., 2007. *Simulating Dependent Credit Migrations.* Working paper.

Trueck, S., 2008. Forecasting credit migration matrices with business cycle effects—A model comparison. *European Journal of Finance* 14(5), 359–379.

Trueck, S., Özturkmen, E., 2004. Estimation, adjustment and application of transition matrices in credit risk models. In Rachev, S. (ed.), *Handbook on Computational and Numerical Methods in Finance*, Birkhauser, Boston, 373–402.

Trueck, S., Rachev, T., 2005. Credit portfolio risk and PD confidence sets through the business cycle. *Journal of Credit Risk* 1(4), 61–88.

Trueck, S., Rachev, T., 2007. *Changes in Migration Matrices and Credit Var—A New Class of Difference Indices.* Working paper.

Tucker, J., 1996. Neural networks versus logistic regression in financial modeling: A methodological comparison. *Proceedings of the 1996 World First Online Workshop on Soft Computing (WSC1)*, Nagoya University (Japan).

Uhrig-Homburg, M., 2002. Valuation of defaultable claims—A survey. *Schmalenbach Business Review* 54(1), 24–57.

Varsany, Z., 2007. *Rating Philosophies—Some Clarifications.* Central Bank of Hungary, Working paper 1660.

Vasicek, O., 1987. *Probability of Loss on a Loan Portfolio.* Working paper, KMV.

Weber, M., Krahnen, J., Vomann, F., 1998. Risikomessung im Kreditgeschaft: Eine empirische Analyse bankinterner Ratingverfahren. *Zeitschrift fr betriebswirtschaftliche Forschung* 41, 117–142.

Wehrspohn, U., 2004. Ausfallwahrscheinlichkeiten im Konjunkturzyklus: Credit Portfolio View. In Romeike, F. (ed.), *Modernes Risikomanagement*, Wiley–VCH, Weinheim, Germany.

Wei, J., 2003. A multi-factor, credit migration model for sovereign and corporate debts. *Journal of International Money and Finance* 22, 709–735.

Willemann, S., 2004. *An Evaluation of the Base Correlation Framework for Synthetic CDOs.* Working paper.

Wilson, R., Sharda, R., 1994. Bankruptcy prediction using neural networks. *Decision Support Systems* 11, 545–557.

Wilson, T., 1997a. *Measuring and Managing Credit Portfolio Risk.* McKinsey & Company.

Wilson, T.C., 1997a. Portfolio credit risk I. *Risk* 10(September) 111–117.

Wilson, T.C., 1997b. Portfolio credit risk II. *Risk* 10(October), 56–61.

Zavgren, C., 1985. Assessing the vulnerability to failure of American industrial firms: A logistic analysis. *Journal of Business Finance and Accounting* 12(1), 19–45.

Zhou, C., 1997. *A Jump-Diffusion Approach to Modeling Credit Risk and Valuing Defautable Securities.* Federal Reserve Board, Washington DC.

Zmijewski, M., 1984. Methodological issues related to the estimation of financial distress prediction models. *Journal of Accounting Research* 22 (Supplement), 59–82.

Index

Printed and bound by CPI Group (UK) Ltd, Croydon, CR0 4YY

08/05/2025

01864768-0002